wet moon

book 1:
feeble wanderings

written & illustrated by
Ross Campbell

Cleo's diary pages by
Jessica Calderwood

design by
Keith Wood

edited by
James Lucas Jones

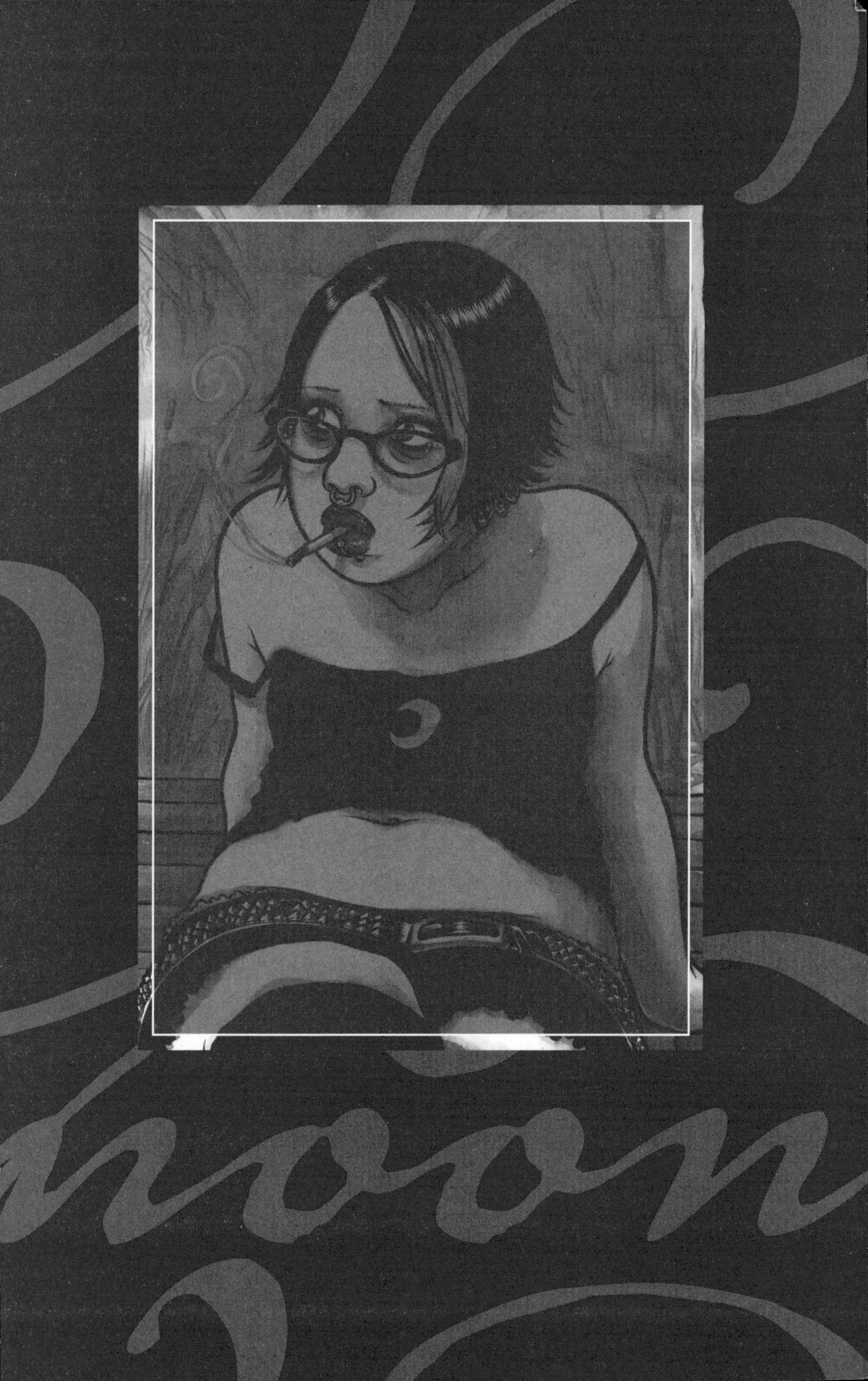
moon

Published by

Oni Press, Inc.

Joe Nozemack, *publisher*

Randal C. Jarrell, *managing editor*

Oni Press, Inc.
6336 SE Milwaukie Ave, PMB 30
Portland, OR 97203

www.onipress.com
www.greenoblivion.com

First Edition: December 2004

ISBN 1-932664-07-6

3 5 7 9 10 8 6 4

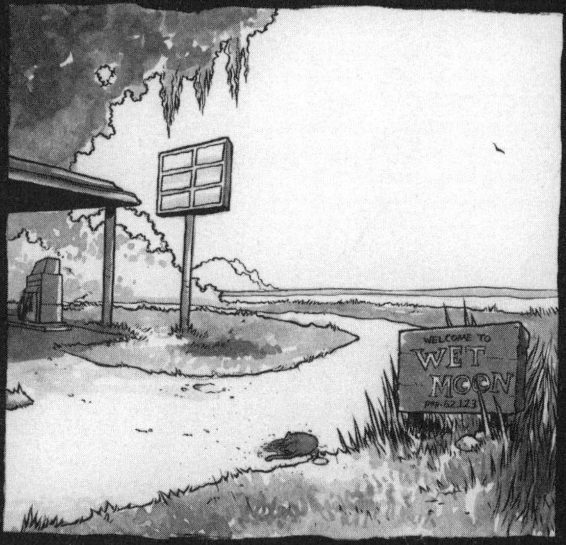
WELCOME TO
WET MOON
pop. 62,123

1

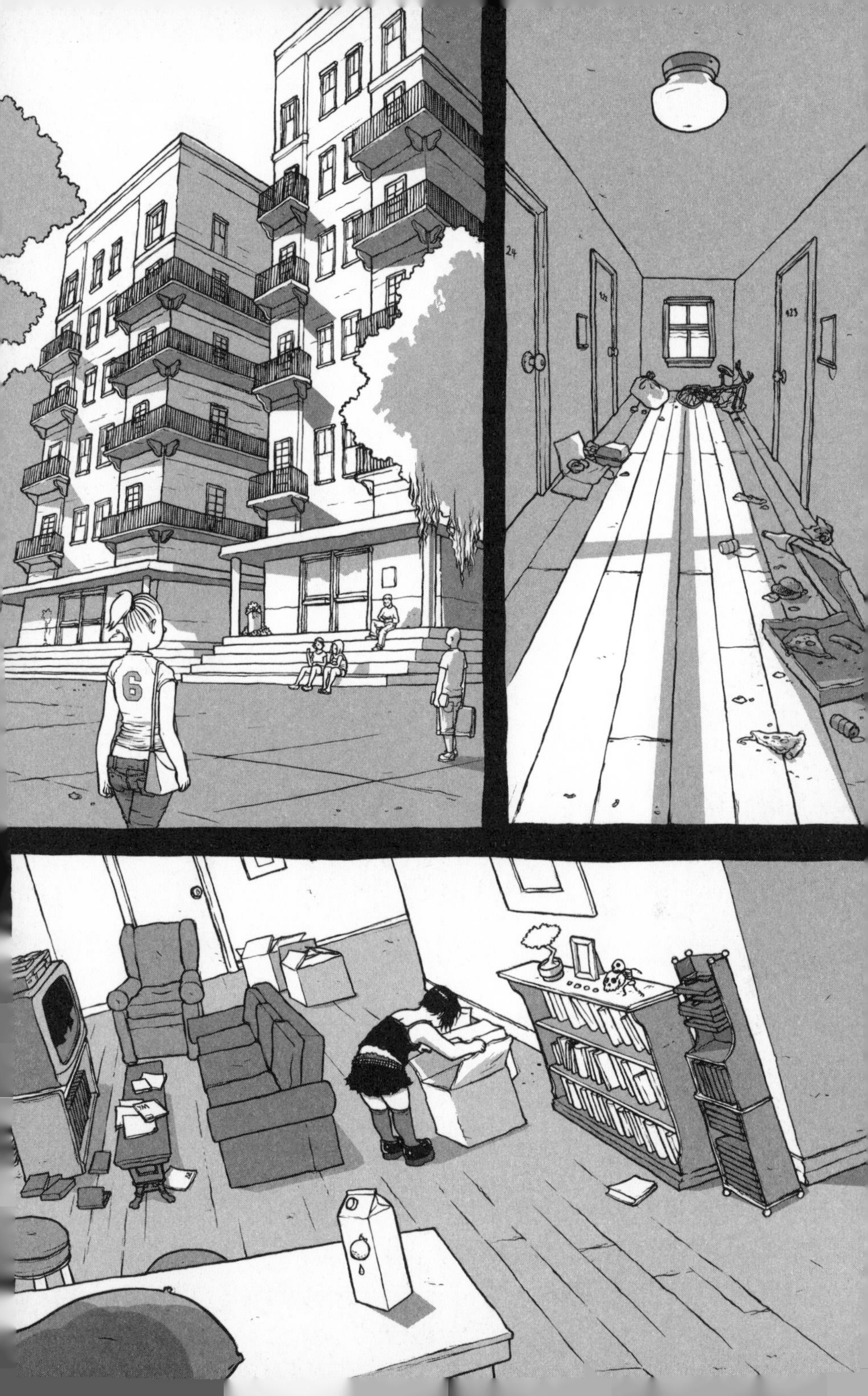

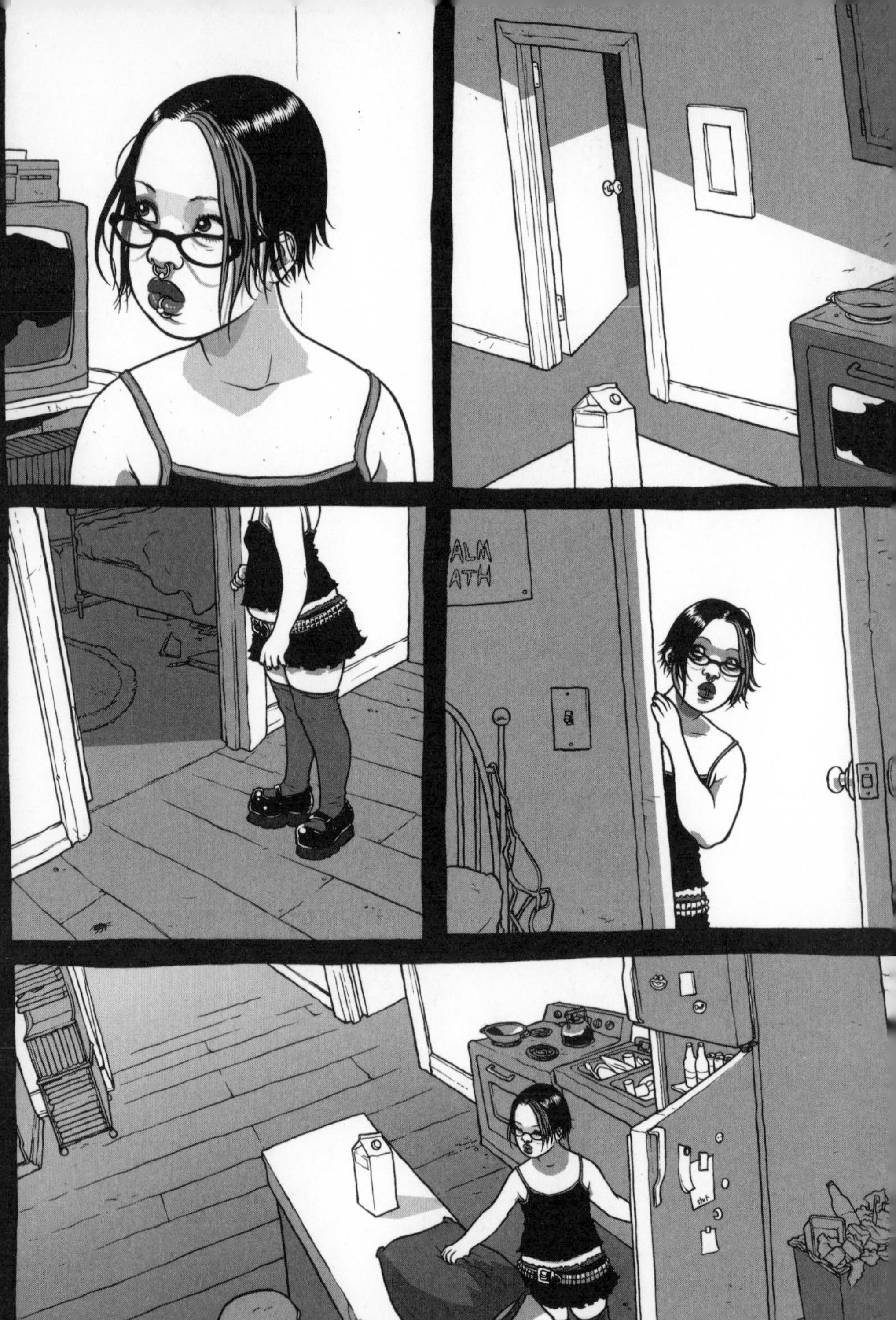

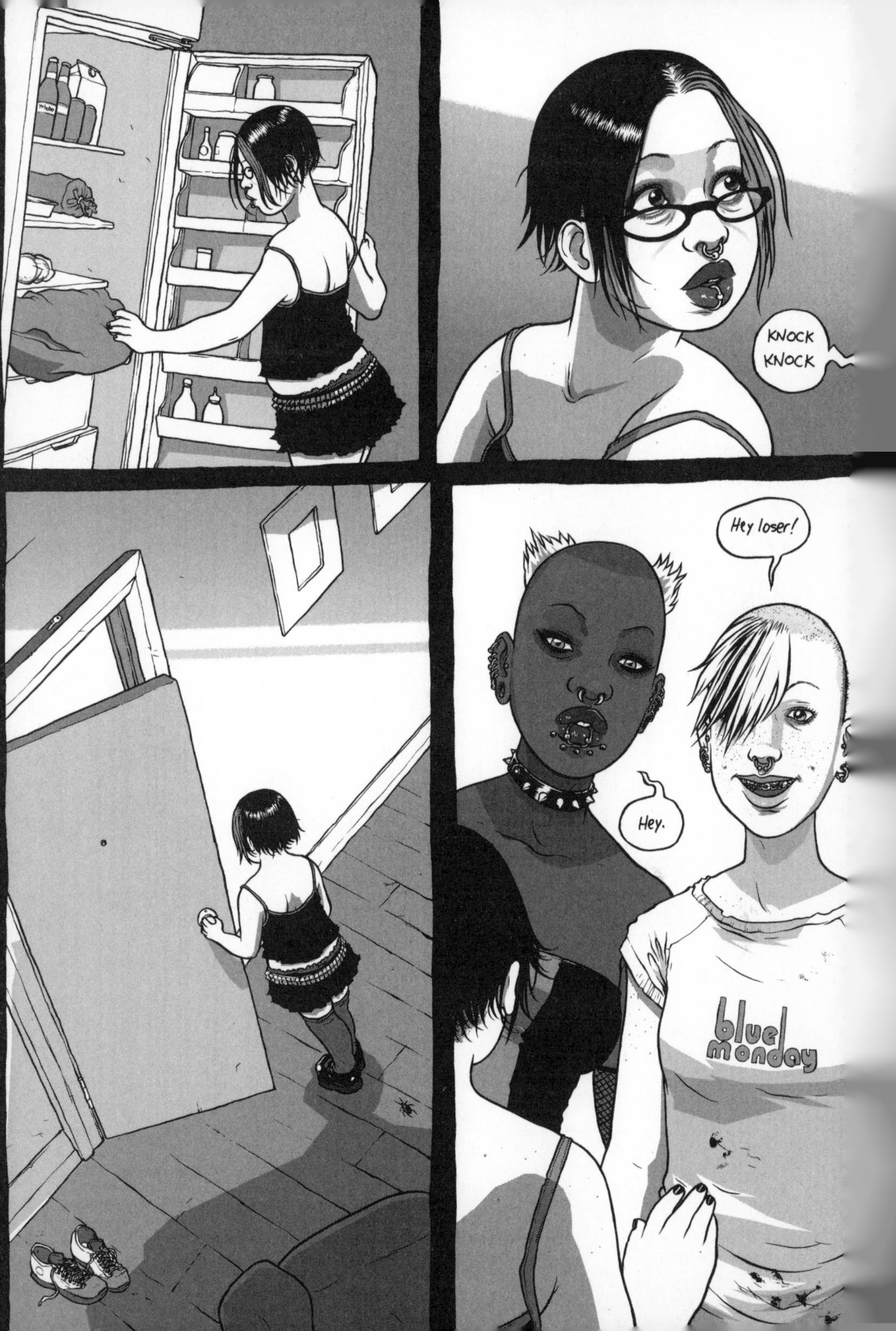
KNOCK KNOCK
Hey loser!
Hey.
blue monday

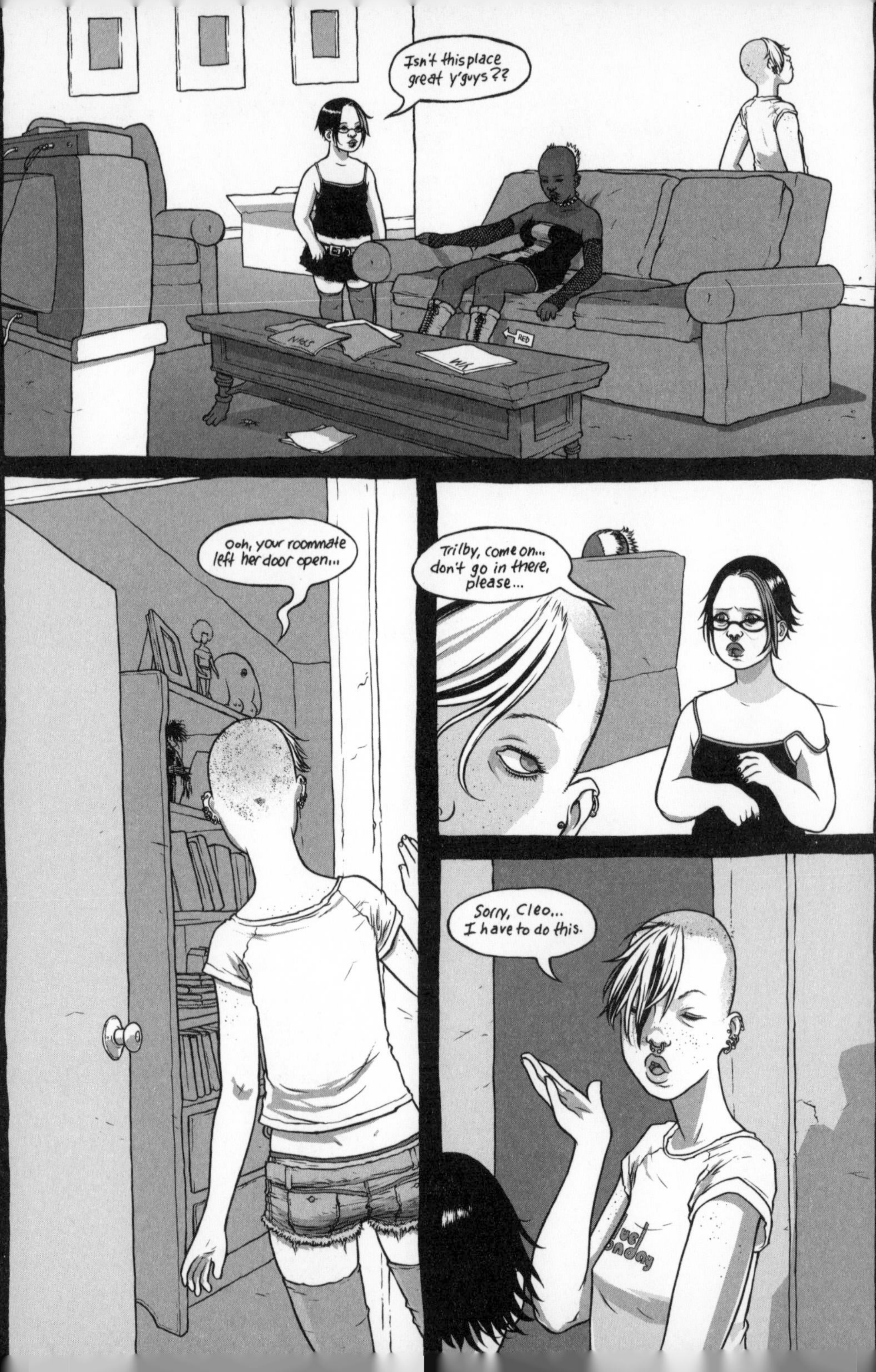
Isn't this place great y'guys??
Ooh, your roommate left her door open...
Trilby, come on... don't go in there, please...
Sorry, Cleo... I have to do this.

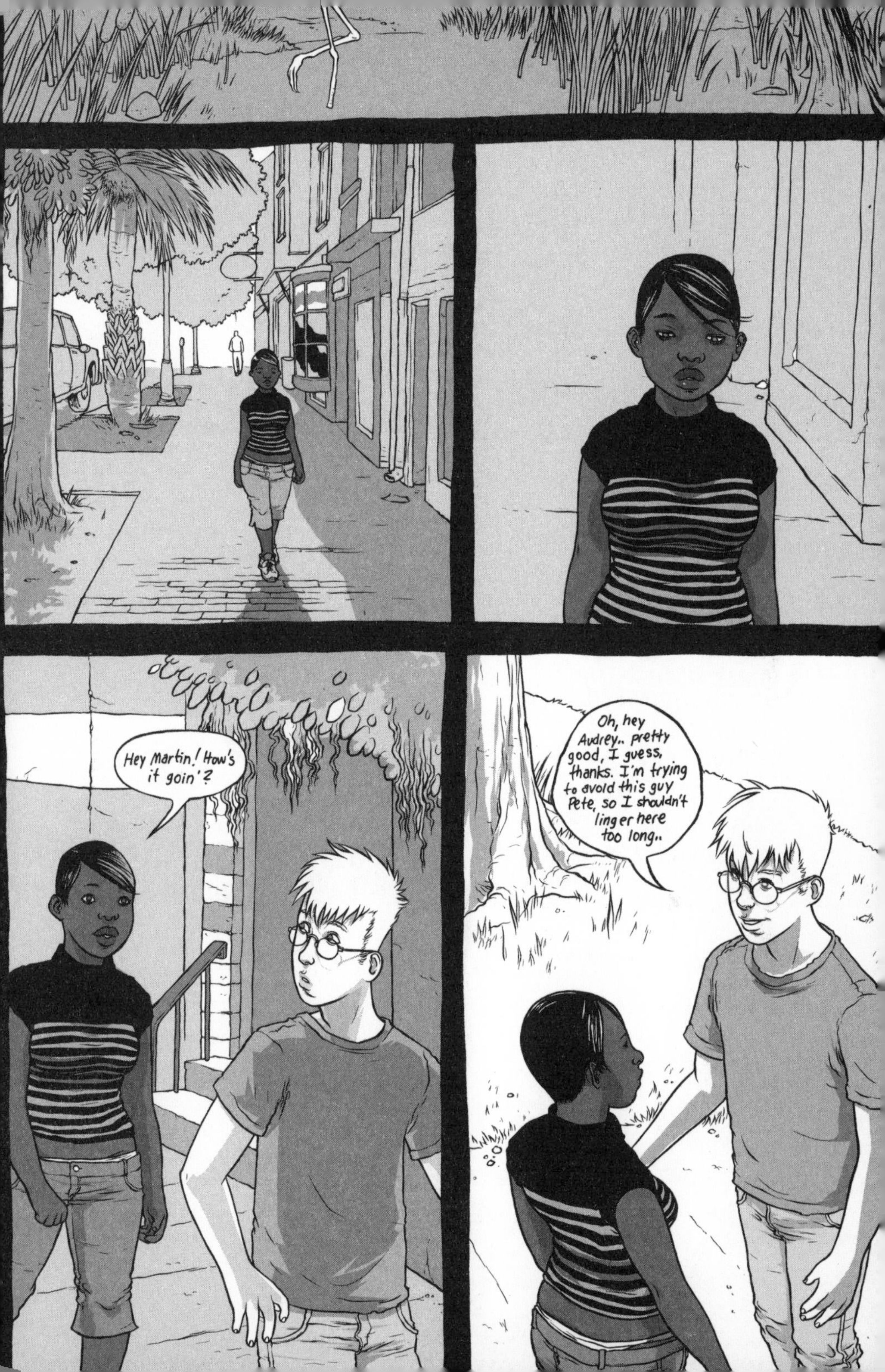
Hey Martin! How's it goin'?
Oh, hey Audrey.. pretty good, I guess, thanks. I'm trying to avoid this guy Pete, so I shouldn't linger here too long..

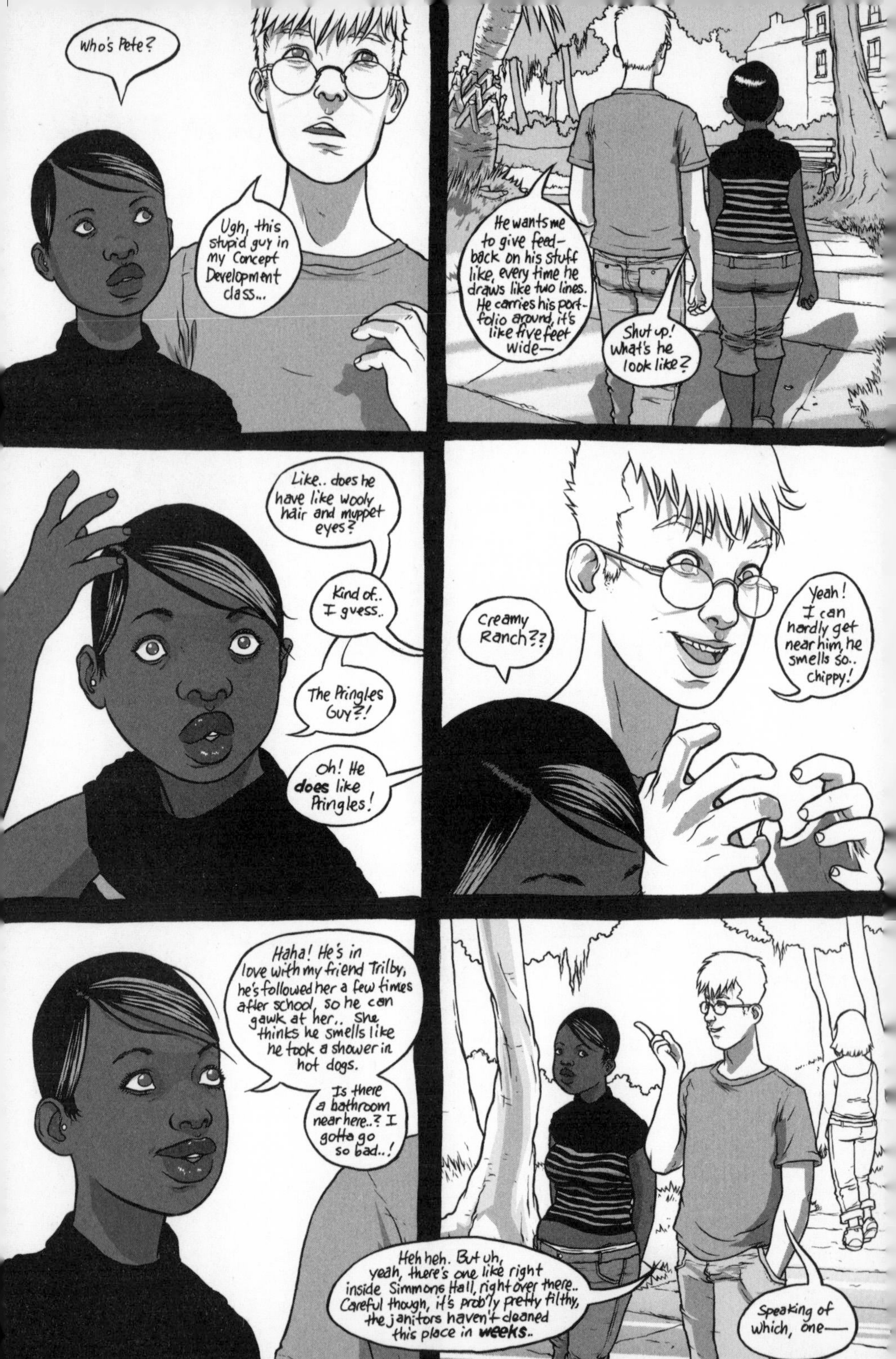
Who's Pete?
Ugh, this stupid guy in my Concept Development class...
He wants me to give feed-back on his stuff like, every time he draws like two lines. He carries his port-folio around, it's like five feet wide—
Shut up! What's he look like?
Like.. does he have like wooly hair and muppet eyes?
Kind of.. I guess..
The Pringles Guy?!
Oh! He **does** like Pringles!
Creamy Ranch??
Yeah! I can hardly get near him, he smells so.. chippy!
Haha! He's in love with my friend Trilby, he's followed her a few times after school, so he can gawk at her.. She thinks he smells like he took a shower in hot dogs.
Is there a bathroom near here..? I gotta go so bad..!
Heh heh. But uh, yeah, there's one like right inside Simmons Hall, right over there.. Careful though, it's prob'ly pretty filthy, the janitors haven't cleaned this place in **weeks**..
Speaking of which, one—

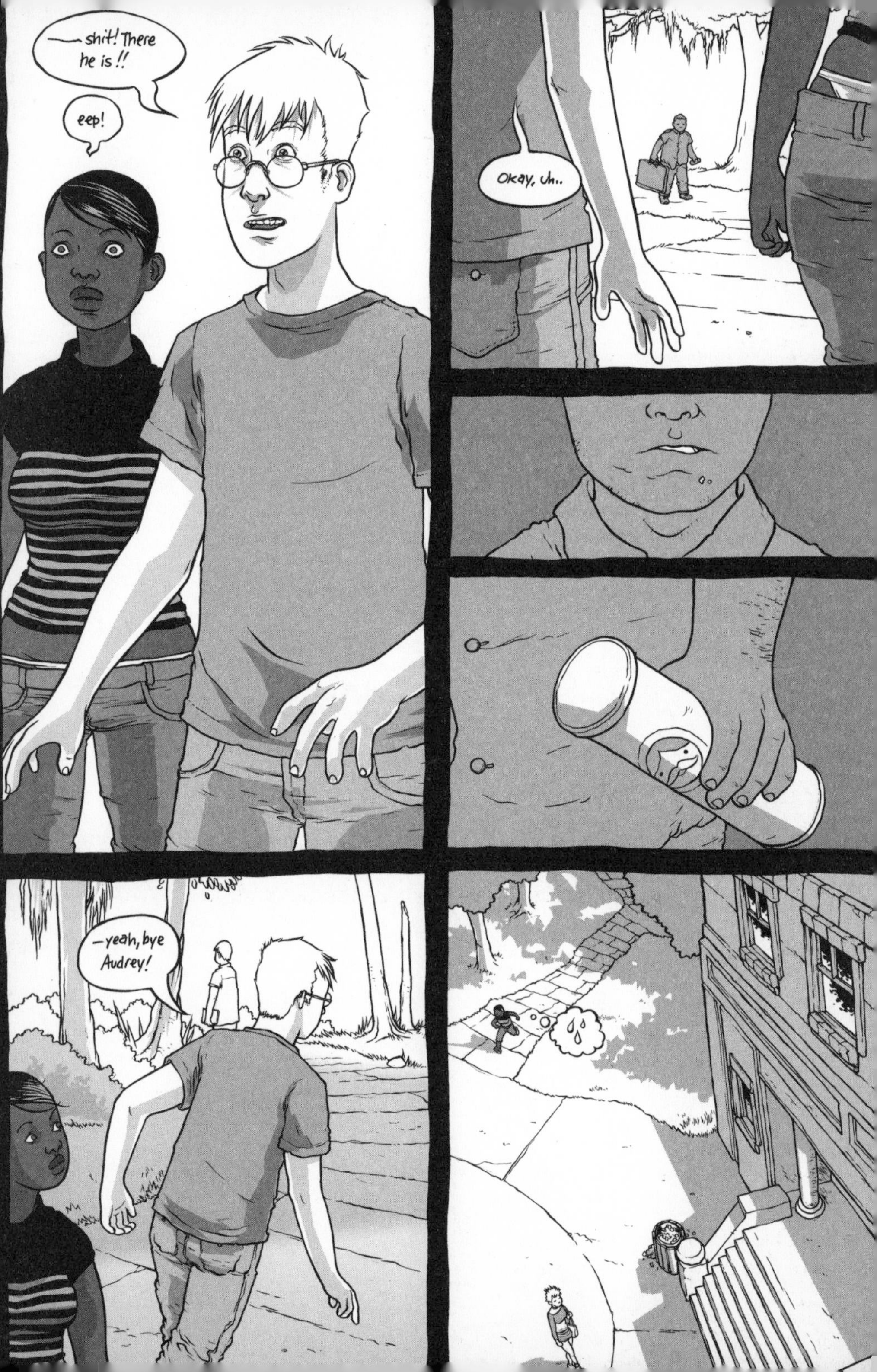
—shit! There he is!!
eep!
Okay, uh..
—yeah, bye Audrey!

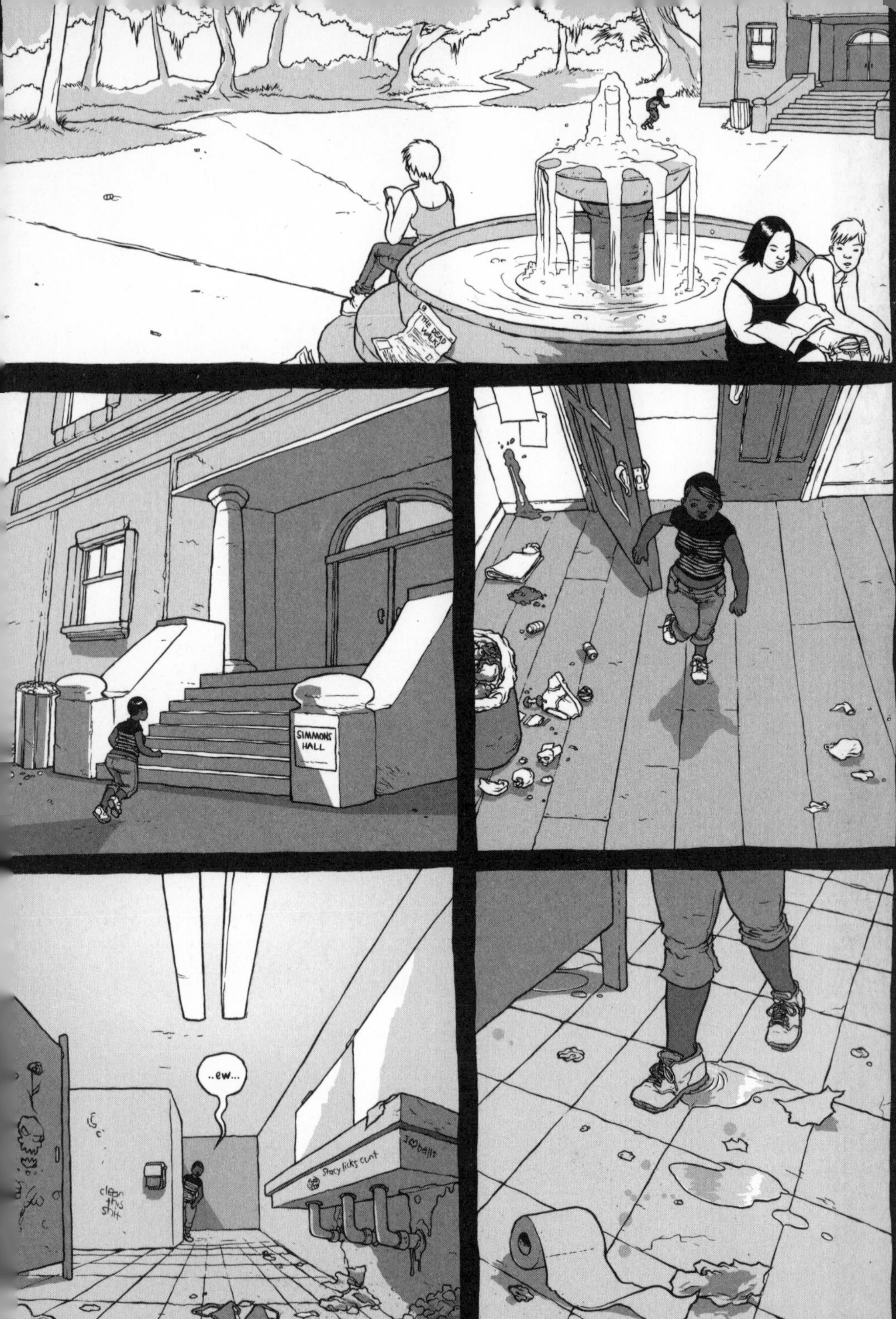
THE DEAD WALK
SIMMONS HALL
..ew...
clean this shit
Stacy licks cunt
I ♡ balls

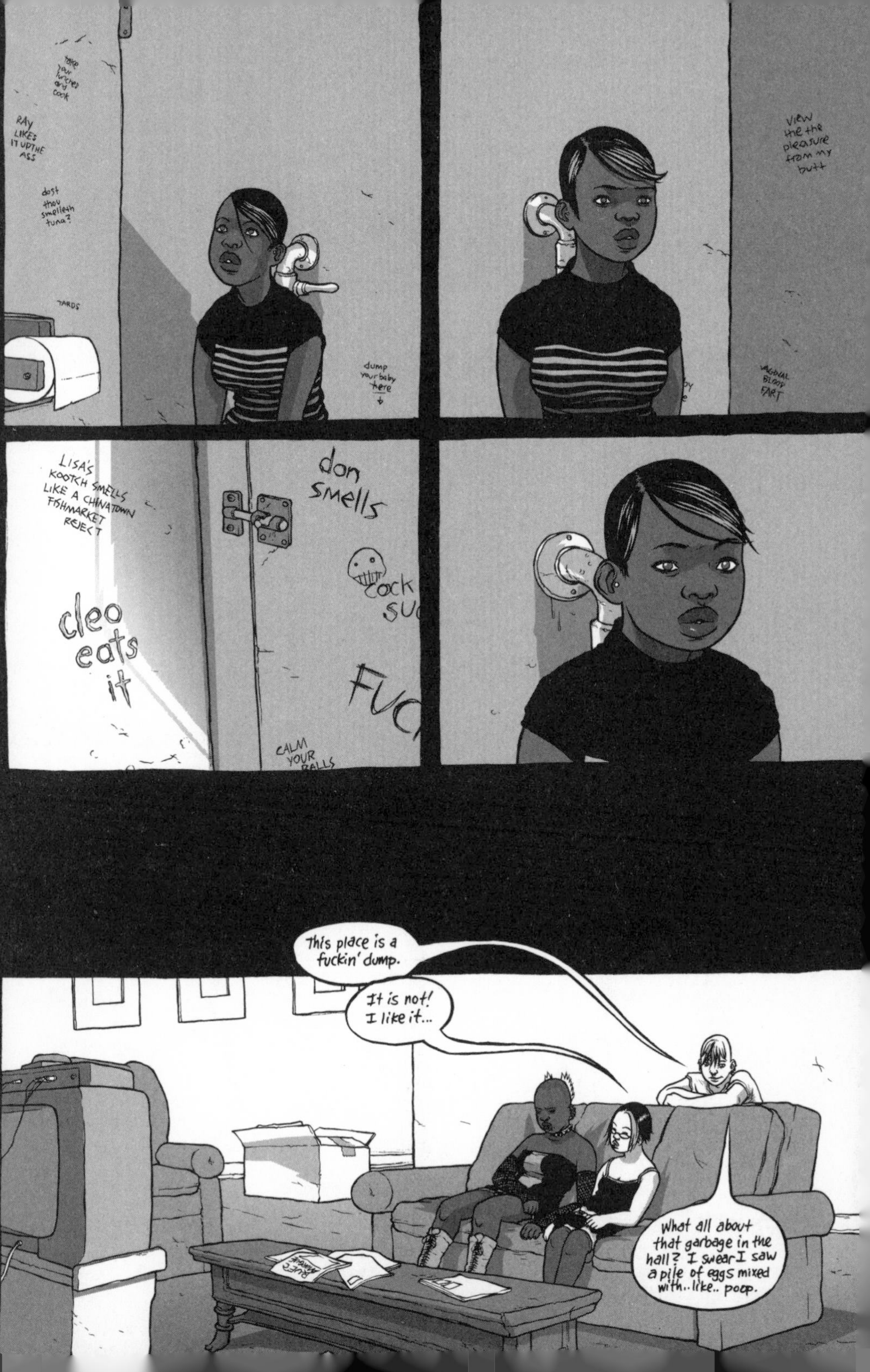

RAY LIKES IT UP THE ASS
dost thou smelleth tuna?
TARDS
dump your baby here
view the the pleasure from my butt
VAGINAL BLOOD FART
LISA'S KOOTCH SMELLS LIKE A CHINATOWN FISHMARKET REJECT
don smells
cleo eats it
CALM YOUR BALLS
This place is a fuckin' dump.
It is not! I like it...
What all about that garbage in the hall? I swear I saw a pile of eggs mixed with.. like.. poop.

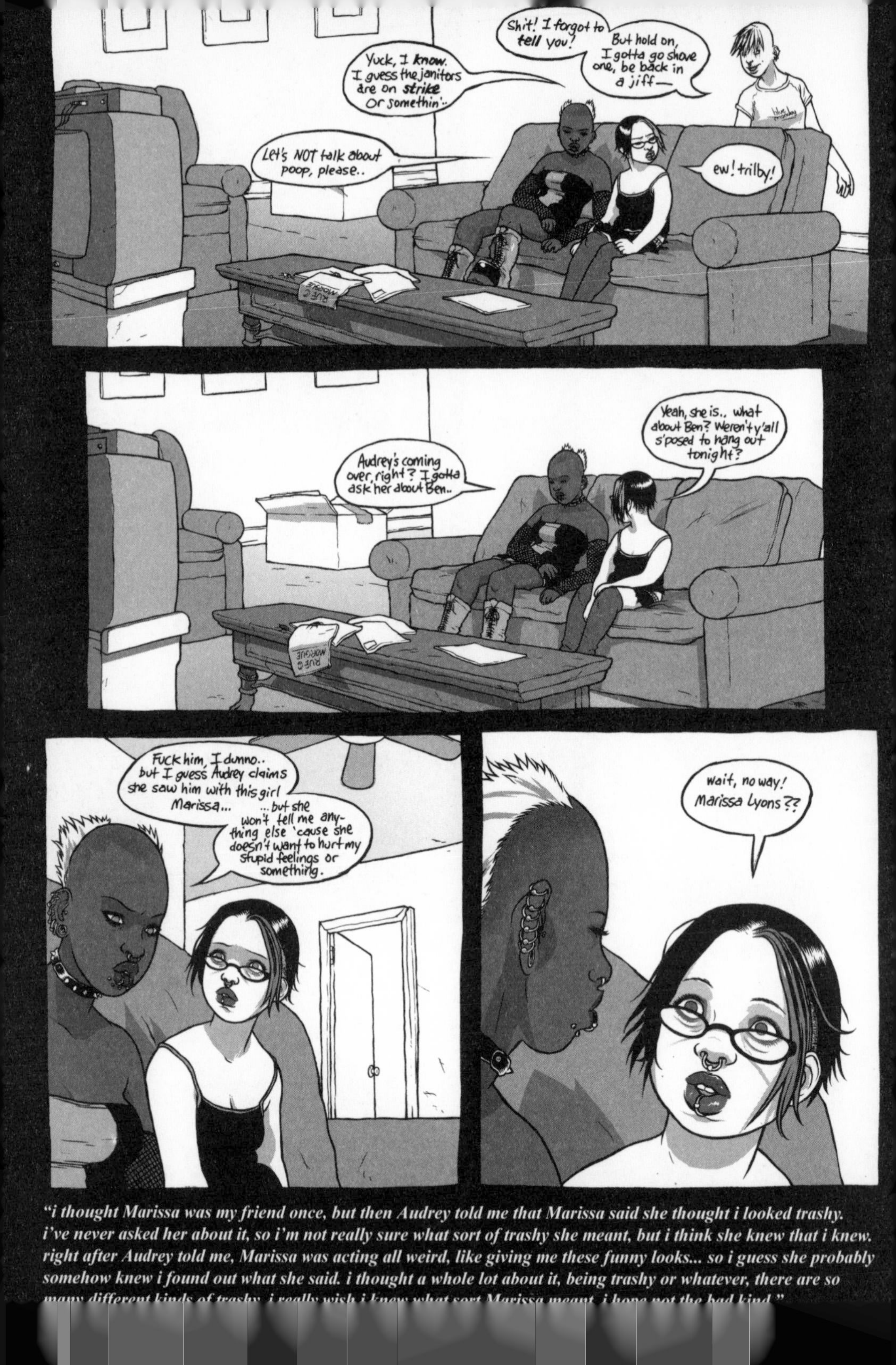
Yuck, I know. I guess the janitors are on strike or somethin'..
Shit! I forgot to tell you!
But hold on, I gotta go shove one, be back in a jiff—
Let's NOT talk about poop, please..
ew! trilby!
Audrey's coming over, right? I gotta ask her about Ben..
Yeah, she is.. what about Ben? Weren't y'all s'posed to hang out tonight?
Fuck him, I dunno.. but I guess Audrey claims she saw him with this girl Marissa...
...but she won't tell me anything else 'cause she doesn't want to hurt my stupid feelings or something.
wait, no way! Marissa Lyons??

"i thought Marissa was my friend once, but then Audrey told me that Marissa said she thought i looked trashy. i've never asked her about it, so i'm not really sure what sort of trashy she meant, but i think she knew that i knew. right after Audrey told me, Marissa was acting all weird, like giving me these funny looks... so i guess she probably somehow knew i found out what she said. i thought a whole lot about it, being trashy or whatever, there are so many different kinds of trashy. i really wish i knew what sort Marissa meant. i hope not the bad kind."

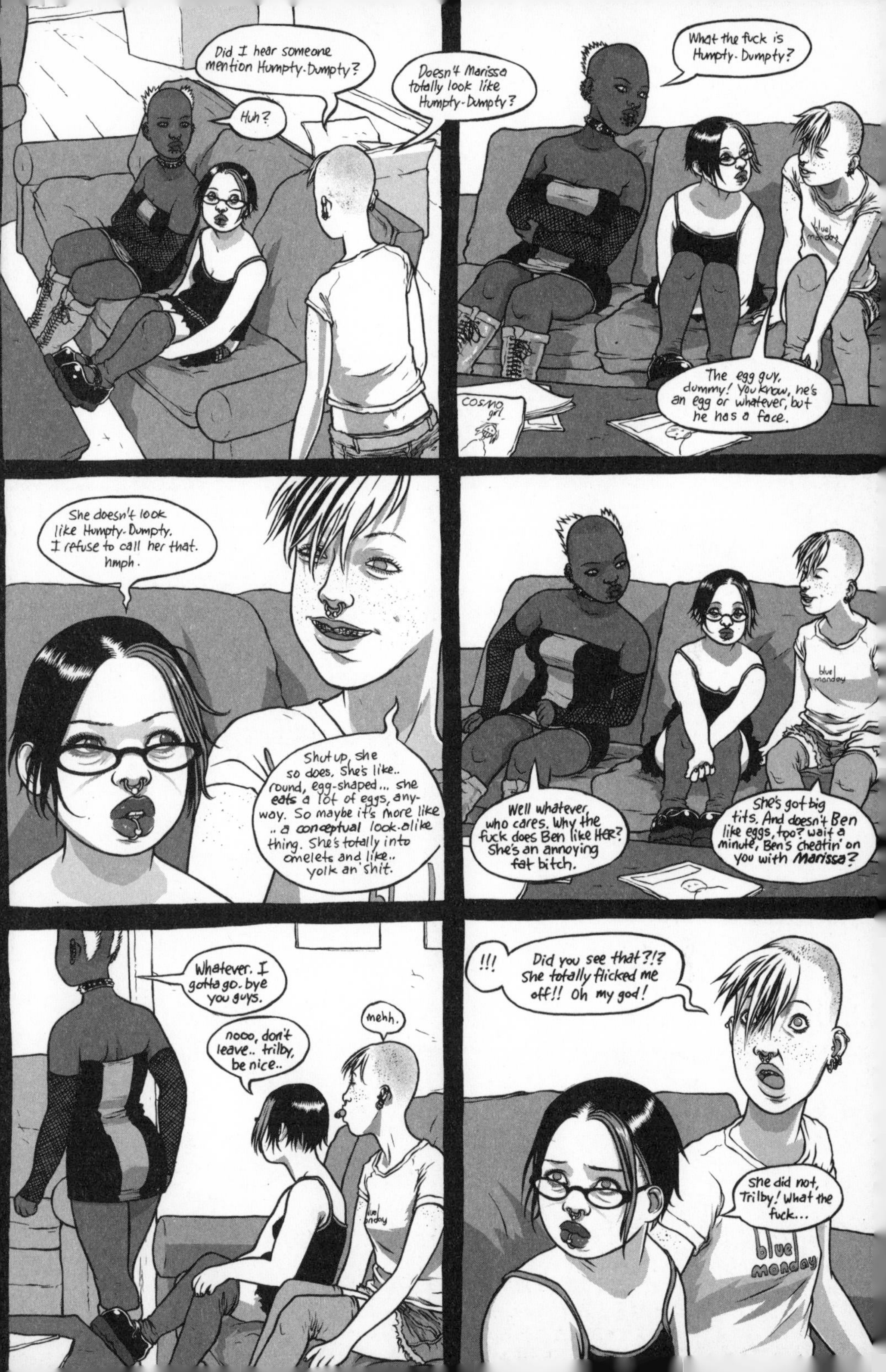
Did I hear someone mention Humpty-Dumpty?
Huh?
Doesn't Marissa totally look like Humpty-Dumpty?
What the fuck is Humpty-Dumpty?
The egg guy, dummy! You know, he's an egg or whatever, but he has a face.
COSMO girl
She doesn't look like Humpty-Dumpty. I refuse to call her that. hmph.
Shut up, she so does. She's like.. round, egg-shaped... she eats a lot of eggs, anyway. So maybe it's more like .. a conceptual look-alike thing. She's totally into omelets and like.. yolk an' shit.
Well whatever, who cares. Why the fuck does Ben like HER? She's an annoying fat bitch.
She's got big tits. And doesn't Ben like eggs, too? wait a minute, Ben's cheatin' on you with Marissa?
Whatever. I gotta go. bye you guys.
nooo, don't leave.. trilby, be nice..
mehh.
!!!
Did you see that?!? She totally flicked me off!! Oh my god!
She did not, Trilby! What the fuck...
blue monday

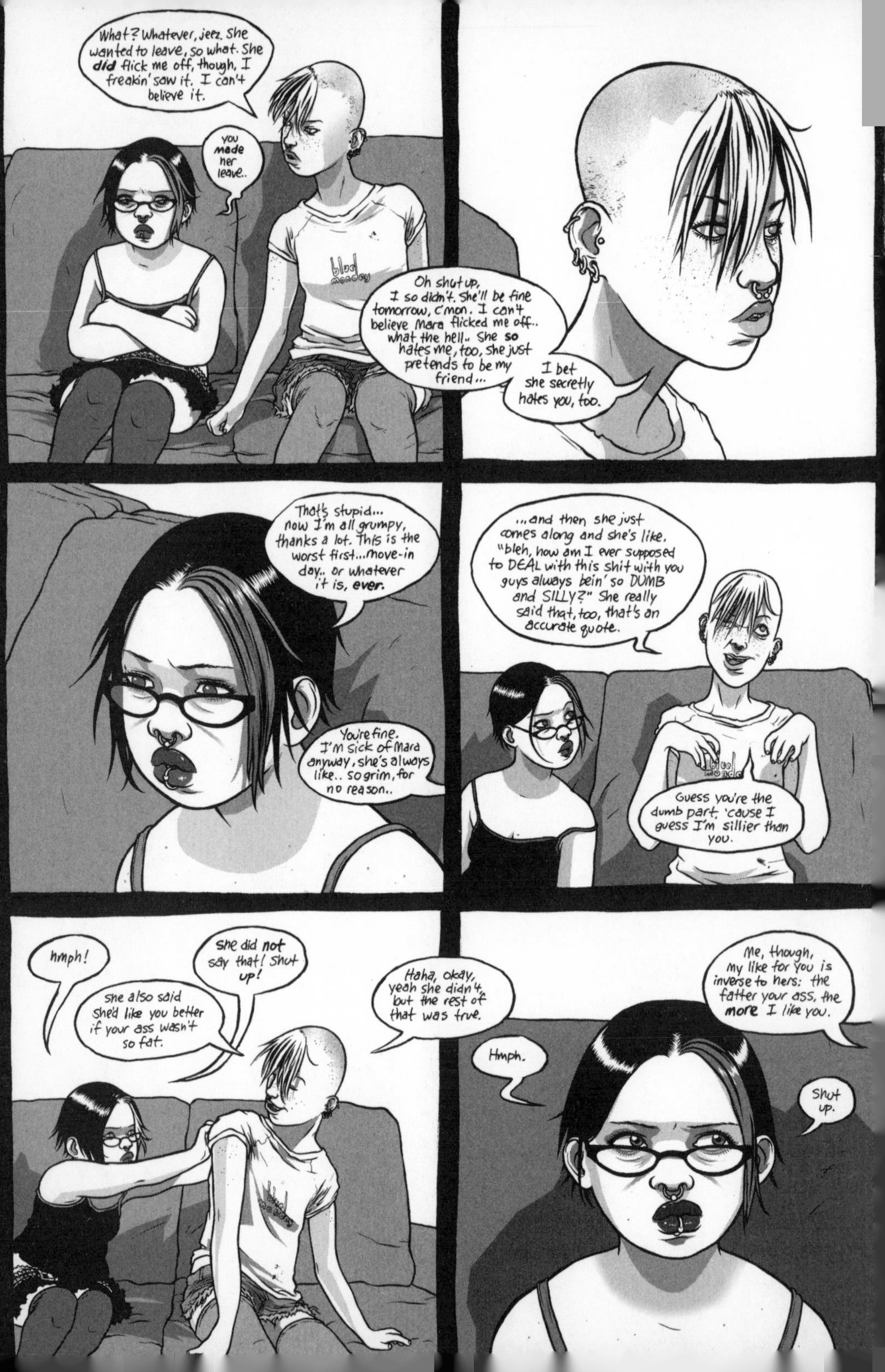
What? Whatever, jeez. She wanted to leave, so what. She **did** flick me off, though. I freakin' saw it. I can't believe it.
you **made** her leave..
Oh shut up, I so didn't. She'll be fine tomorrow, c'mon. I can't believe Mara flicked me off.. what the hell.. She **so** hates me, too, she just pretends to be my friend...
I bet she secretly hates you, too.
That's stupid... now I'm all grumpy, thanks a lot. This is the worst first...move-in day.. or whatever it is, **ever.**
You're fine. I'm sick of Mara anyway, she's always like.. so grim, for no reason..
...and then she just comes along and she's like, "bleh, how am I ever supposed to DEAL with this shit with you guys always bein' so DUMB and SILLY?" She really said that, too, that's an accurate quote.
Guess you're the dumb part, 'cause I guess I'm sillier than you.
hmph!
she also said she'd like you better if your ass wasn't so fat.
she did **not** say that! Shut **up**!
Haha, okay, yeah she didn't, but the rest of that was true.
Hmph.
Me, though, my like for you is inverse to hers: the fatter your ass, the **more** I like you.
Shut up.

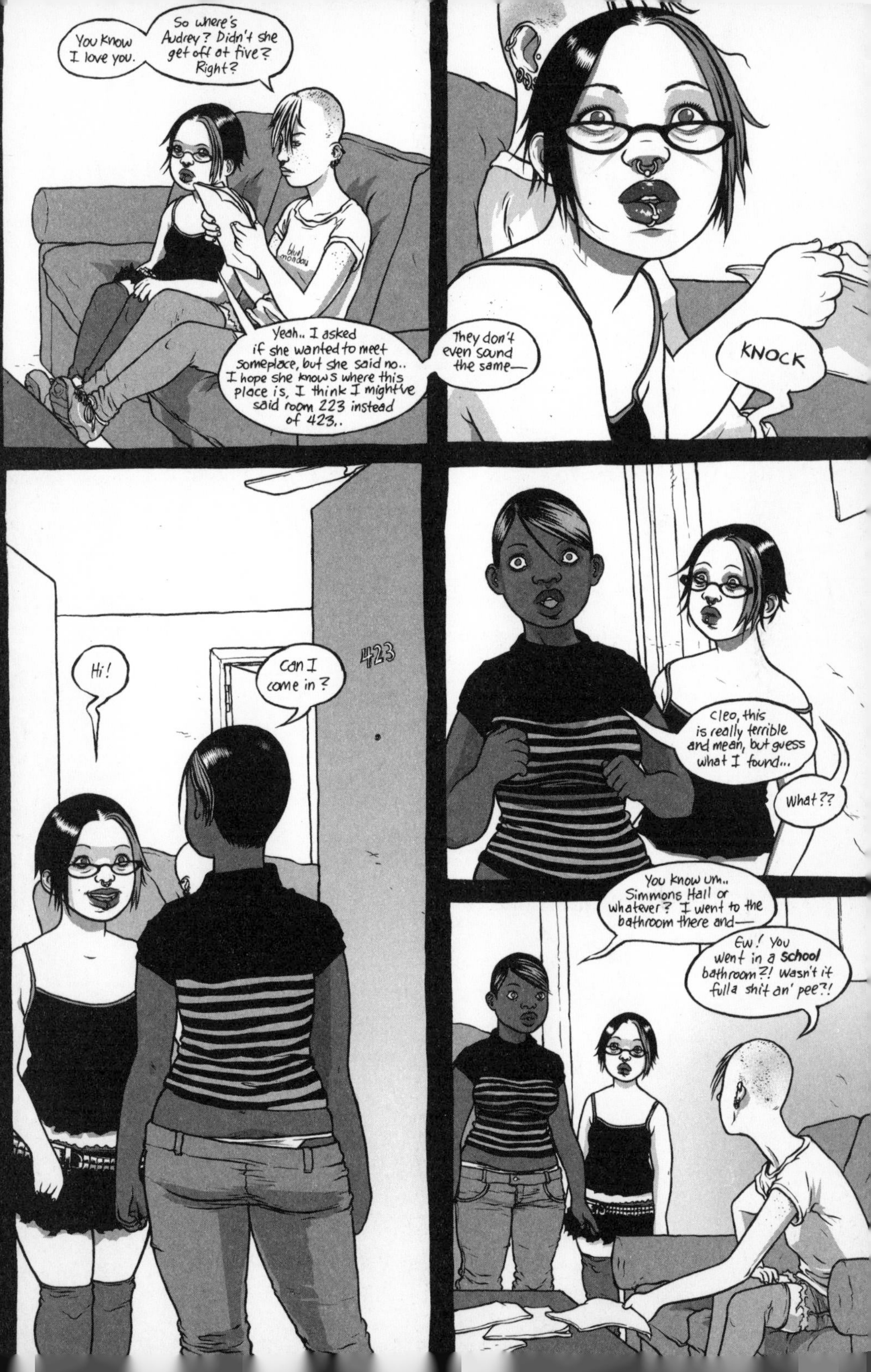
You know I love you.
So where's Audrey? Didn't she get off at five? Right?
blue monday
Yeah.. I asked if she wanted to meet someplace, but she said no.. I hope she knows where this place is, I think I might've said room 223 instead of 423..
They don't even sound the same—
KNOCK
Hi!
Can I come in?
423
Cleo, this is really terrible and mean, but guess what I found...
What??
You know um.. Simmons Hall or whatever? I went to the bathroom there and—
Ew! You went in a school bathroom?! Wasn't it fulla shit an' pee?!

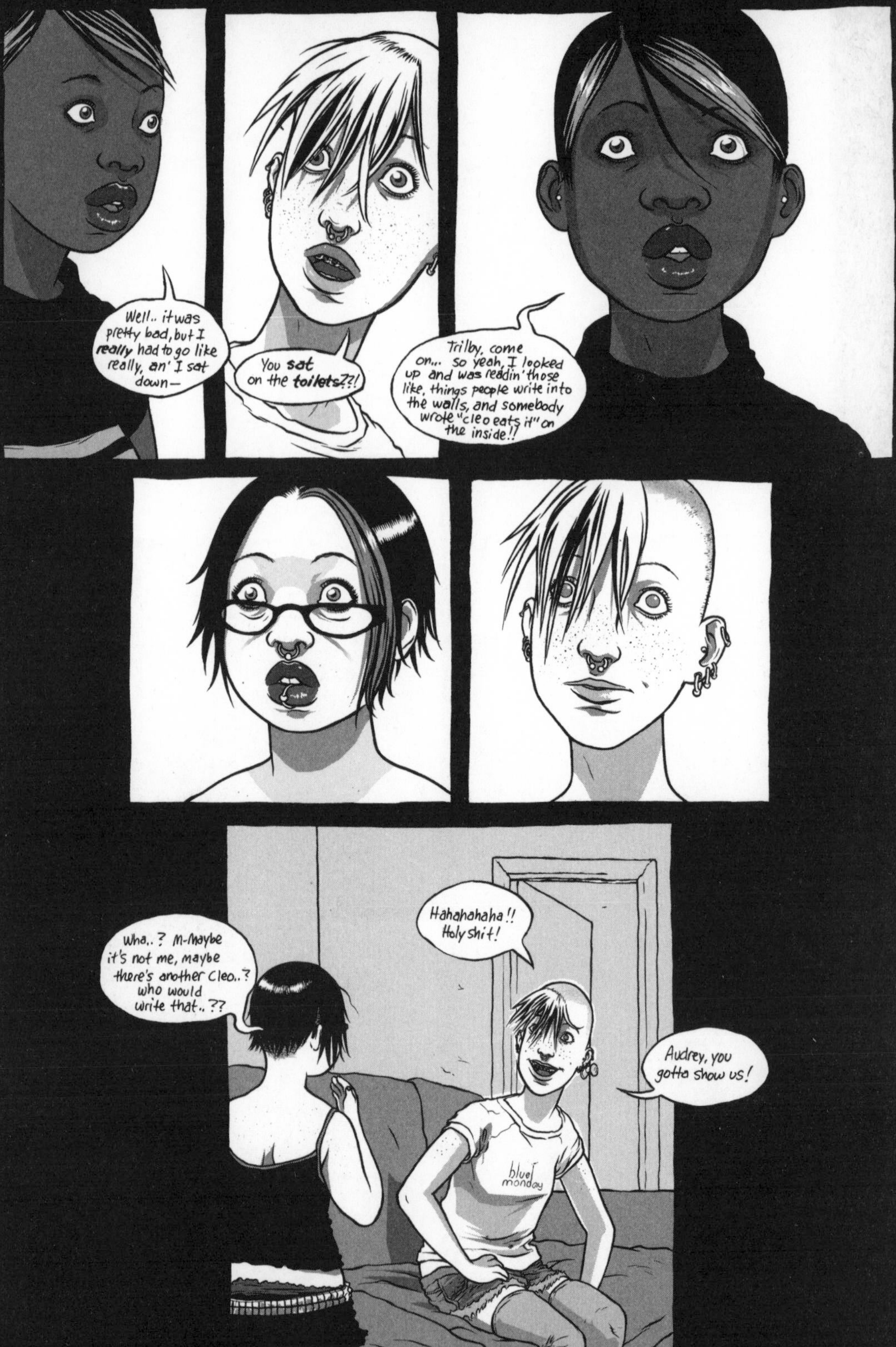
Well.. it was pretty bad, but I really had to go like really, an' I sat down—
You sat on the toilets??!
Trilby, come on... so yeah, I looked up and was readin' those like, things people write into the walls, and somebody wrote "cleo eats it" on the inside!!
Wha..? M-Maybe it's not me, maybe there's another Cleo..? who would write that..??
Hahahahaha!! Holy shit!
Audrey, you gotta show us!
blue monday

September 17th

this is the first time I've had the chance to write, since we visited Uncle Dwight and Aunt Annie, in Birmingham. I really didn't want to go, because I knew that as soon as I'd get back from it, I'd have to rush off to my new dorm room, without any respite from the trip. Dad said I should pack before the trip, but of course I didn't, so I had to run around and pack up everything super quick. And now that I'm all moved in, I can finally write. The trip: It kinda sucked; Annie was sick so she wasn't

much fun, but we made some green tea together and told school stories, so that was kinda cool... My cousins were there this time, usually Jason's off at college and Amber's visiting with her real mother. But they were there, and Jason totally has a crush on Trilby, it's so annoying. So all he talked about the whole time was her, like asking me questions about her, saying how pretty she was, and on and on. And Amber was a total bitch, she practically refused to talk to me, and I'm 99% positive she stole three of my barrettes, the ones I just got: the little

spider ones, and the one with the cute rattlesnake on it. I can't believe it. So now I'm even more depressed. I've moved into this uninviting dorm room, my roommates apparently avoiding me. I thought roommates were supposed to greet you when you moved in, and make you feel at home. But all I get is an empty room. I know they're avoiding me.

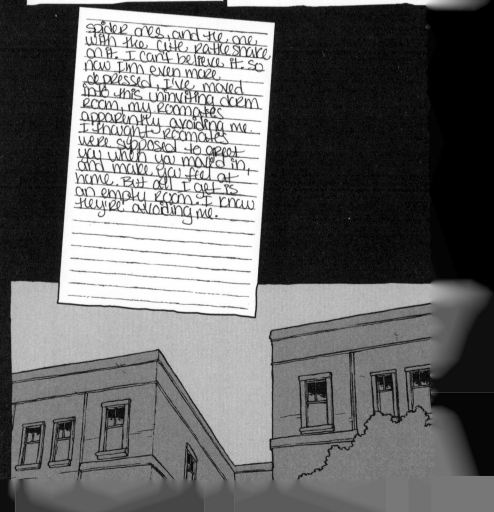

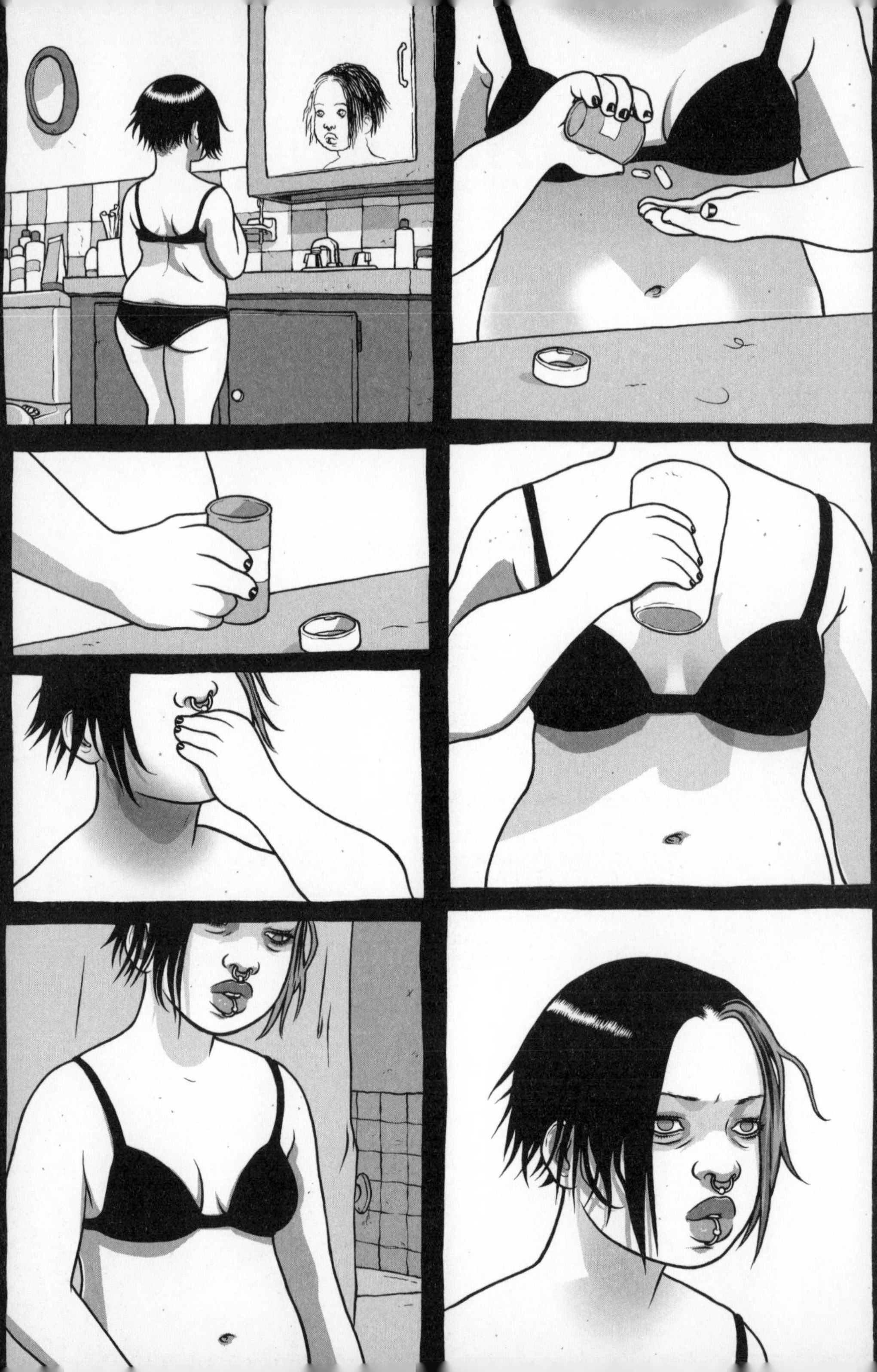

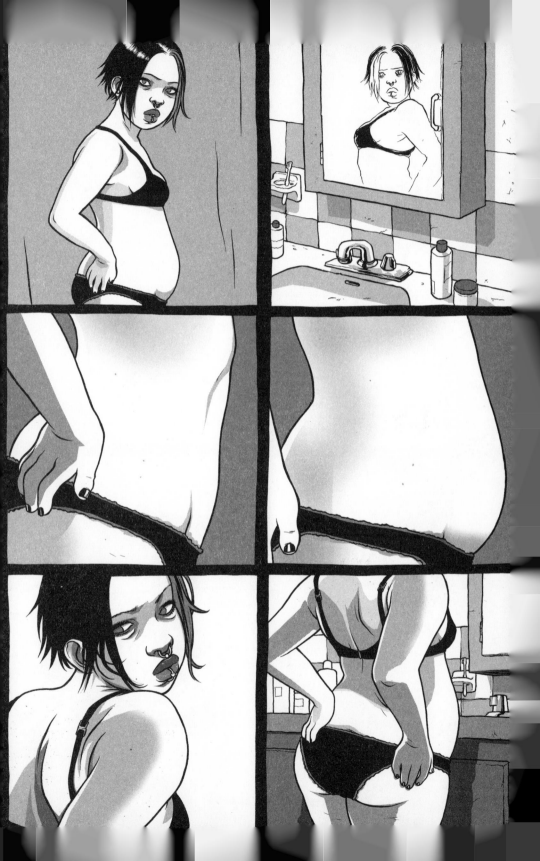

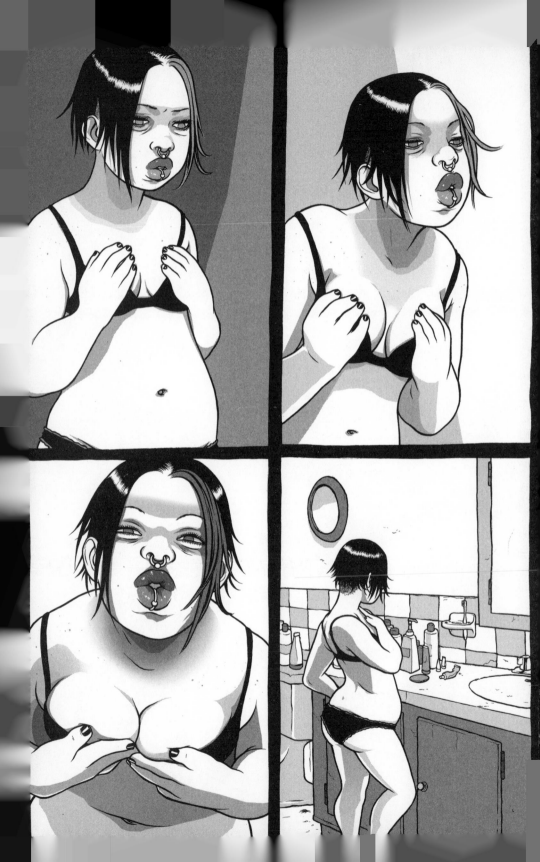

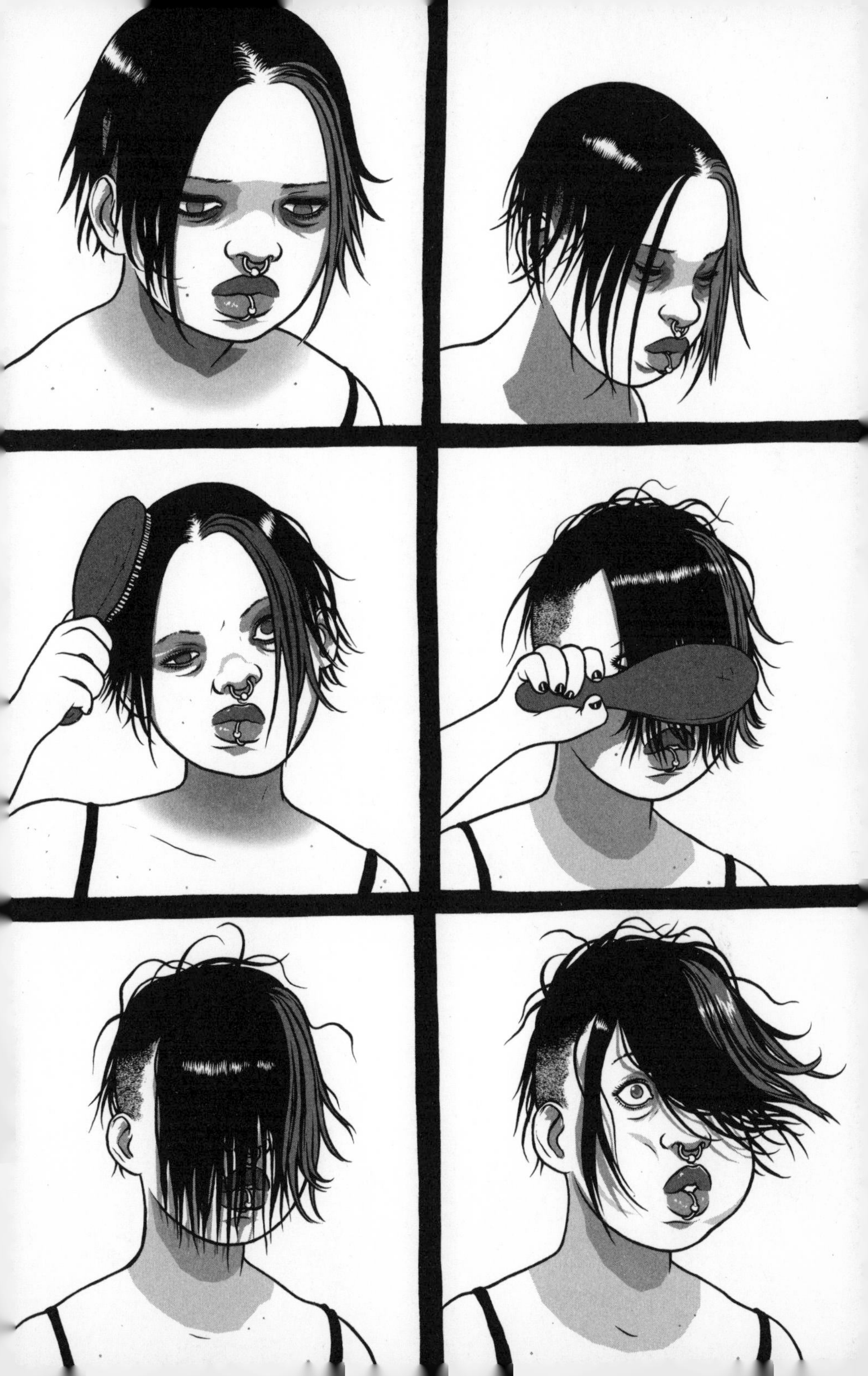

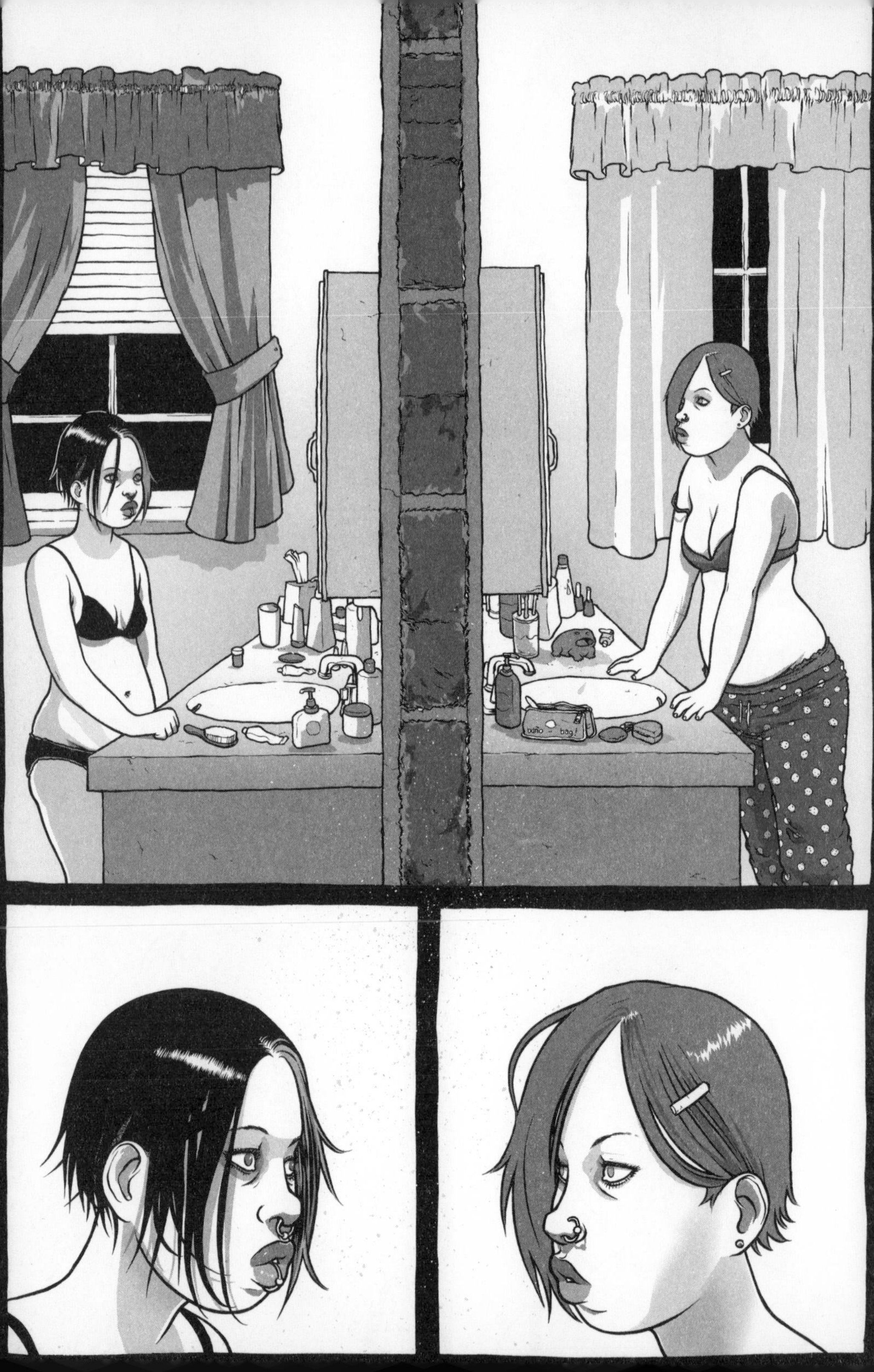
baño bag!

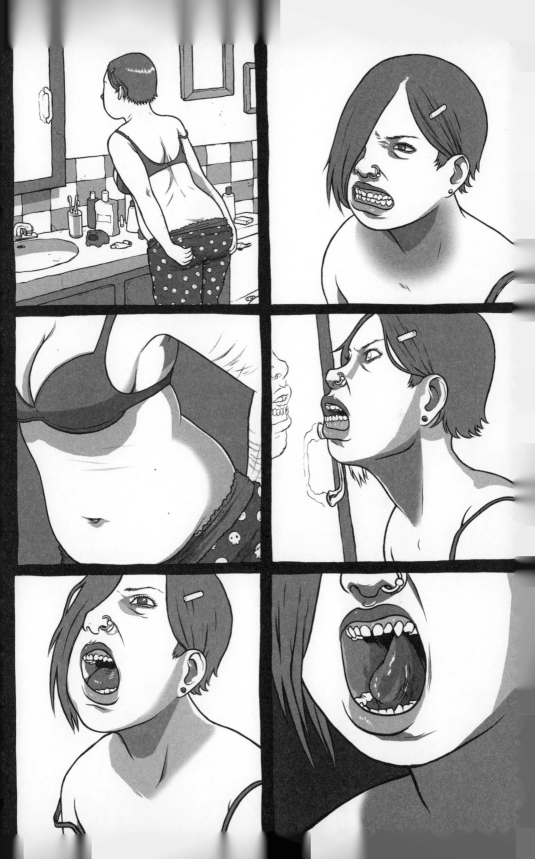

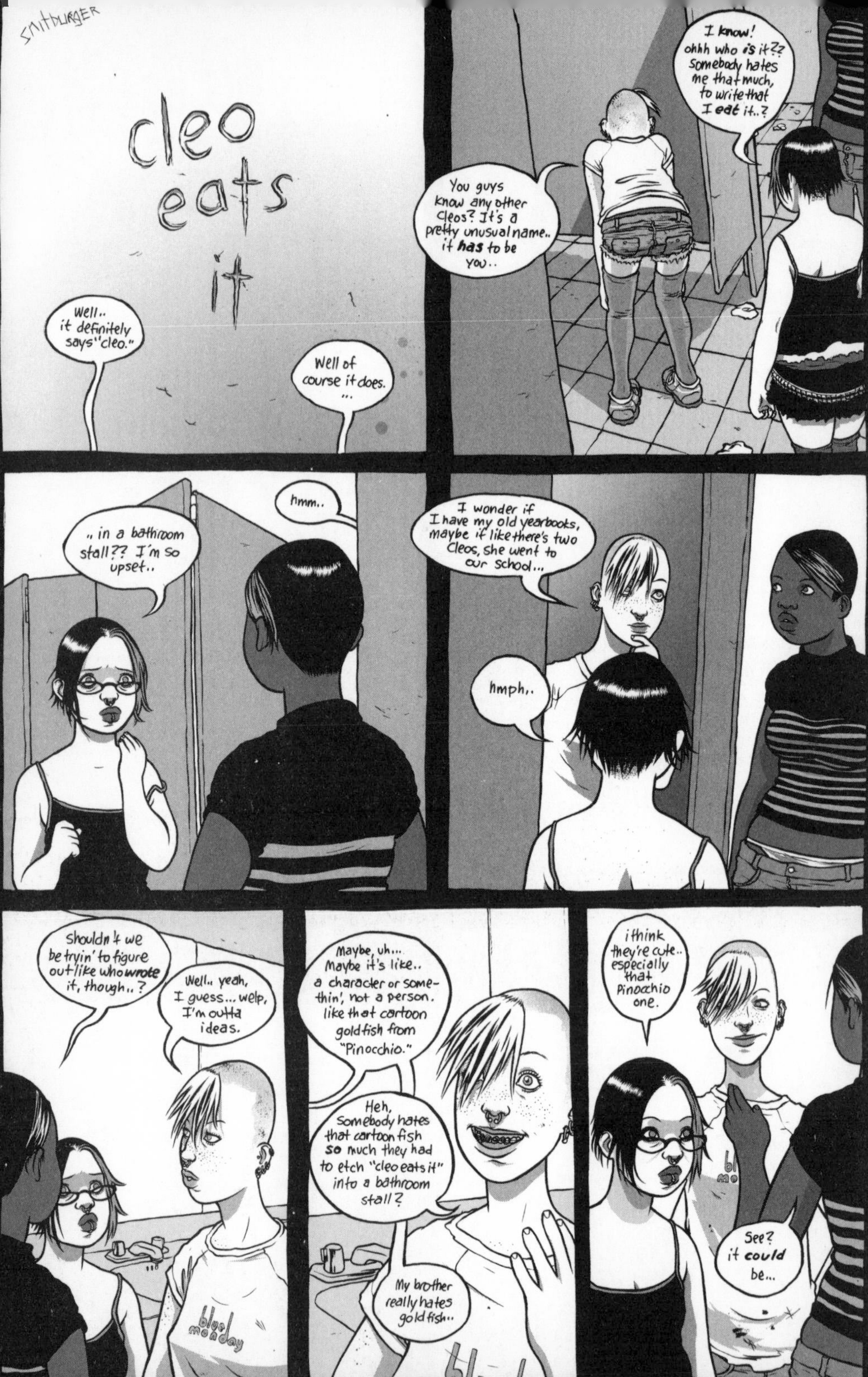
snitburger
cleo eats it
Well.. it definitely says "cleo."
Well of course it does. ...
You guys know any other Cleos? It's a pretty unusual name.. it has to be you..
I know! ohhh who is it?? Somebody hates me that much, to write that I eat it..?
.. in a bathroom stall?? I'm so upset..
hmm..
I wonder if I have my old yearbooks, maybe if like there's two Cleos, she went to our school...
hmph..
Shouldn't we be tryin' to figure out like who wrote it, though..?
Well.. yeah, I guess... welp, I'm outta ideas.
blue monday
Maybe, uh... Maybe it's like.. a character or somethin', not a person. like that cartoon goldfish from "Pinocchio."
Heh, Somebody hates that cartoon fish so much they had to etch "cleo eats it" into a bathroom stall?
My brother really hates goldfish..
i think they're cute.. especially that Pinocchio one.
See? it could be...

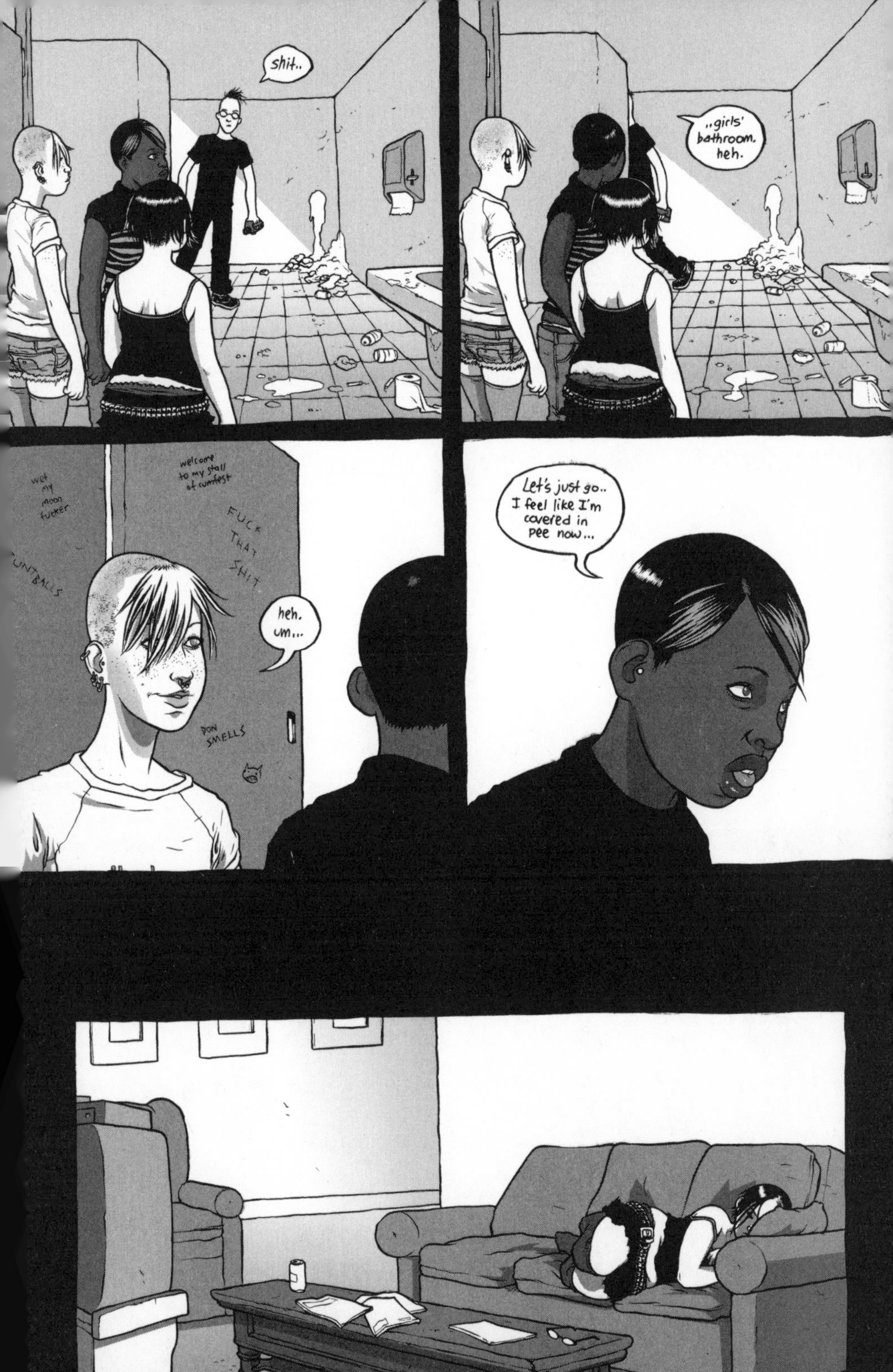
shit..
..girls' bathroom. heh.
welcome to my stall of cumfest
FUCK THAT SHIT
heh. um...
DON SMELLS
Let's just go.. I feel like I'm covered in pee now...

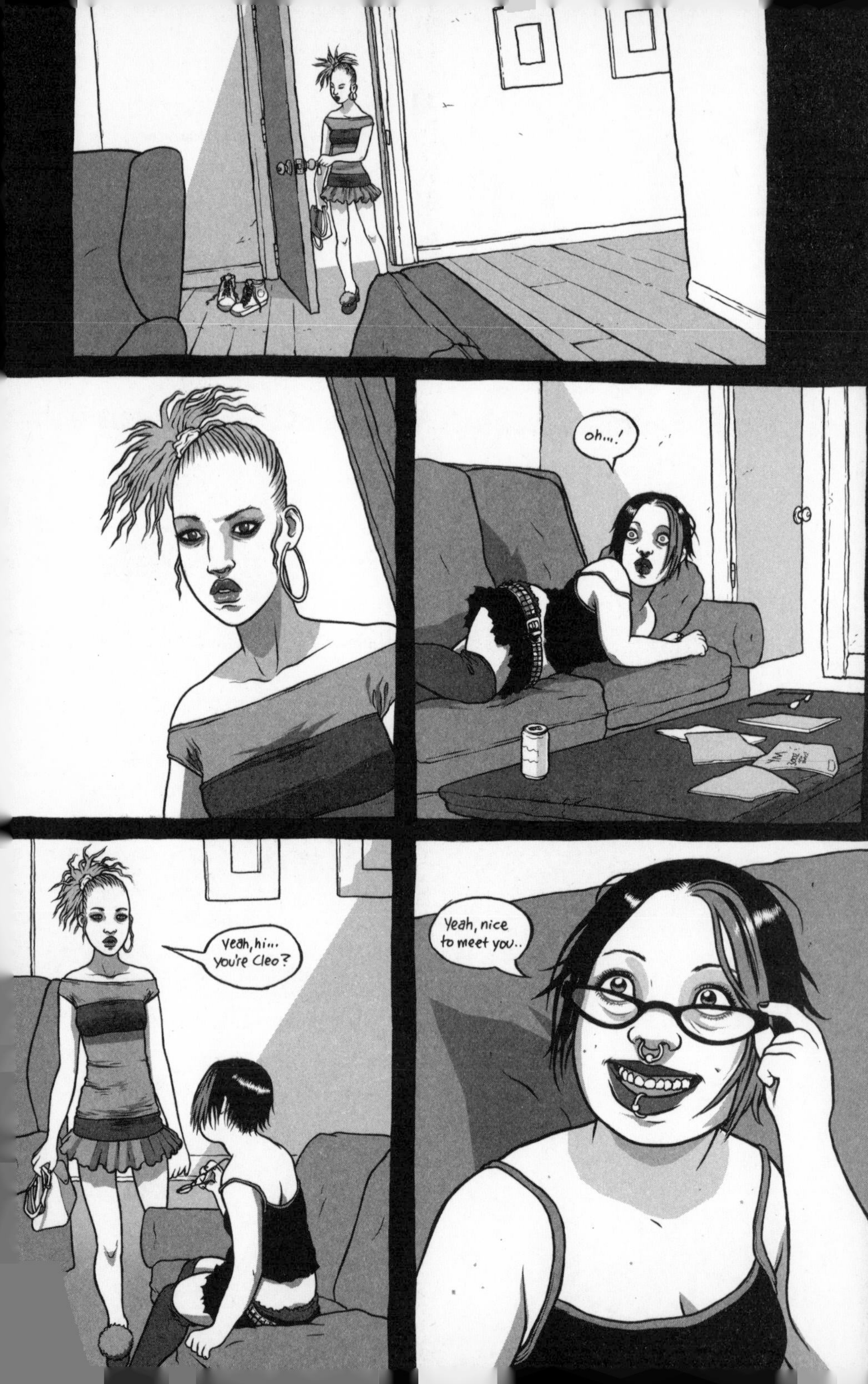
oh...!
Yeah, hi... you're Cleo?
Yeah, nice to meet you..

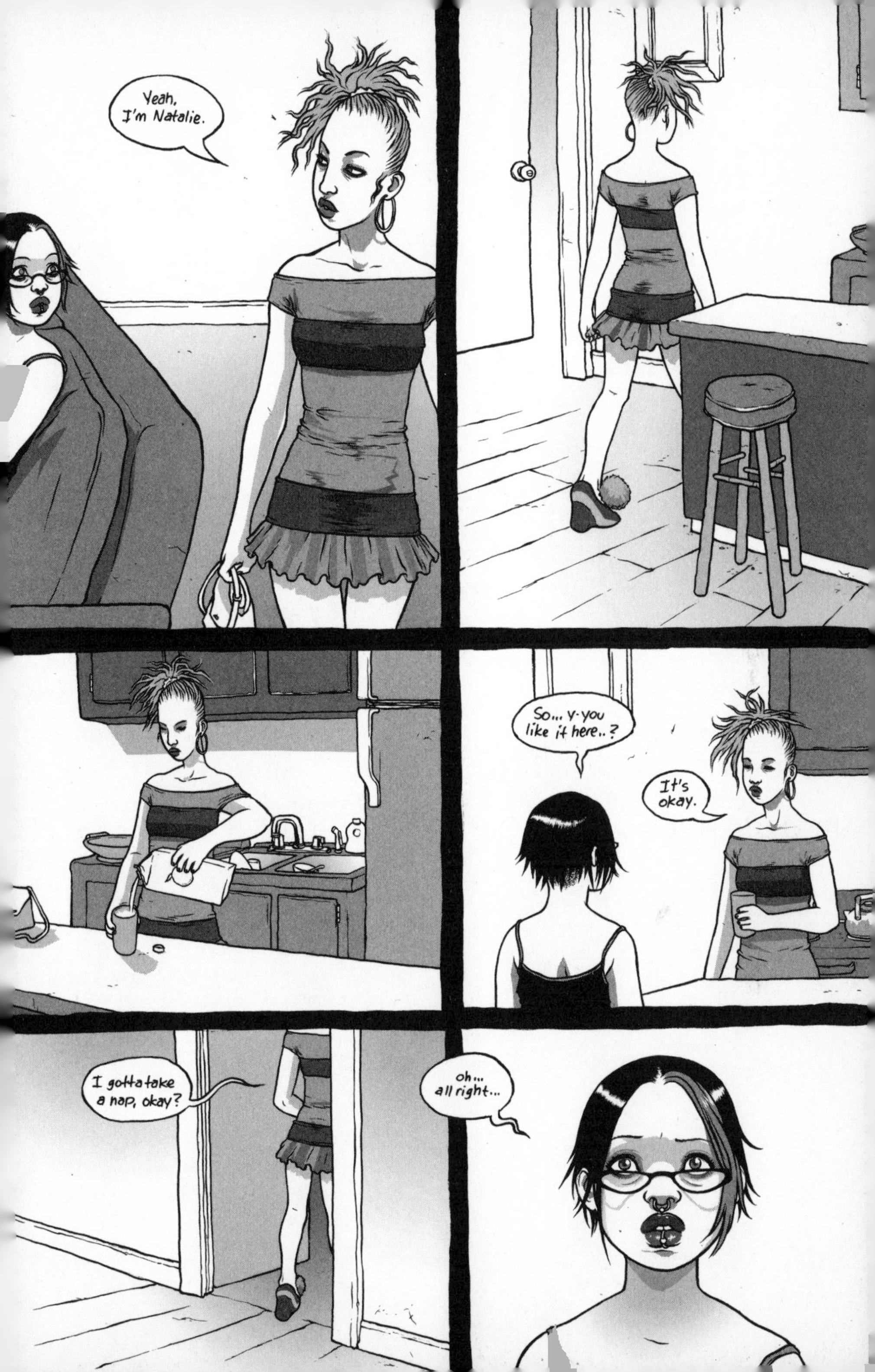
Yeah, I'm Natalie.
So... y-you like it here..?
It's okay.
I gotta take a nap, okay?
oh... all right...

"Strange, the reasons that we met
Stranger now the ending rests
In a place where fires burn forever more."

-Bella Morte

2

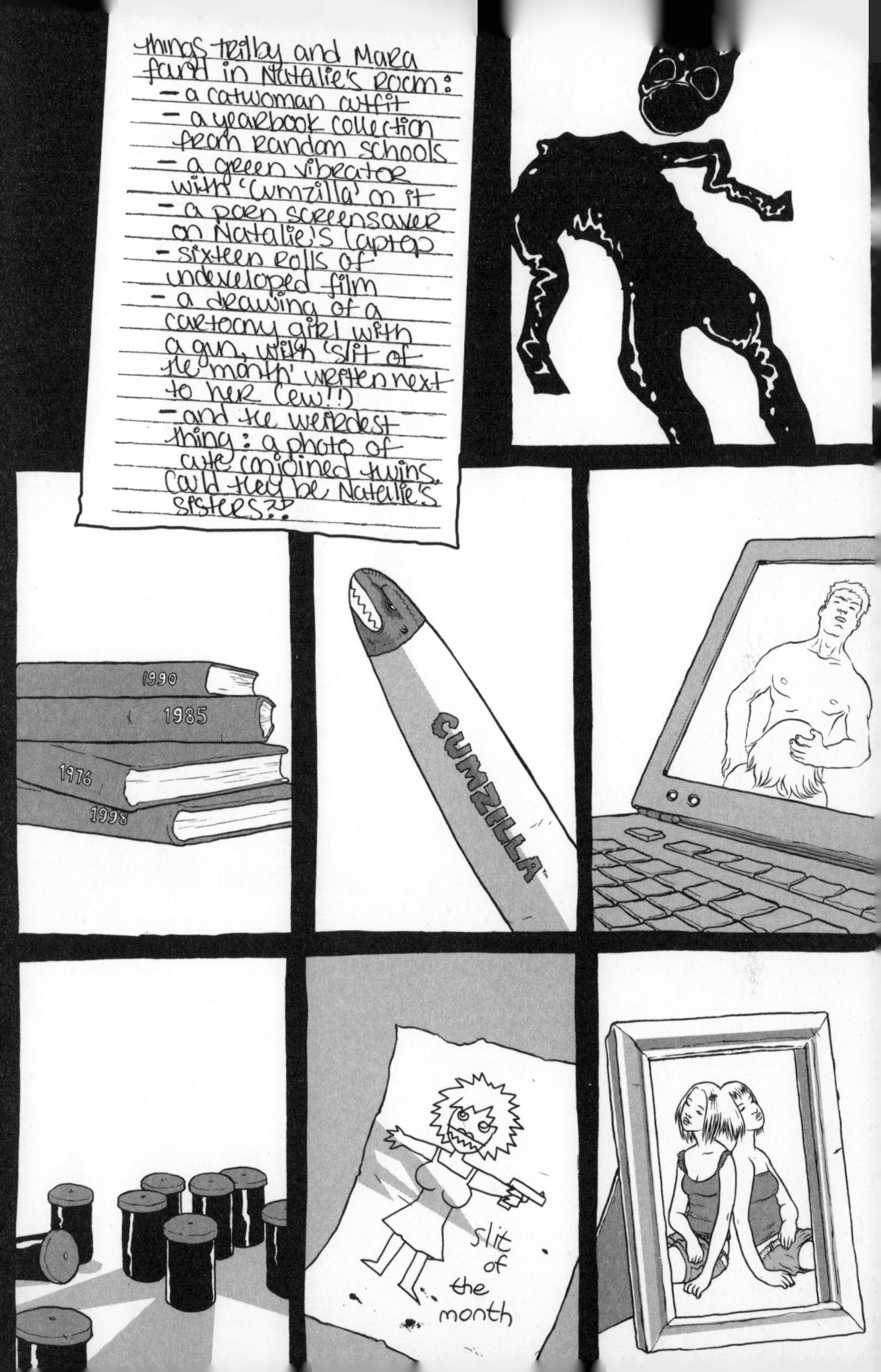
things Trilby and Mara found in Natalie's room:
– a catwoman outfit
– a yearbook collection from random schools
– a green vibrator with 'Cumzilla' on it
– a porn screensaver on Natalie's laptop
– sixteen rolls of undeveloped film
– a drawing of a cartoony girl with a gun, with 'slit of the month' written next to her (ew!!)
– and the weirdest thing: a photo of cute conjoined twins. Could they be Natalie's sisters?!
1990
1985
1976
1998
CUMZILLA™
slit of the month

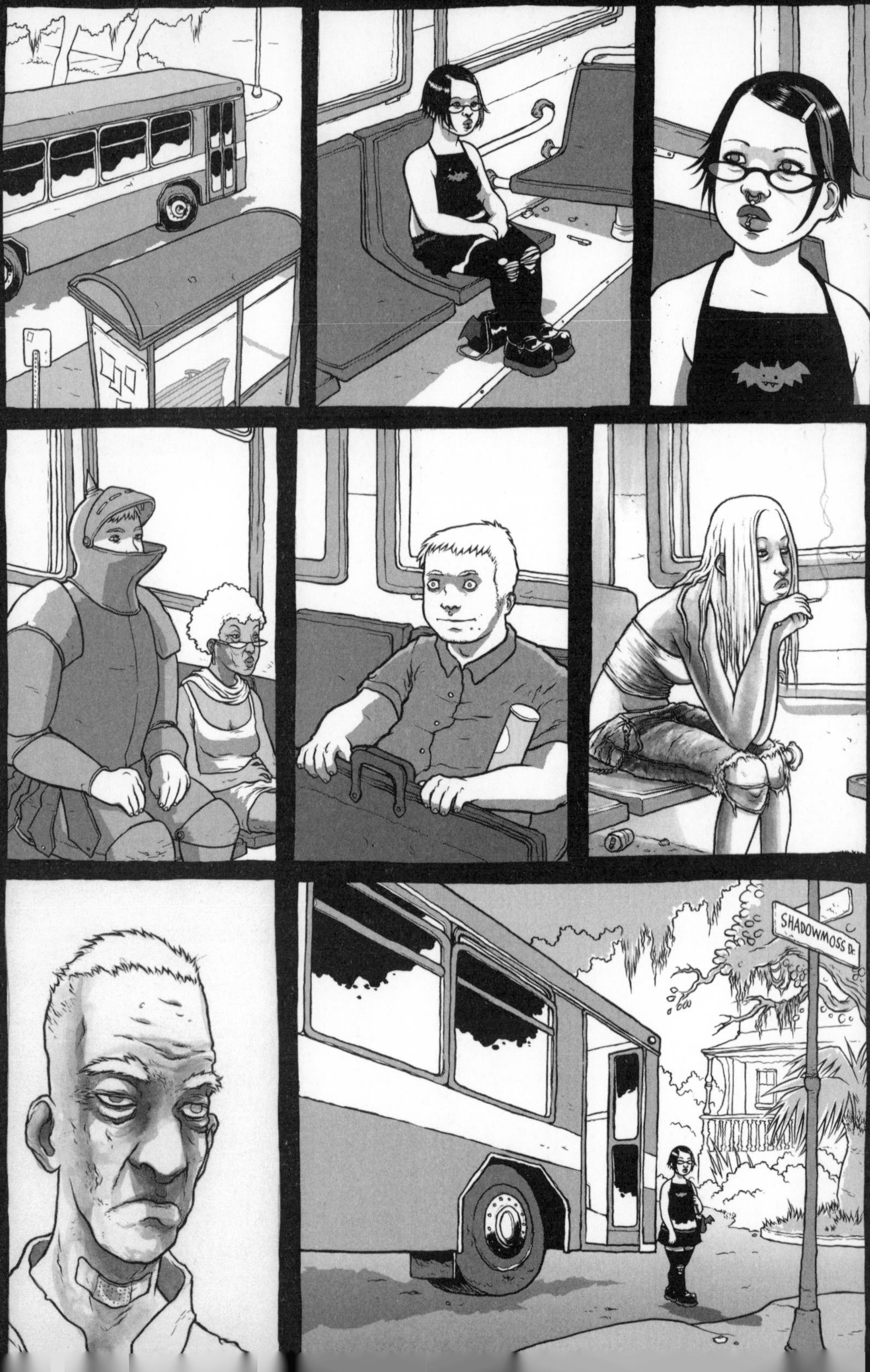
SHADOWMOSS Dr.

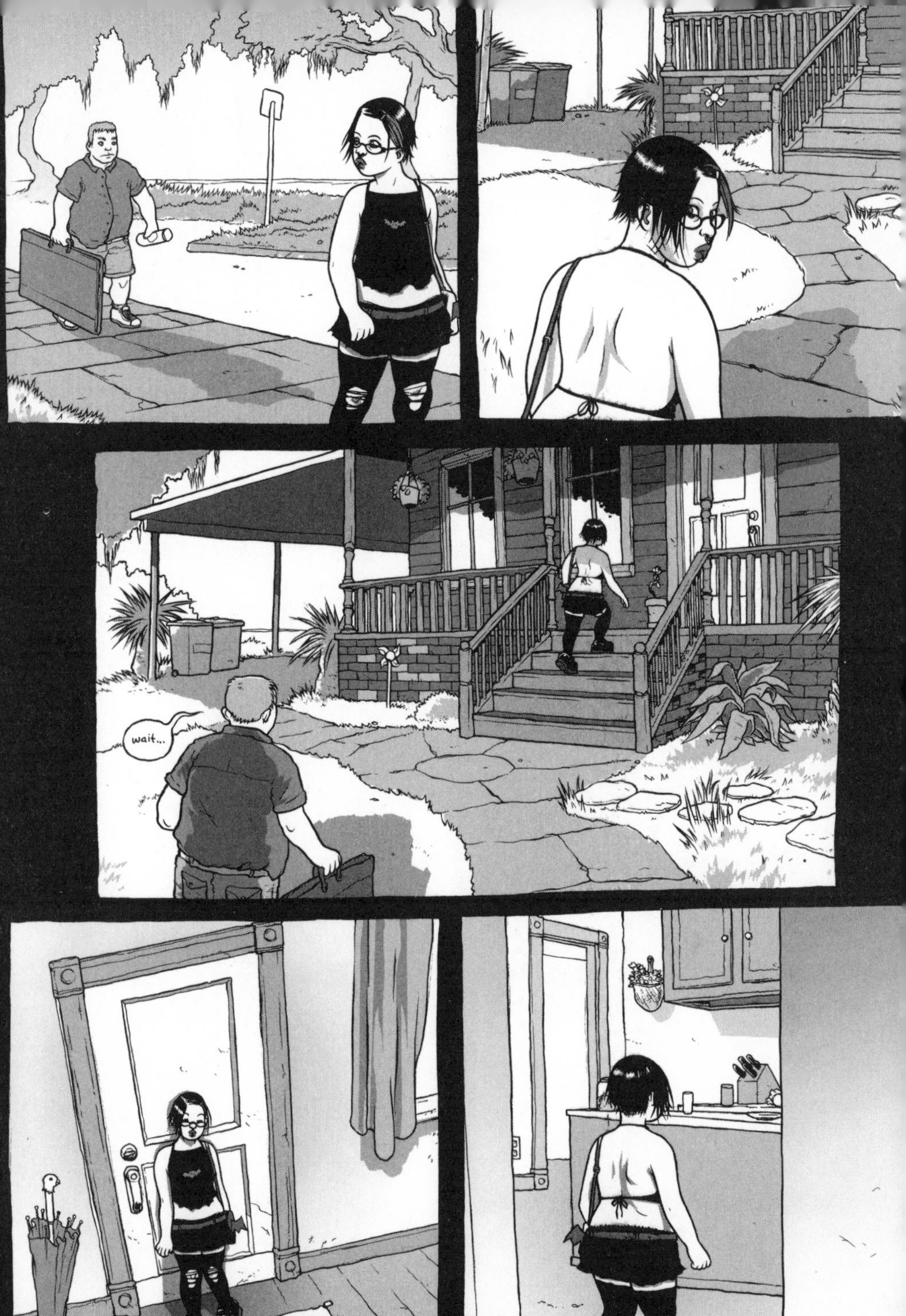
wait...

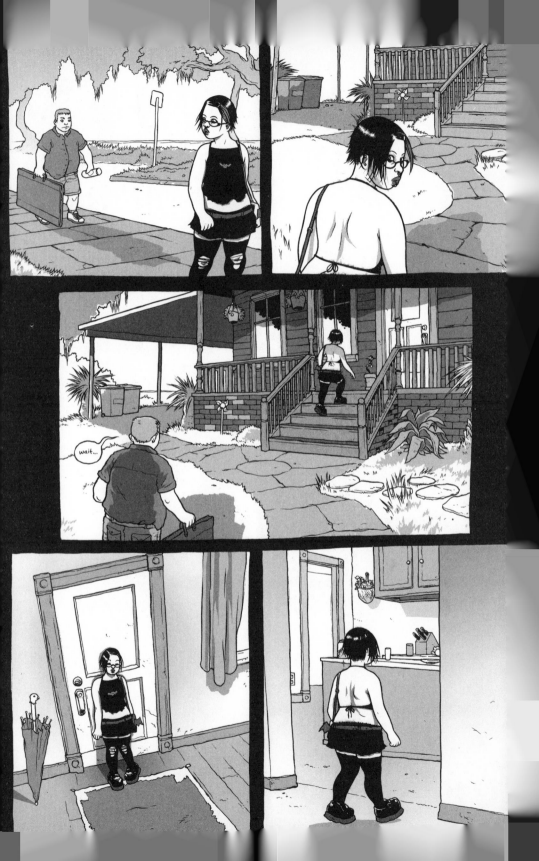

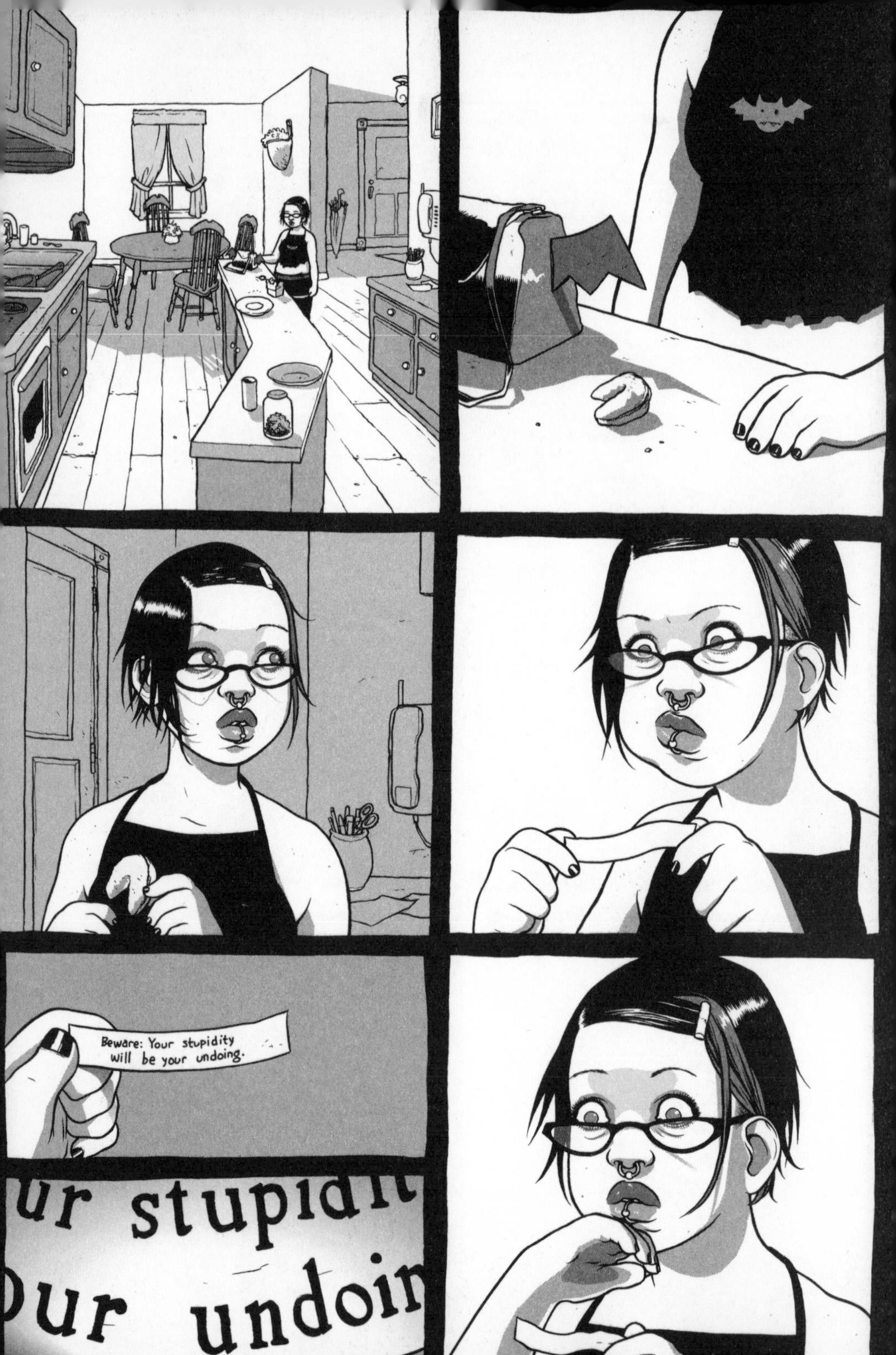
Beware: Your stupidity
will be your undoing.

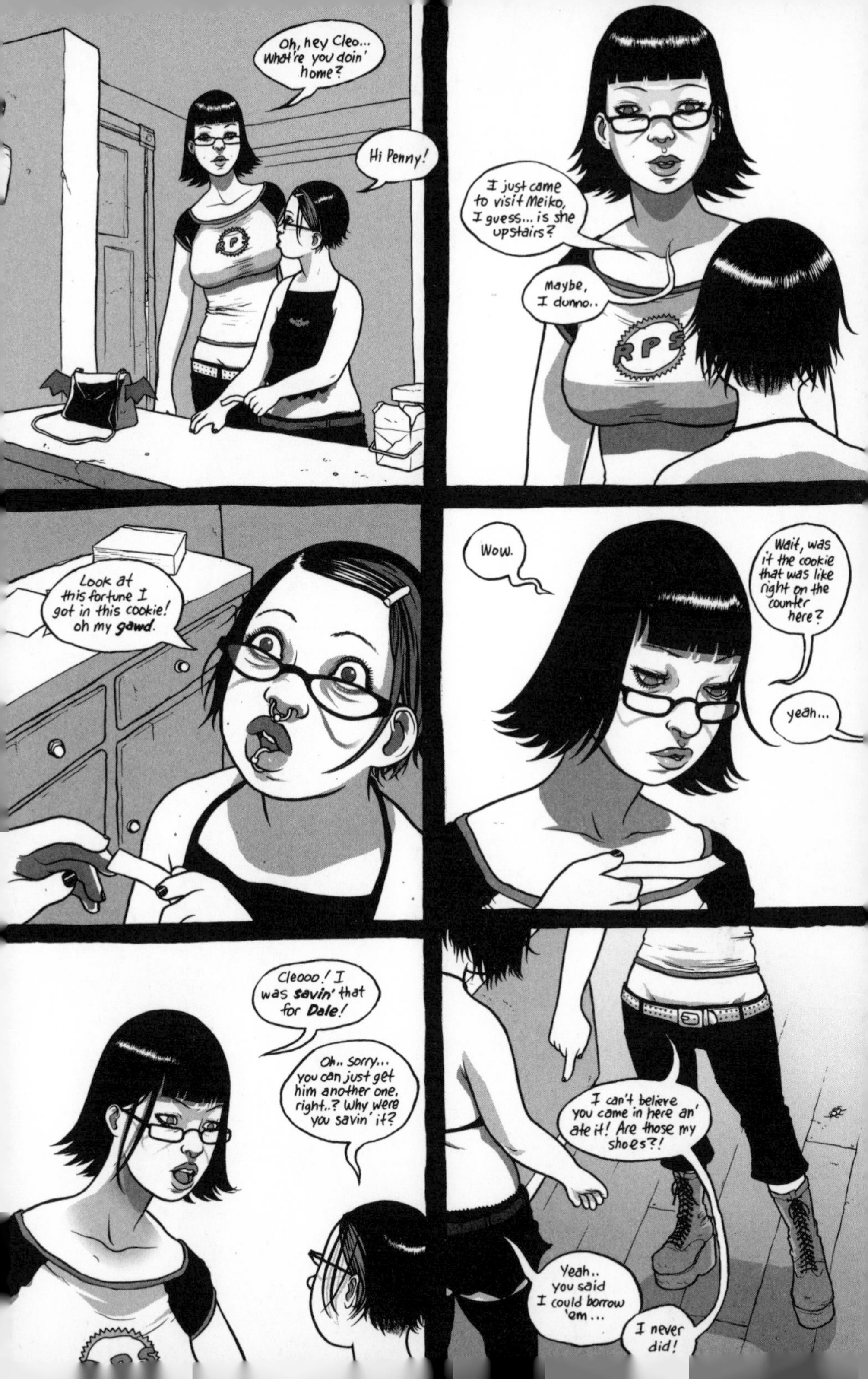

Oh, hey Cleo... What're you doin' home?
Hi Penny!
I just came to visit Meiko, I guess... is she upstairs?
Maybe, I dunno..
Look at this fortune I got in this cookie! oh my **gawd**.
Wow.
Wait, was it the cookie that was like right on the counter here?
yeah...
Cleooo! I was **savin'** that for **Dale**!
Oh.. sorry... you can just get him another one, right..? Why were you savin' it?
I can't believe you came in here an' ate it! Are those my shoes?!
Yeah.. you said I could borrow 'em...
I never did!

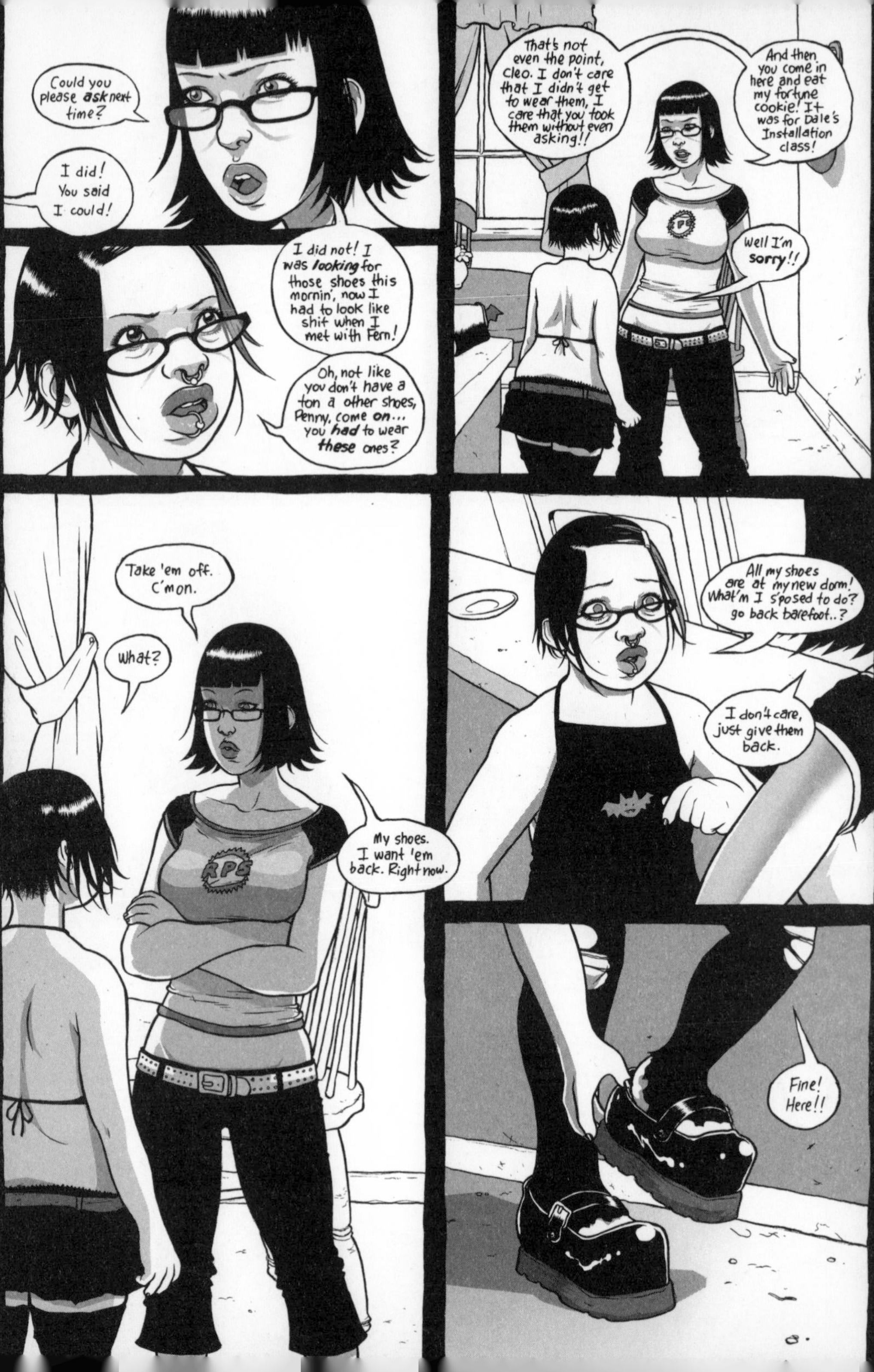

Could you please ask next time?
I did! You said I could!
I did not! I was looking for those shoes this mornin', now I had to look like shit when I met with Fern!
Oh, not like you don't have a ton a other shoes, Penny, come on... you had to wear these ones?
That's not even the point, Cleo. I don't care that I didn't get to wear them, I care that you took them without even asking!!
And then you come in here and eat my fortune cookie! It was for Dale's Installation class!
Well I'm sorry!!
Take 'em off. C'mon.
What?
My shoes. I want 'em back. Right now.
All my shoes are at my new dorm! What'm I s'posed to do? go back barefoot..?
I don't care, just give them back.
Fine! Here!!

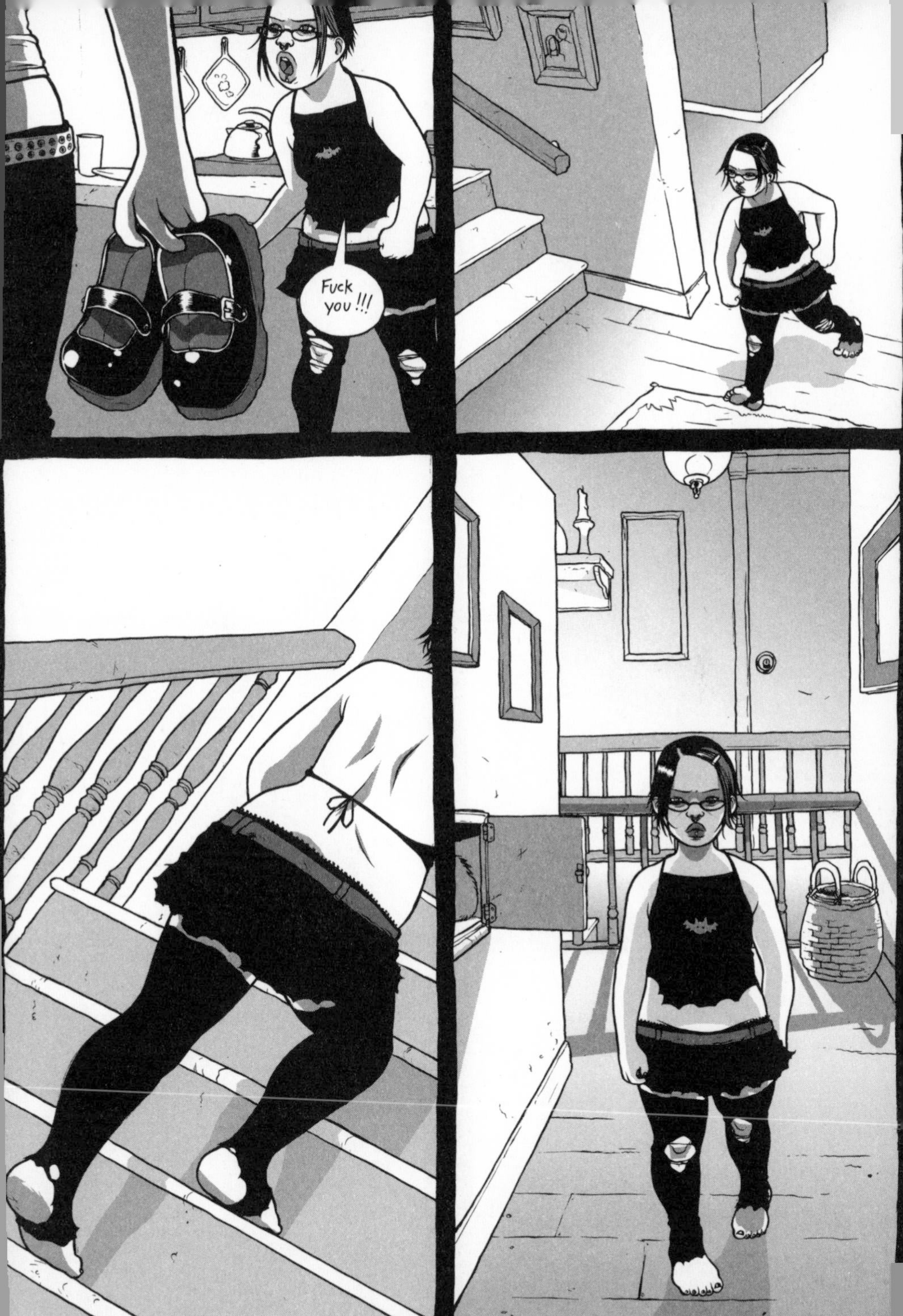
Fuck you!!!

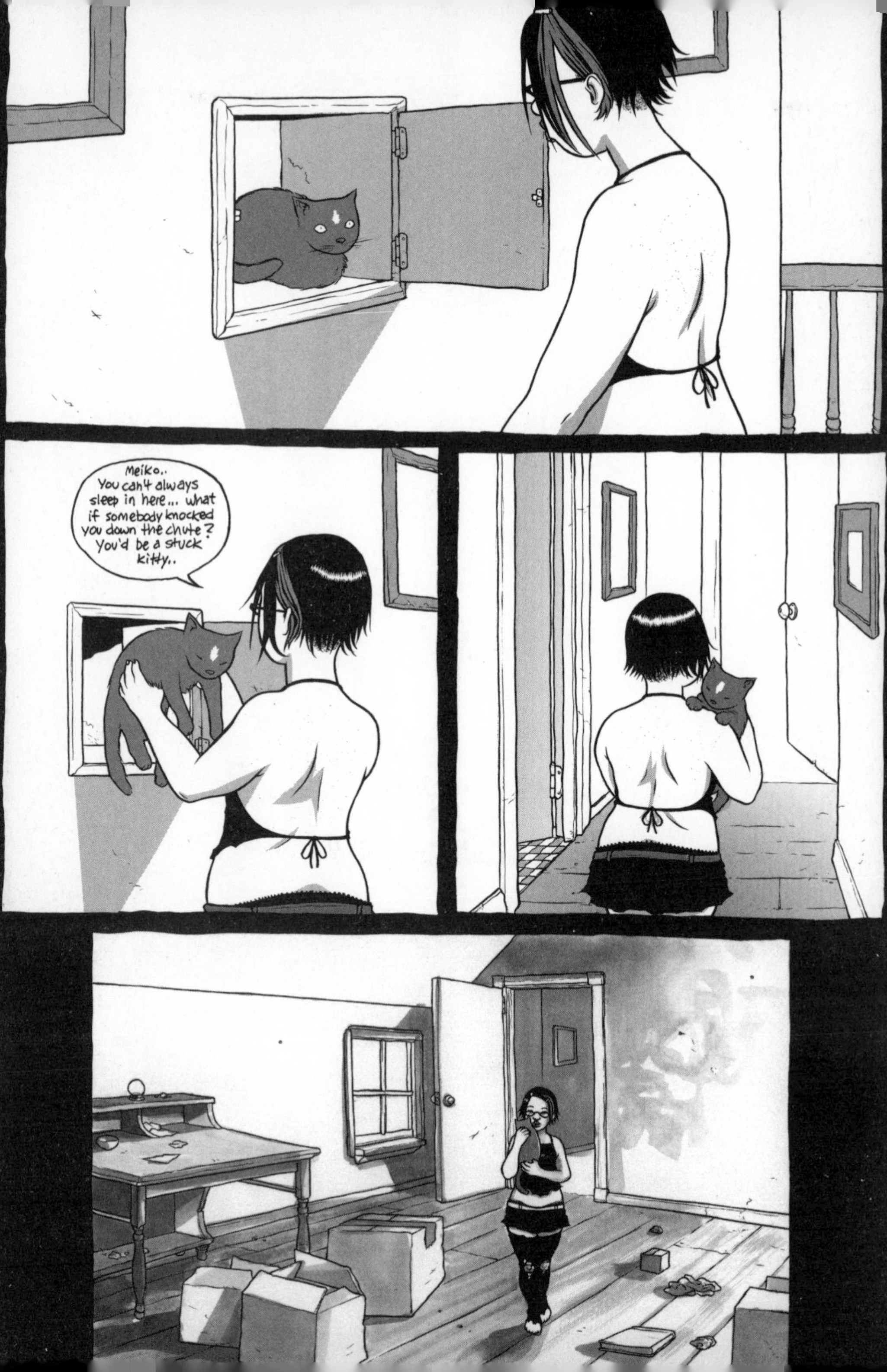
Meiko.. You can't always sleep in here... what if somebody knocked you down the chute? You'd be a stuck kitty..

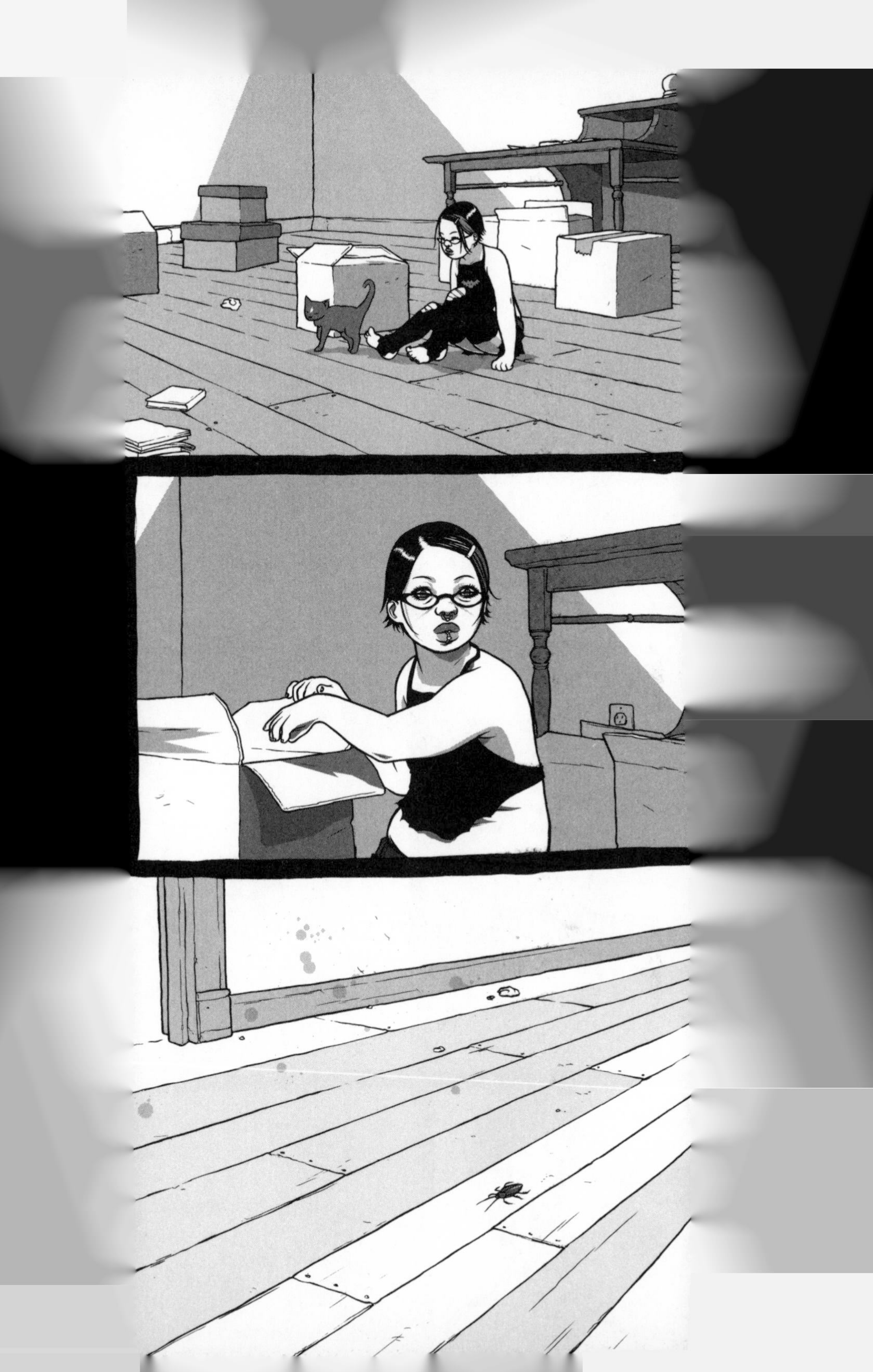

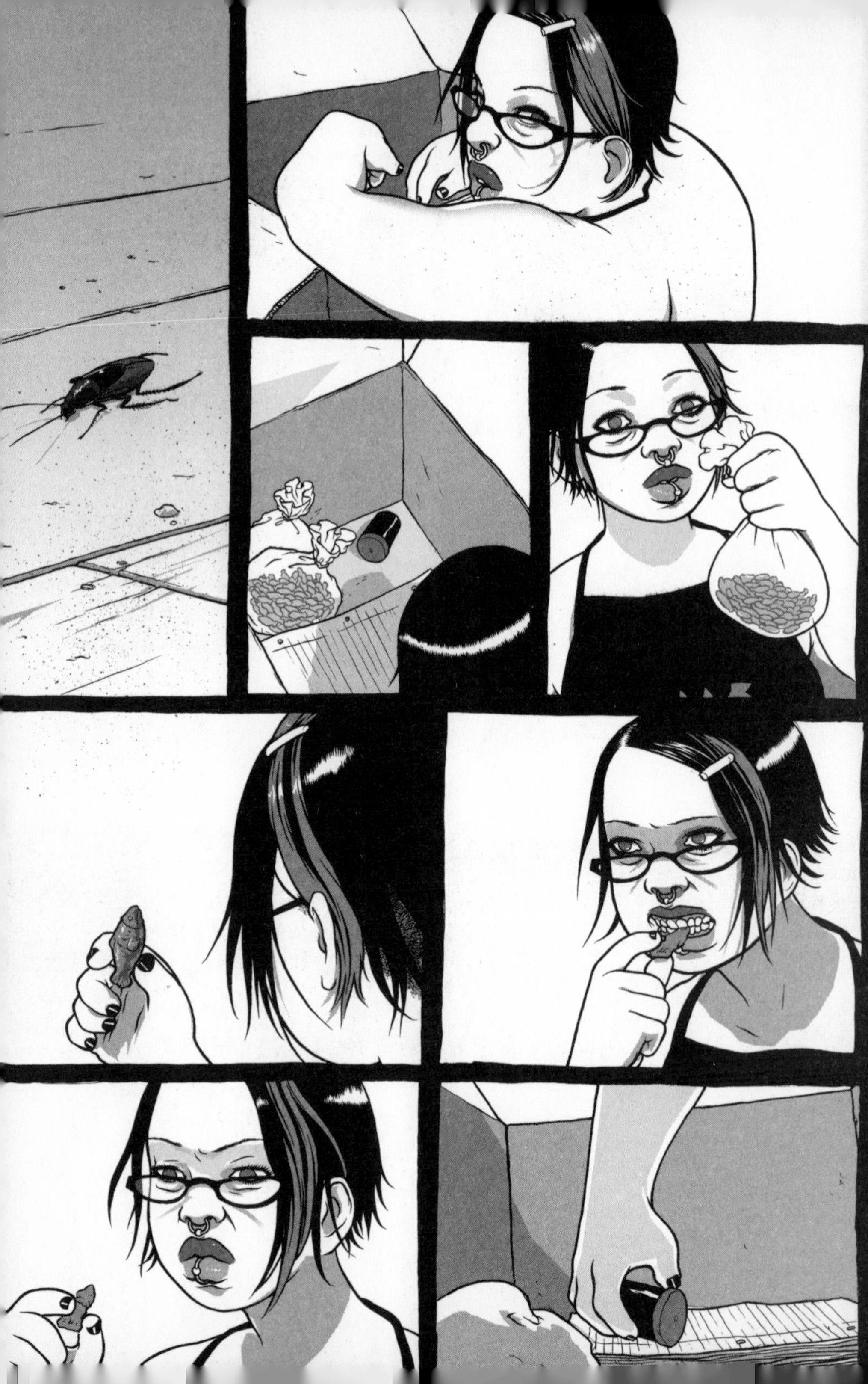

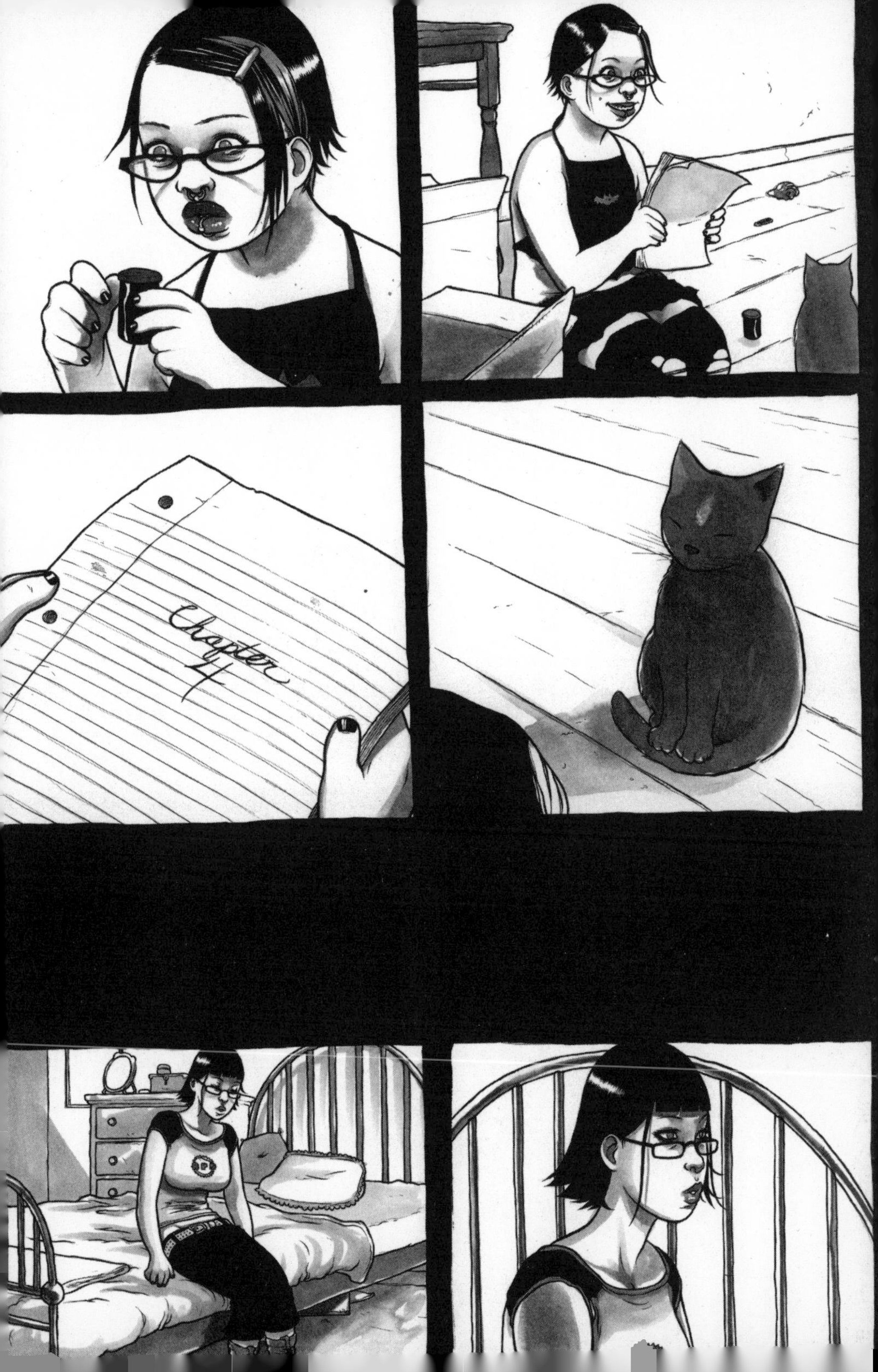
Chapter 4

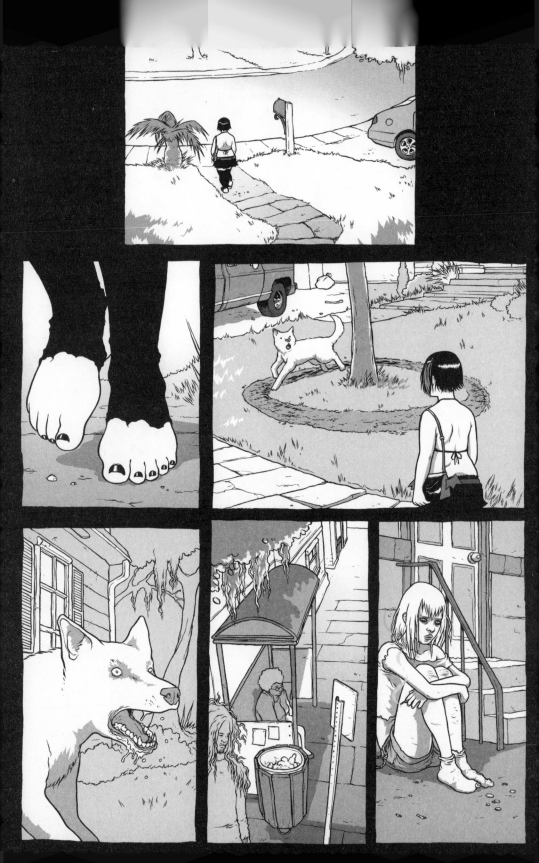

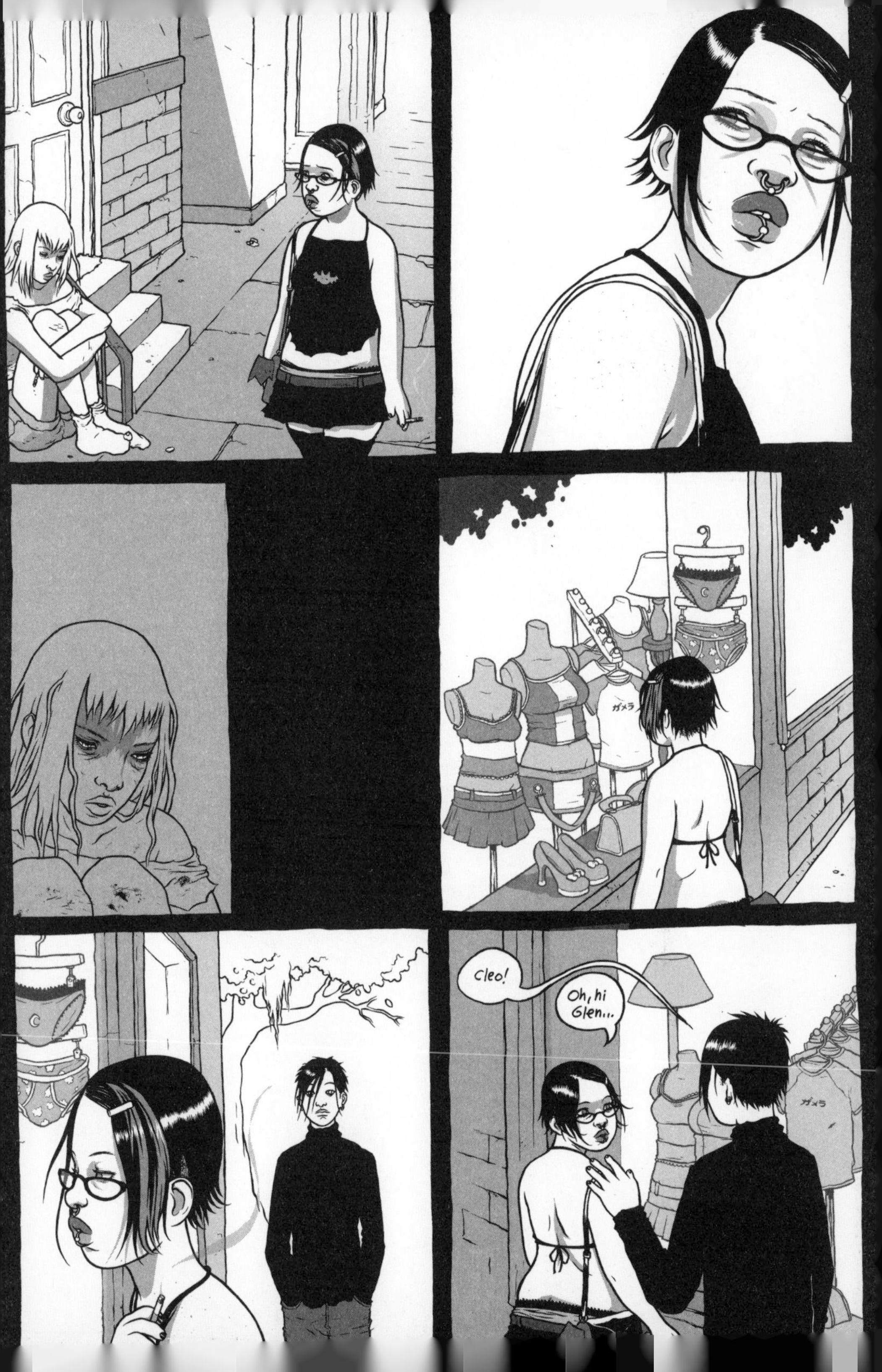
ガメラ
Cleo!
Oh, hi Glen...
ガメラ

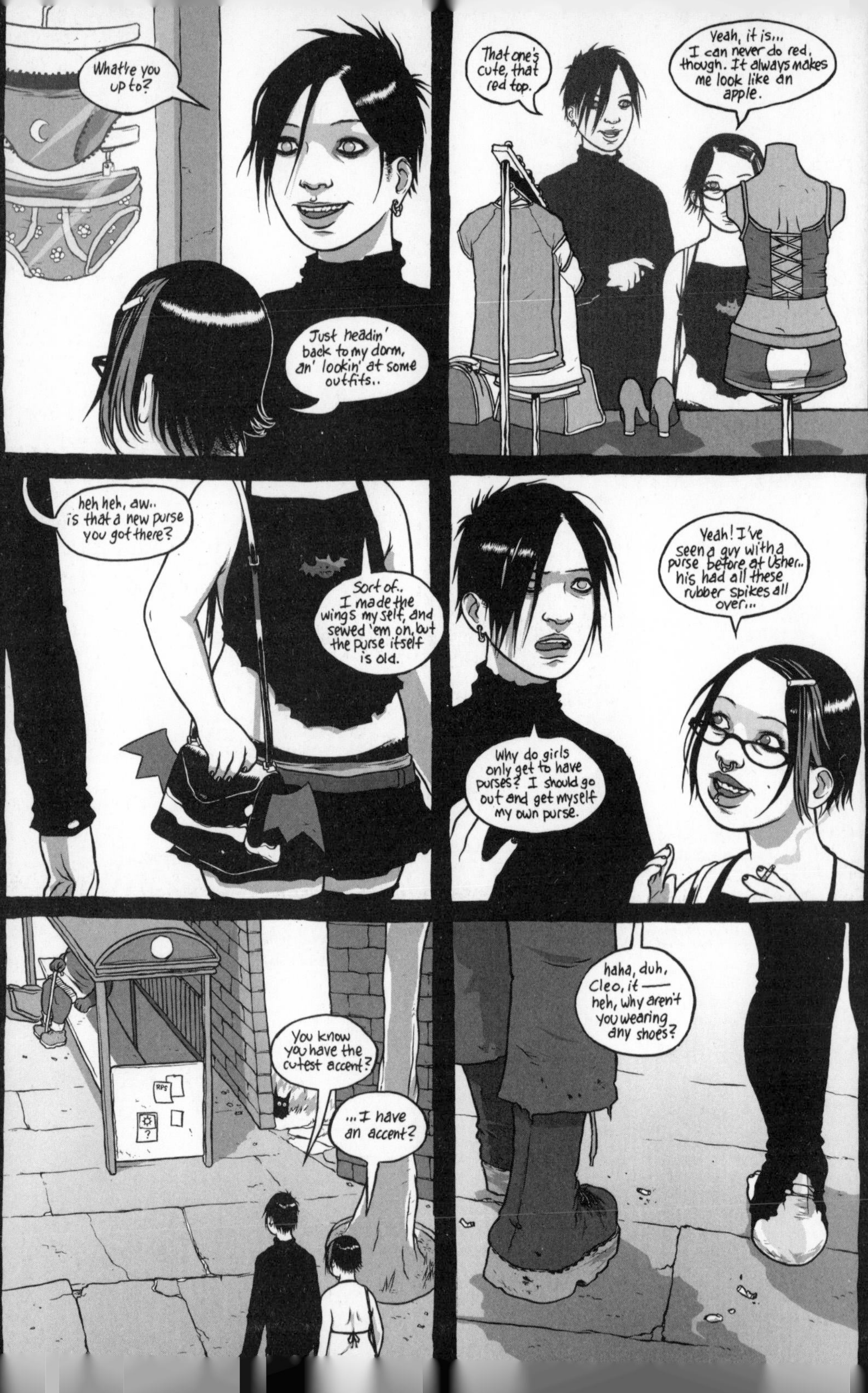
What're you up to?
Just headin' back to my dorm, an' lookin' at some outfits..
That one's cute, that red top.
Yeah, it is... I can never do red, though. It always makes me look like an apple.
heh heh, aw.. is that a new purse you got there?
Sort of.. I made the wings my self, and sewed 'em on, but the purse itself is old.
Yeah! I've seen a guy with a purse before at Usher.. his had all these rubber spikes all over...
Why do girls only get to have purses? I should go out and get myself my own purse.
You know you have the cutest accent?
...I have an accent?
haha, duh, Cleo, it— heh, why aren't you wearing any shoes?

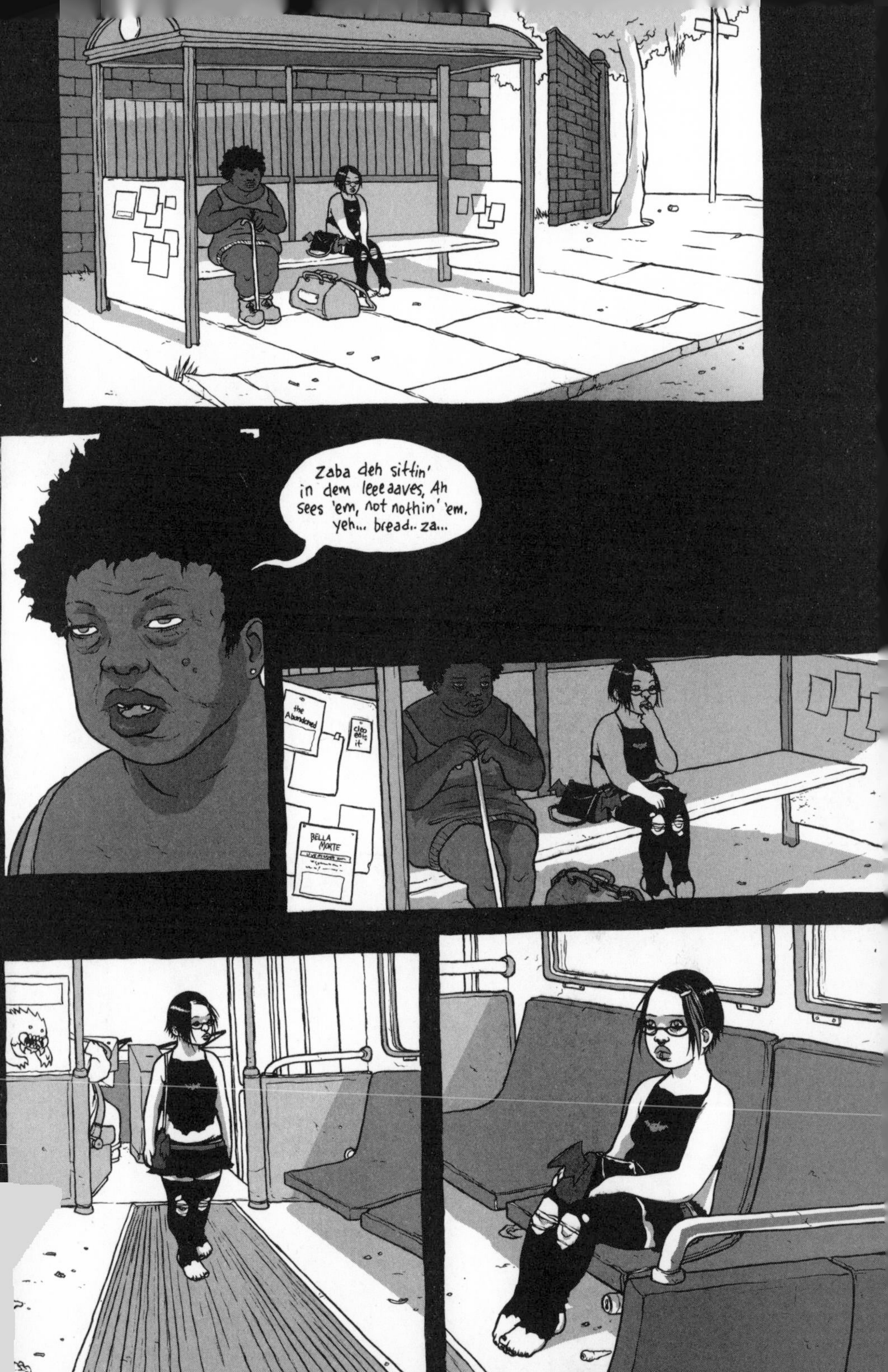
Zaba deh sittin' in dem leeeaaves, Ah sees 'em, not nothin' 'em. yeh... bread.. za...
the Abandoned
cleo eats it
BELLA MORTE

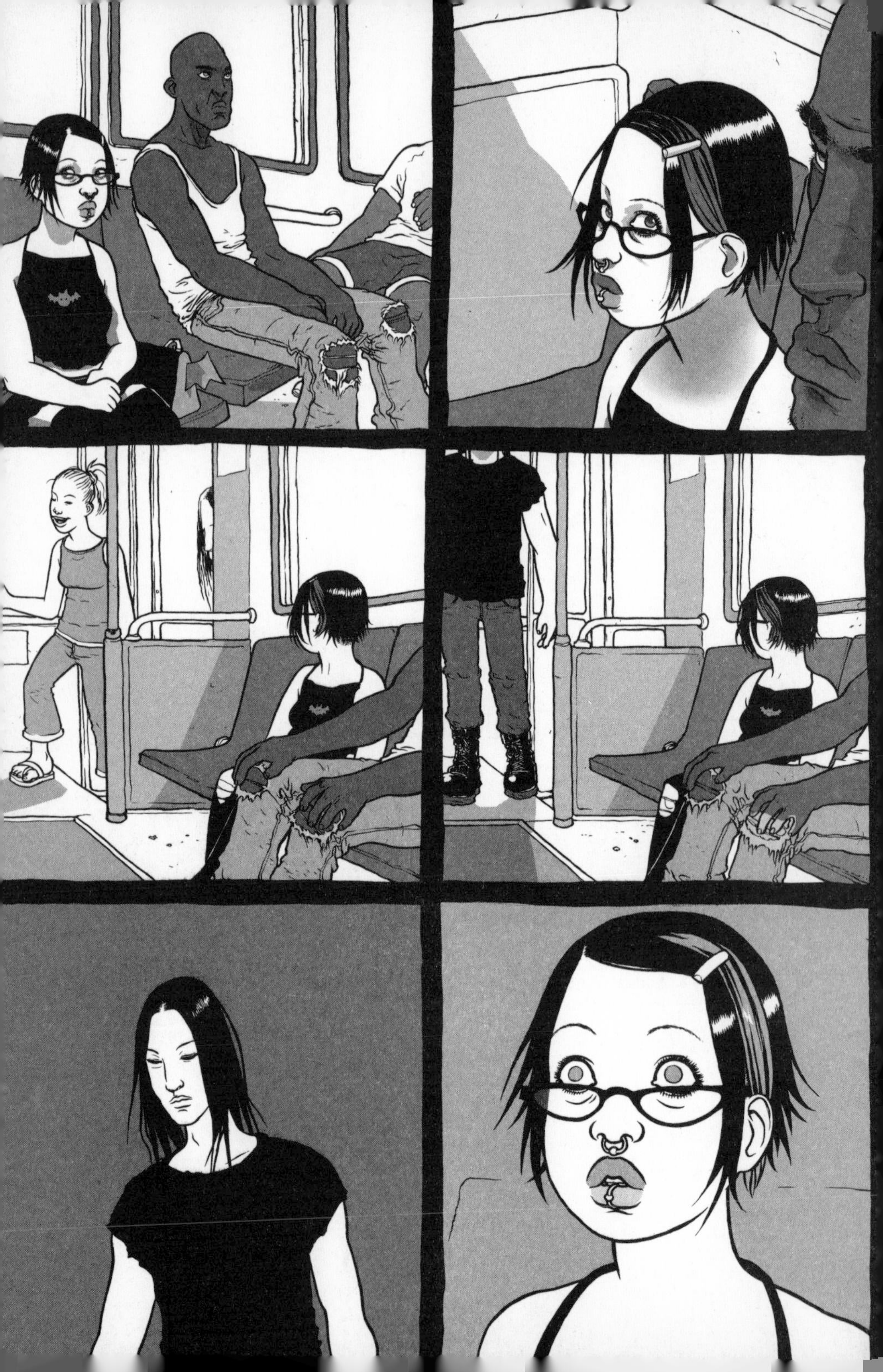

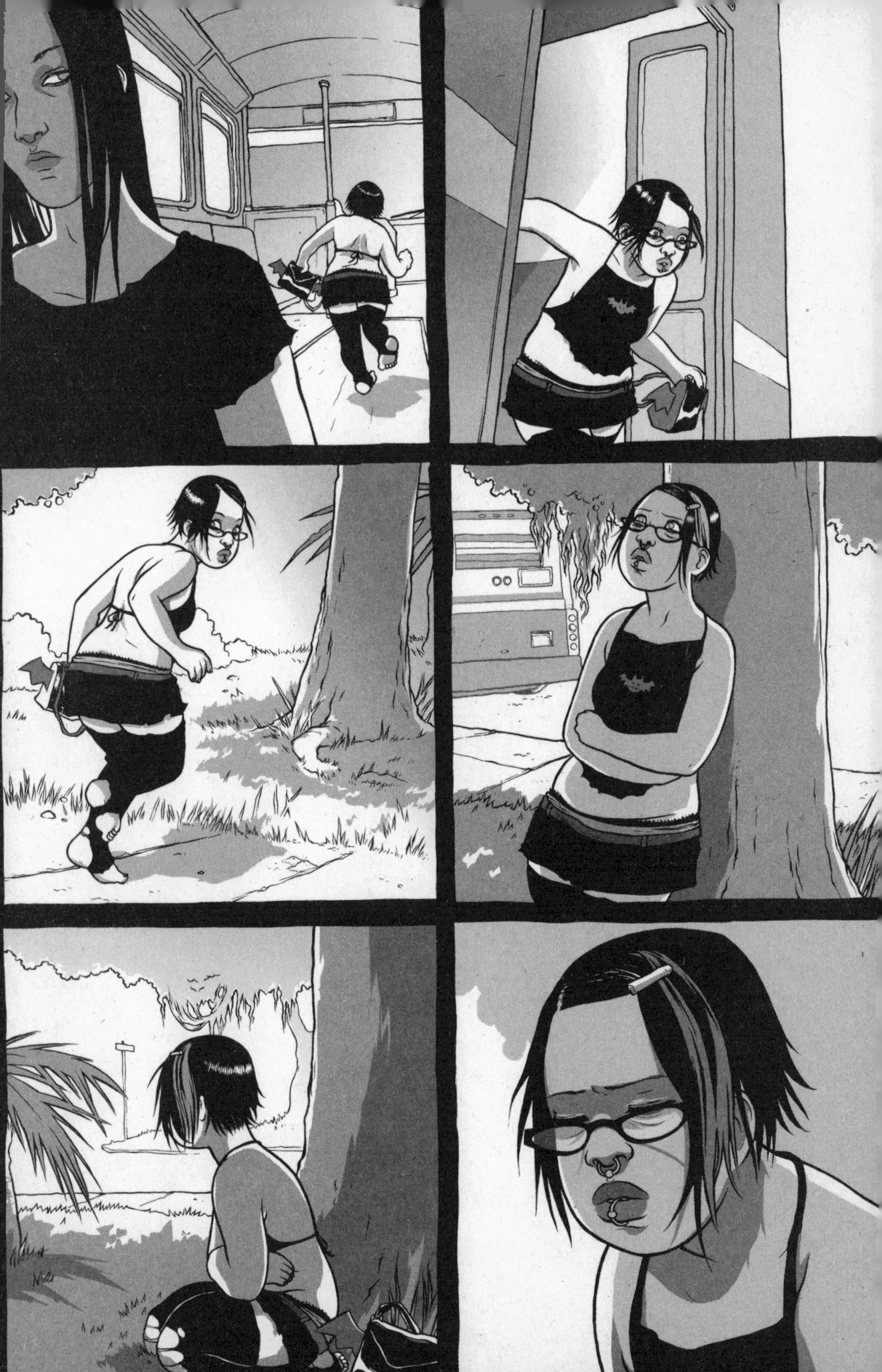

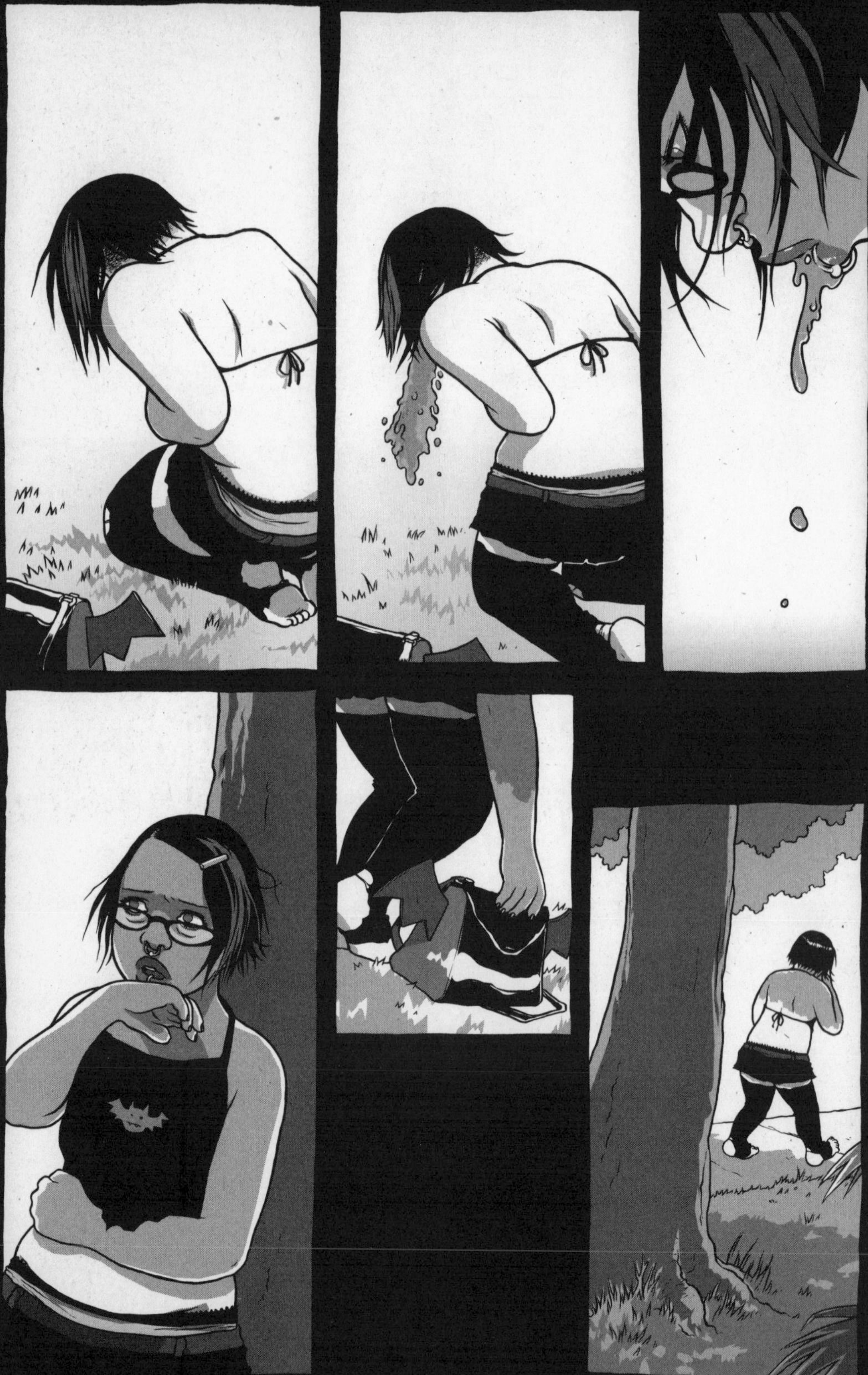

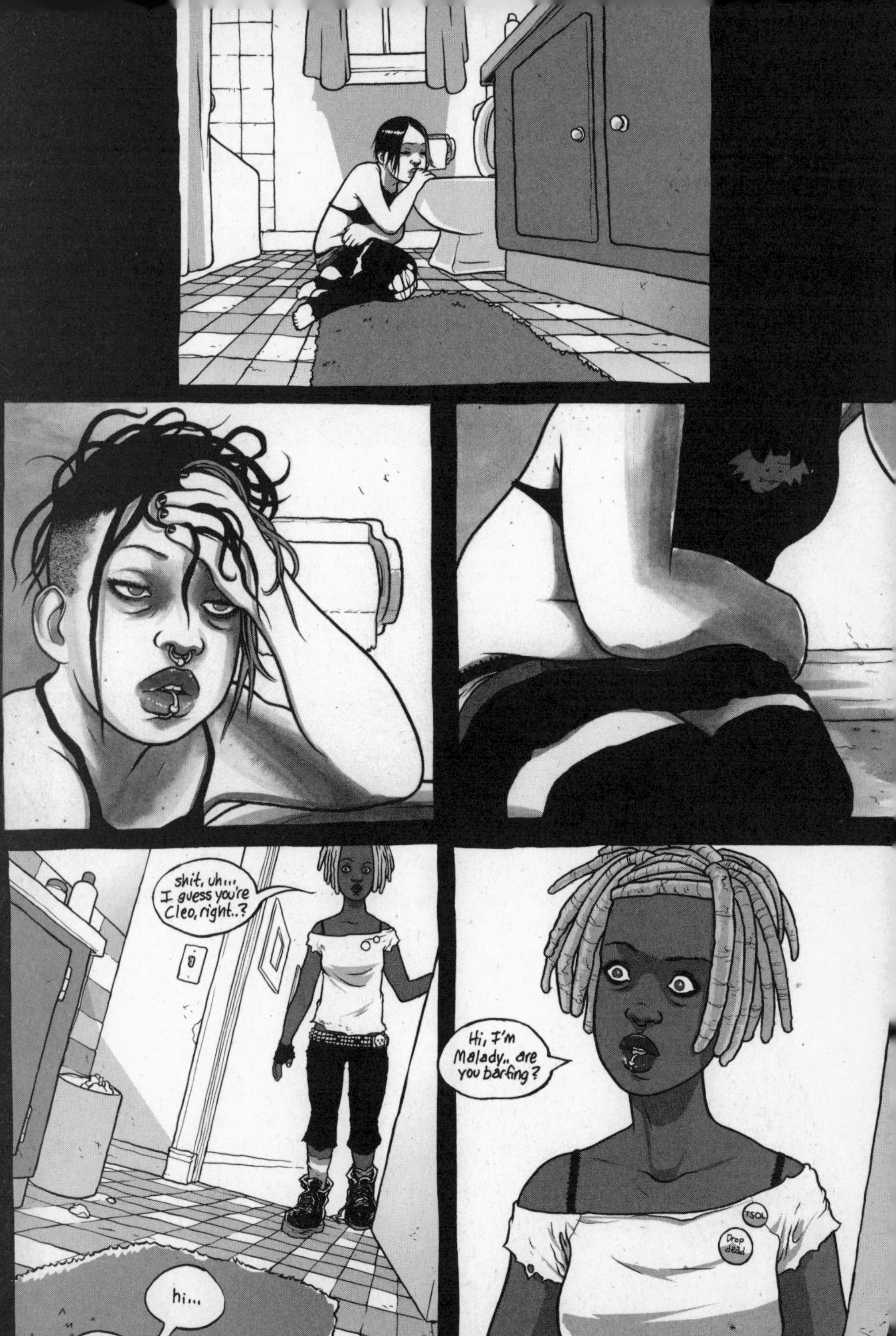
shit, uh... I guess you're Cleo, right..?
hi...
Hi, I'm Malady.. are you barfing?
TSOL
Drop dead

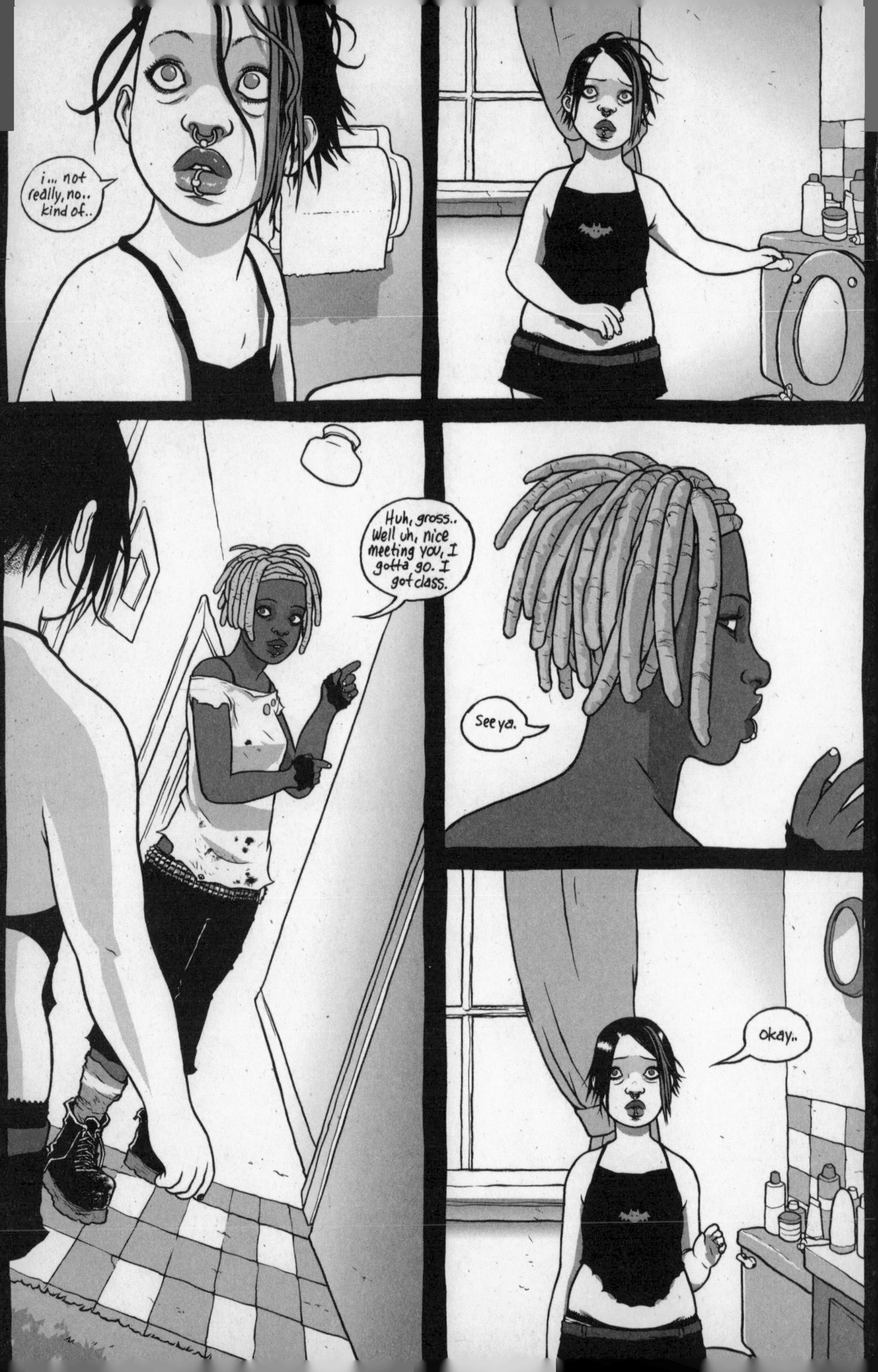
i... not really, no.. kind of..
Huh, gross.. Well uh, nice meeting you, I gotta go. I got class.
See ya.
okay..

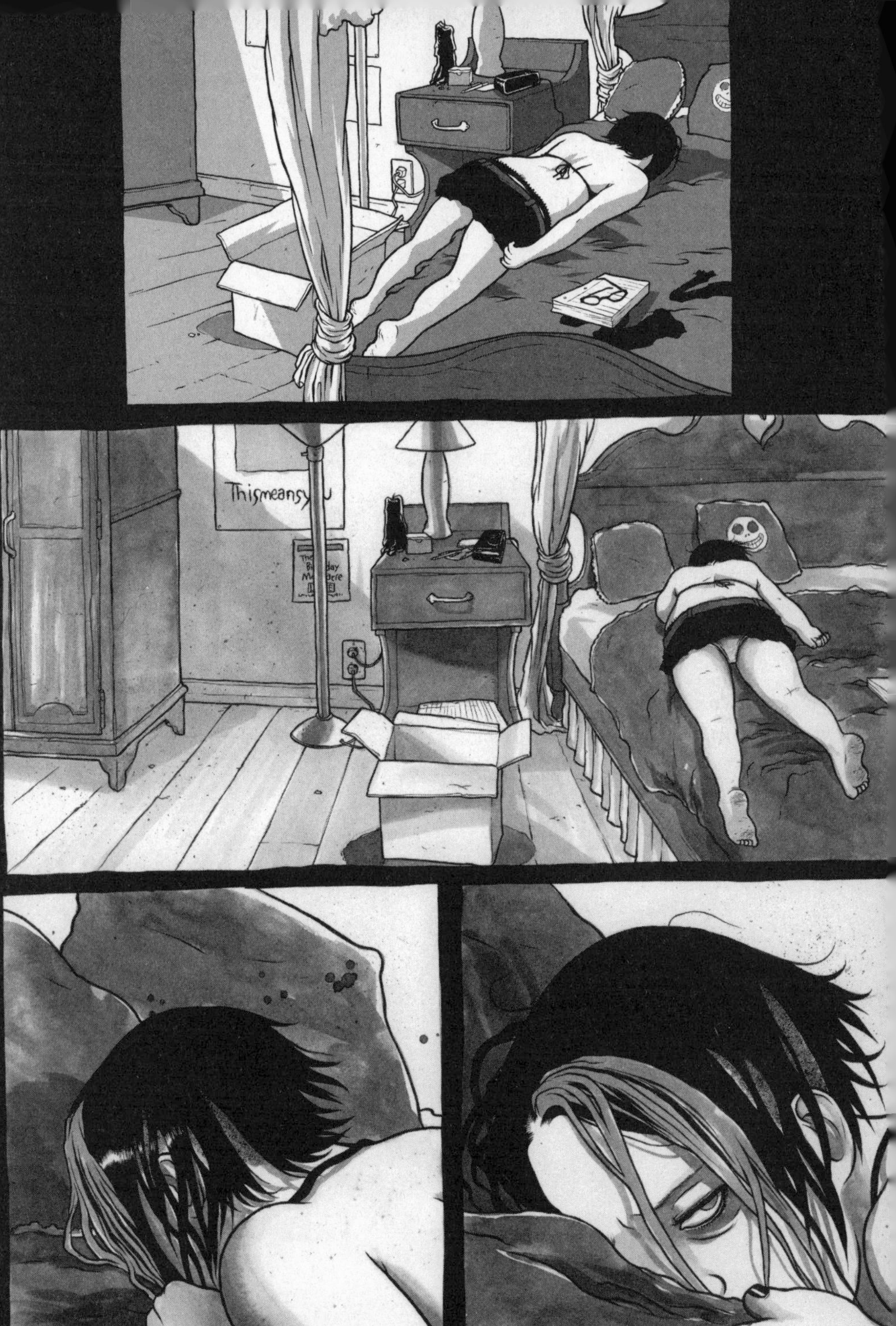
Thismeansy u

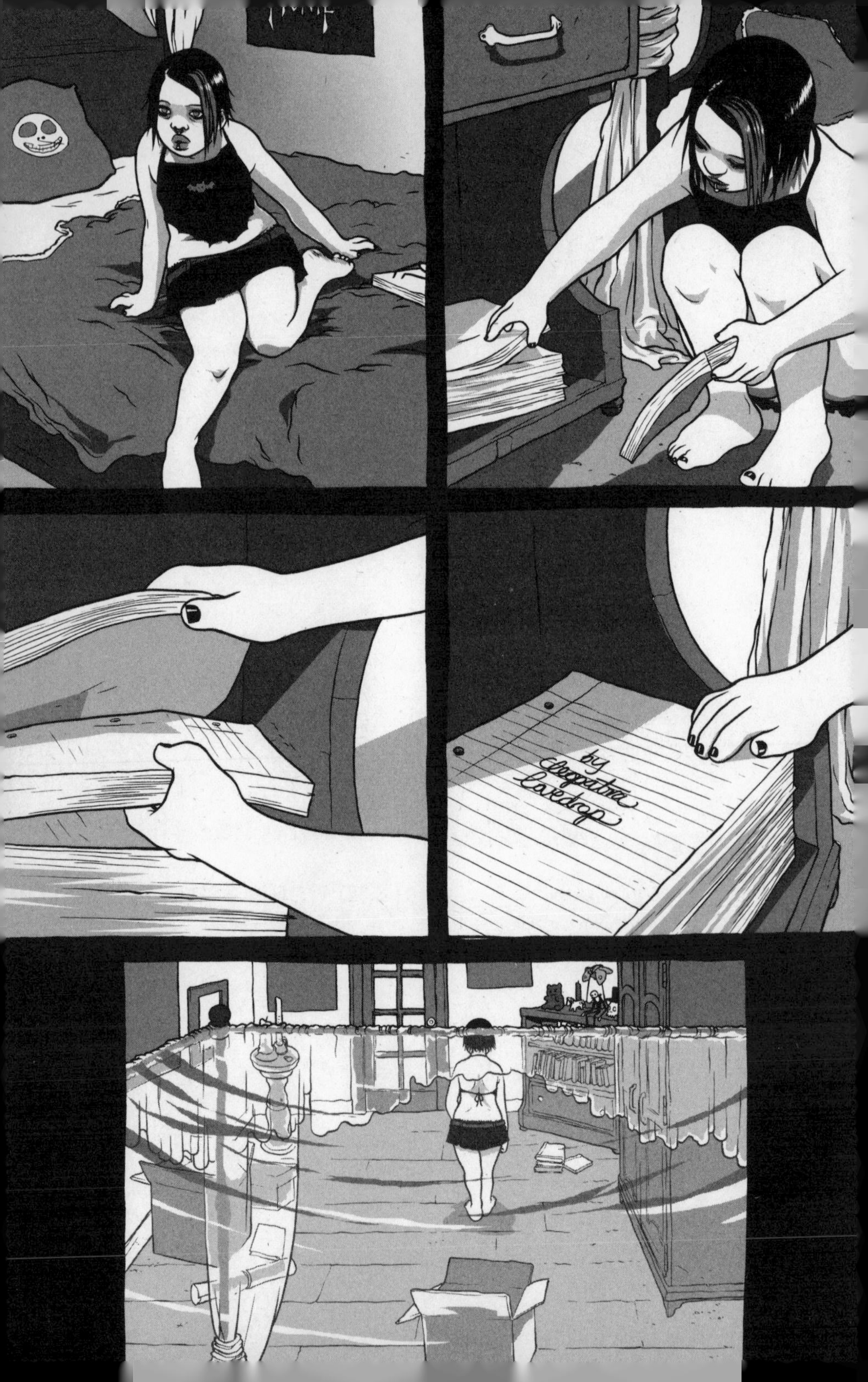
by
Cleopatra
Lovedrop

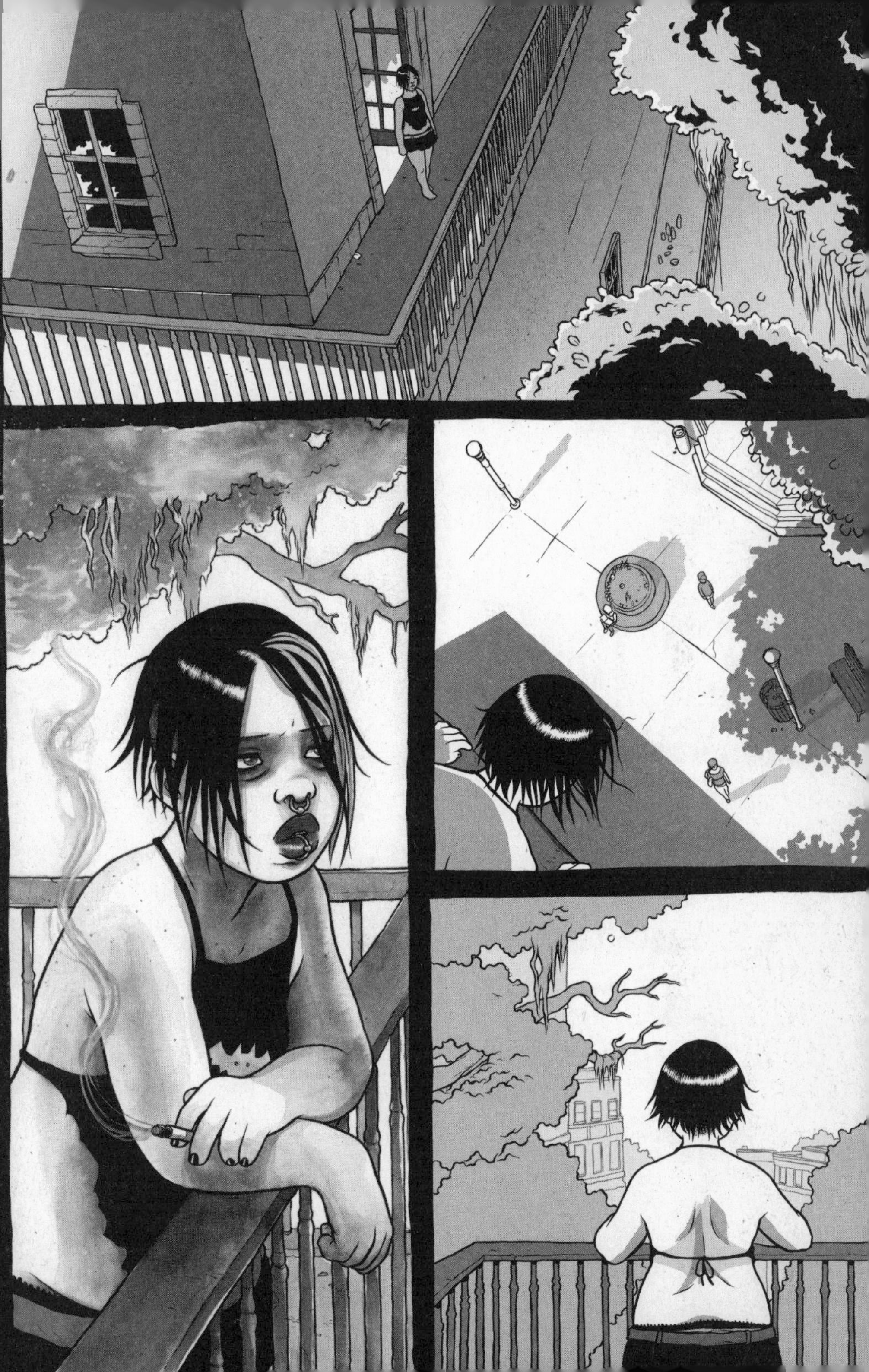

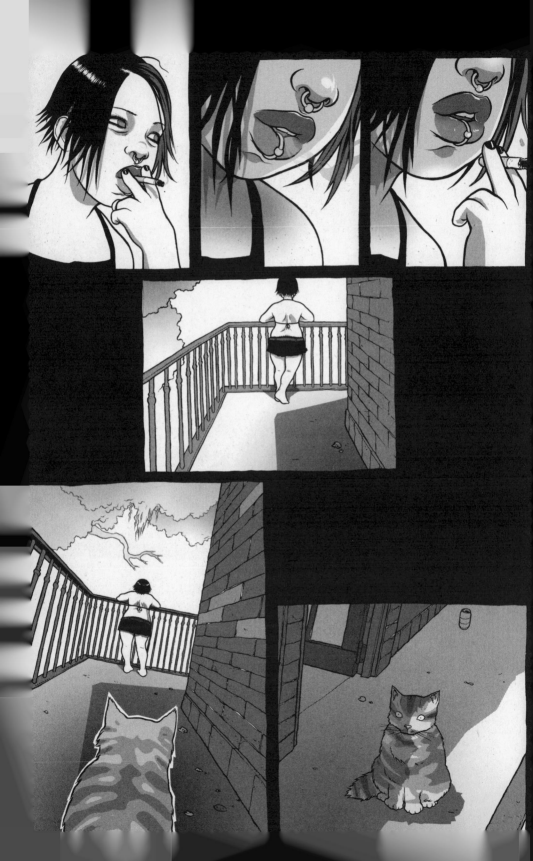

"And boys are so cruel,
so don't let them find you
tonight.
And girls are so vain,
so put them behind you
tonight.
I'll cast you a spell,
a magic where everyone
plays dead forever.
And after tonight,
they'll never remind you."

-the Birthday Massacre

3

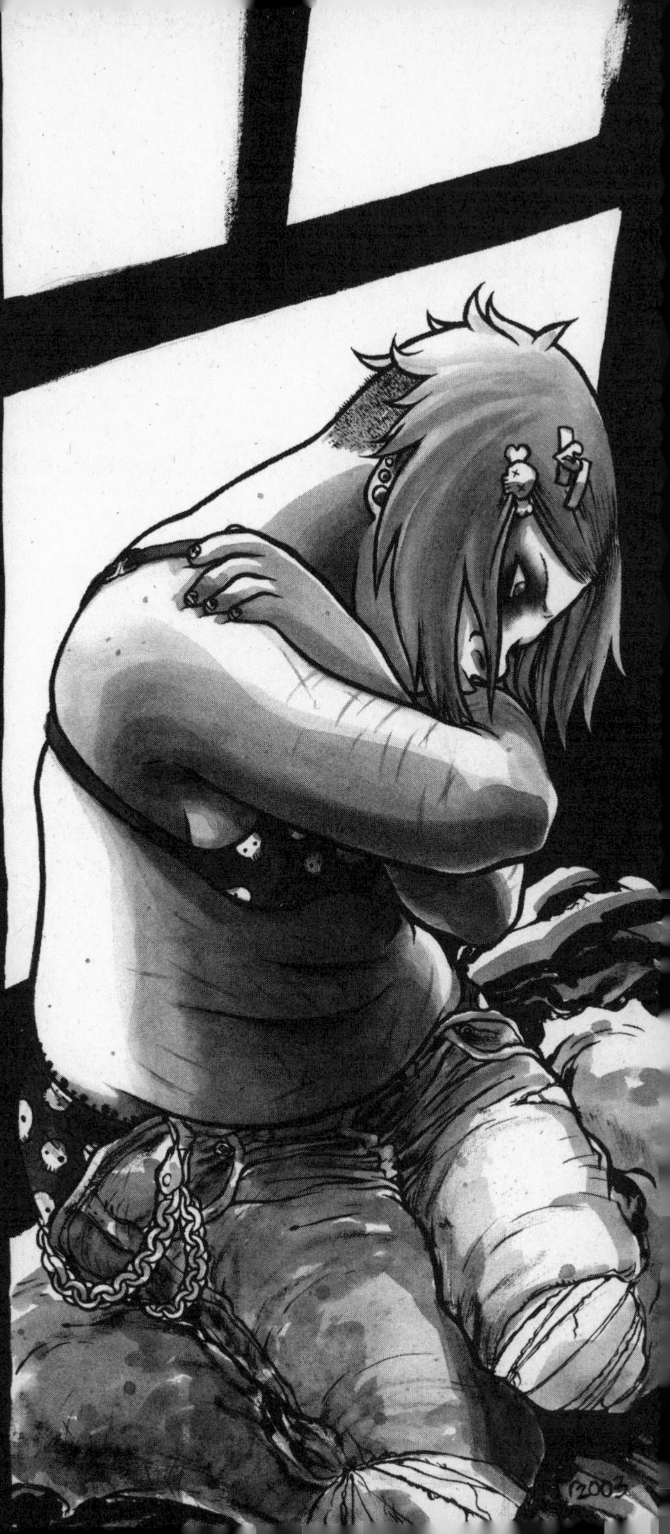

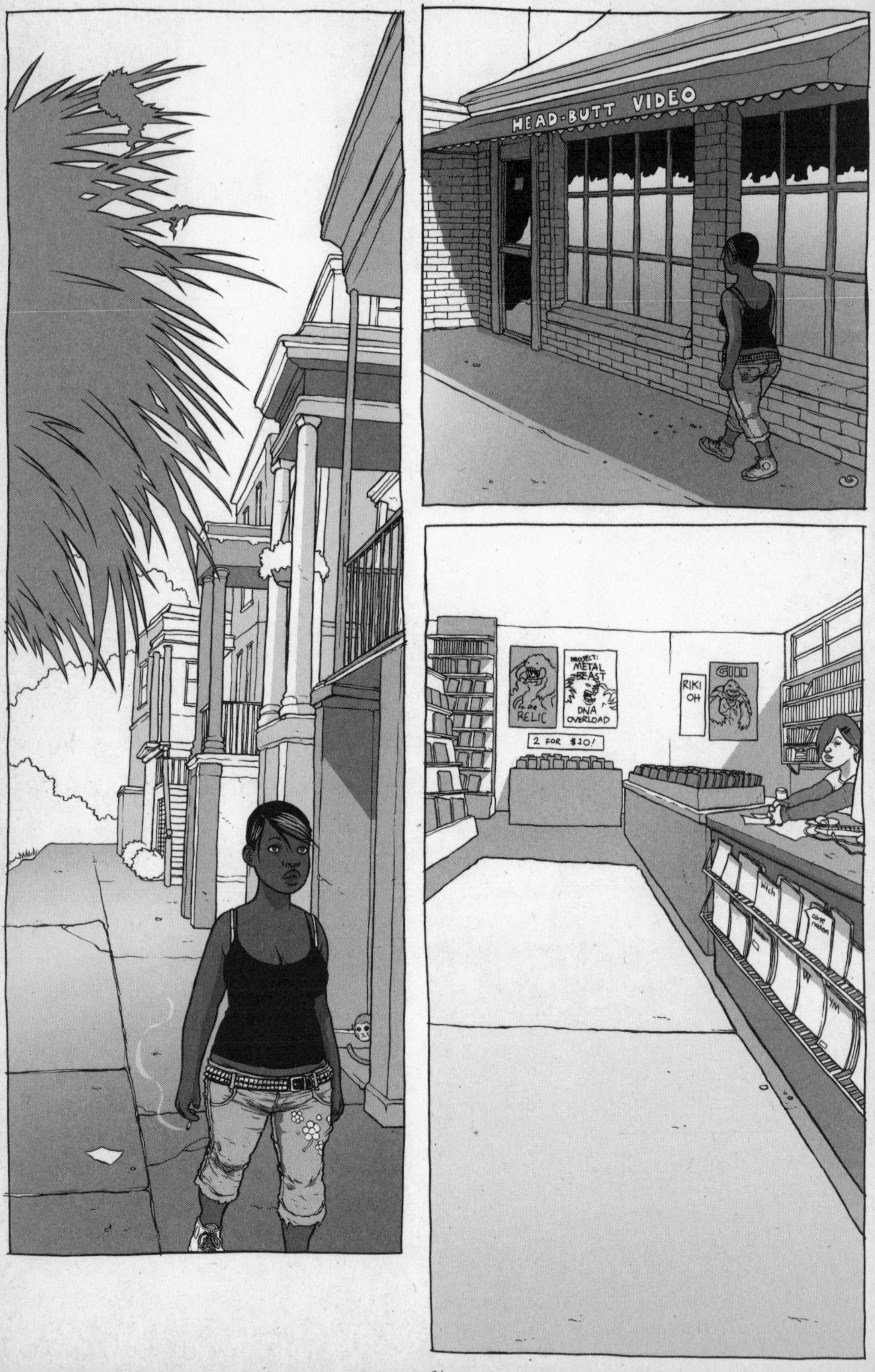
HEAD-BUTT VIDEO
RELIC
PROJECT: METAL BEAST
DNA OVERLOAD
RIKI OH
2 FOR $10!

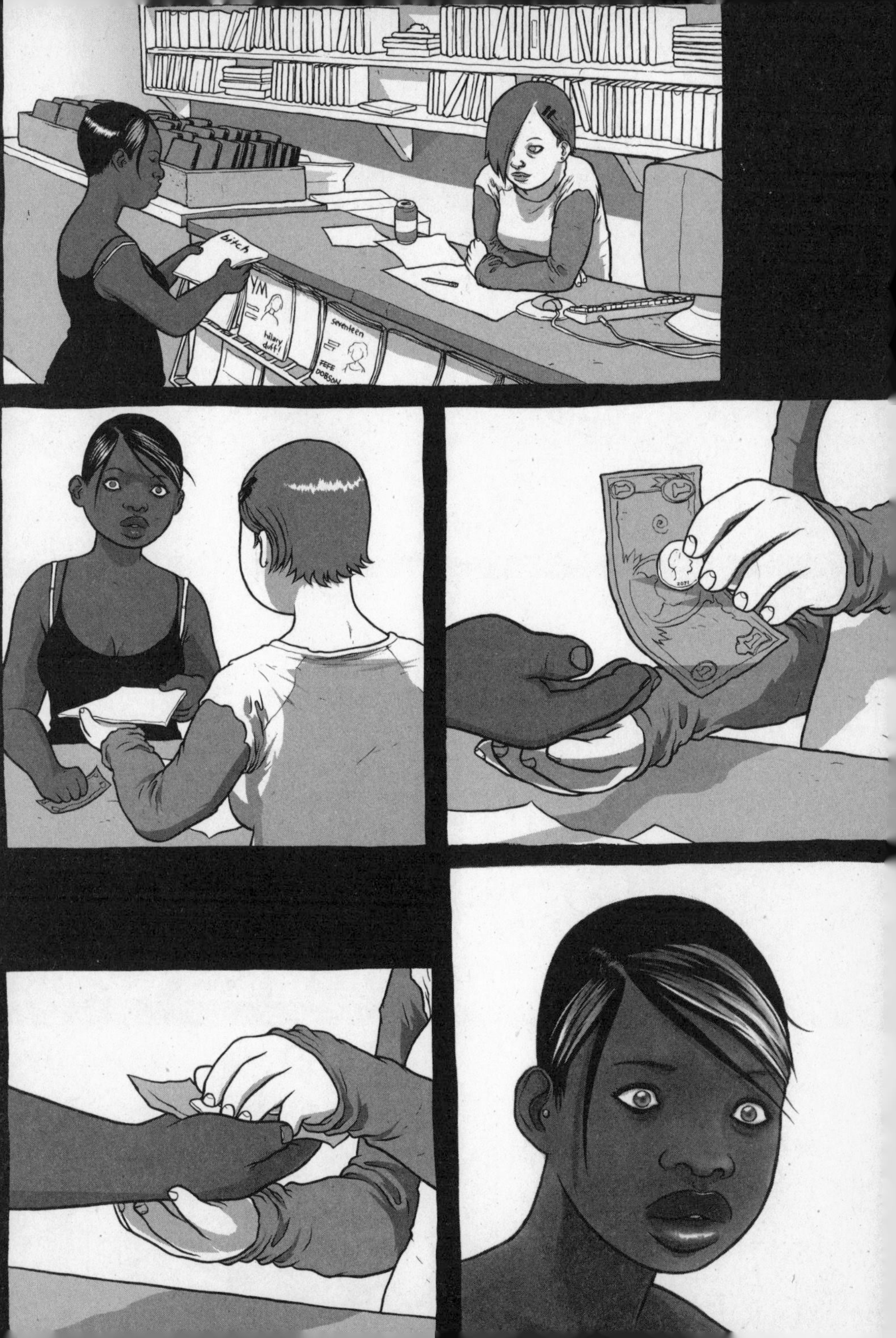
bitch
YM
hilary duff!
seventeen
FEFE DOBSON

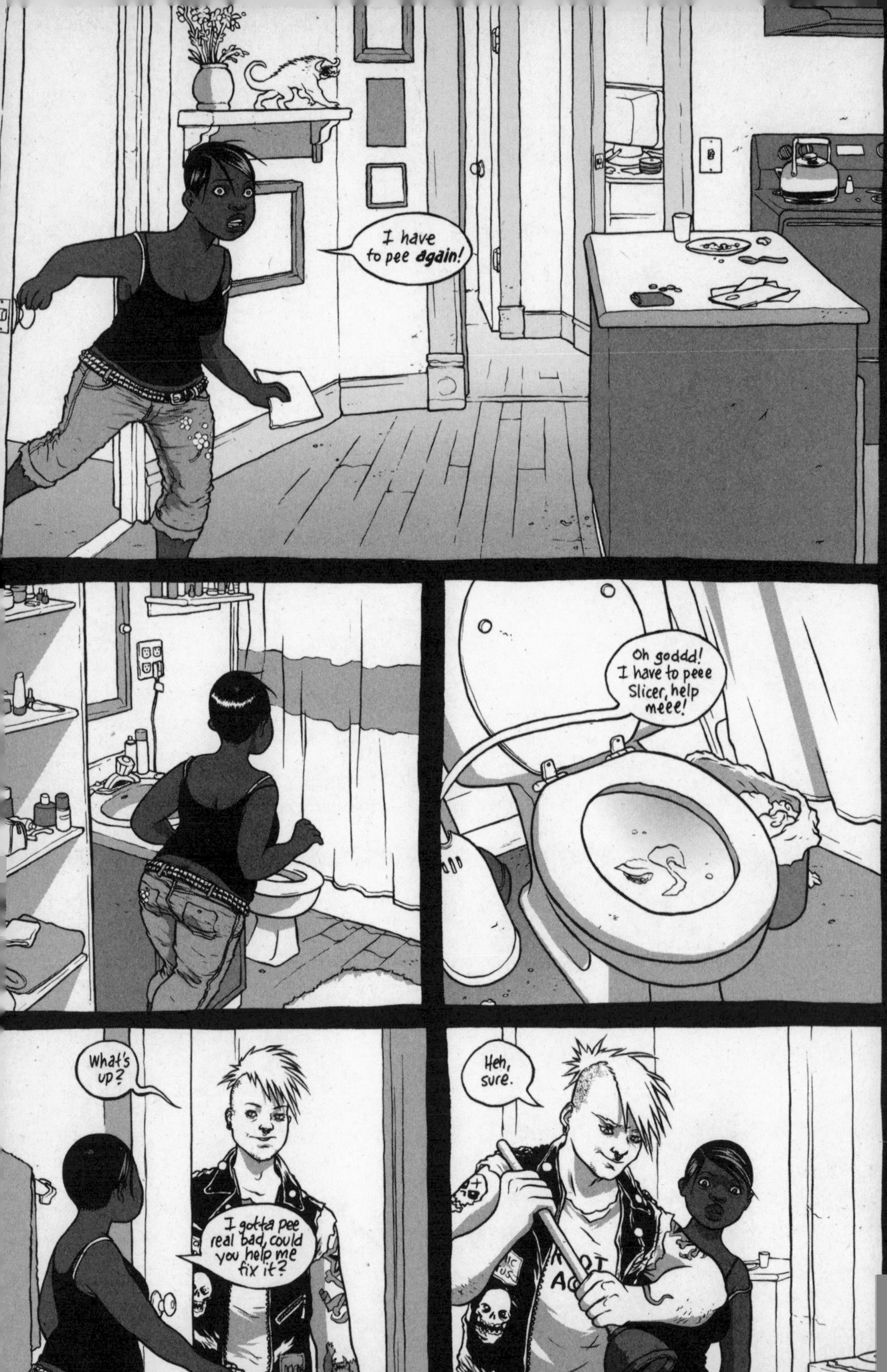
I have to pee again!
Oh goddd! I have to peee Slicer, help meee!
What's up?
I gotta pee real bad, could you help me fix it?
Heh, sure.

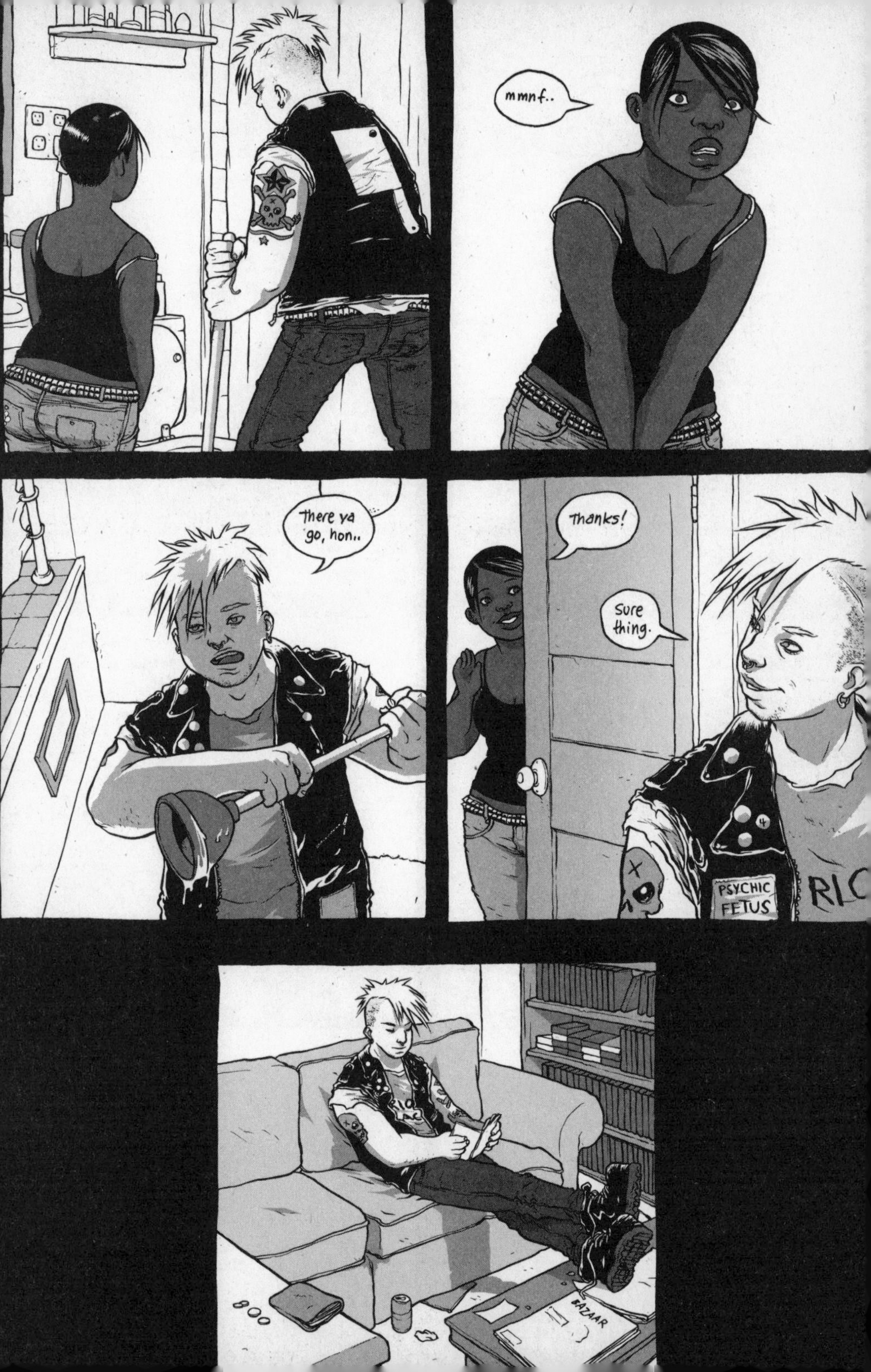
mmnf..
There ya go, hon..
Thanks!
Sure thing.
PSYCHIC FETUS
BAZAAR

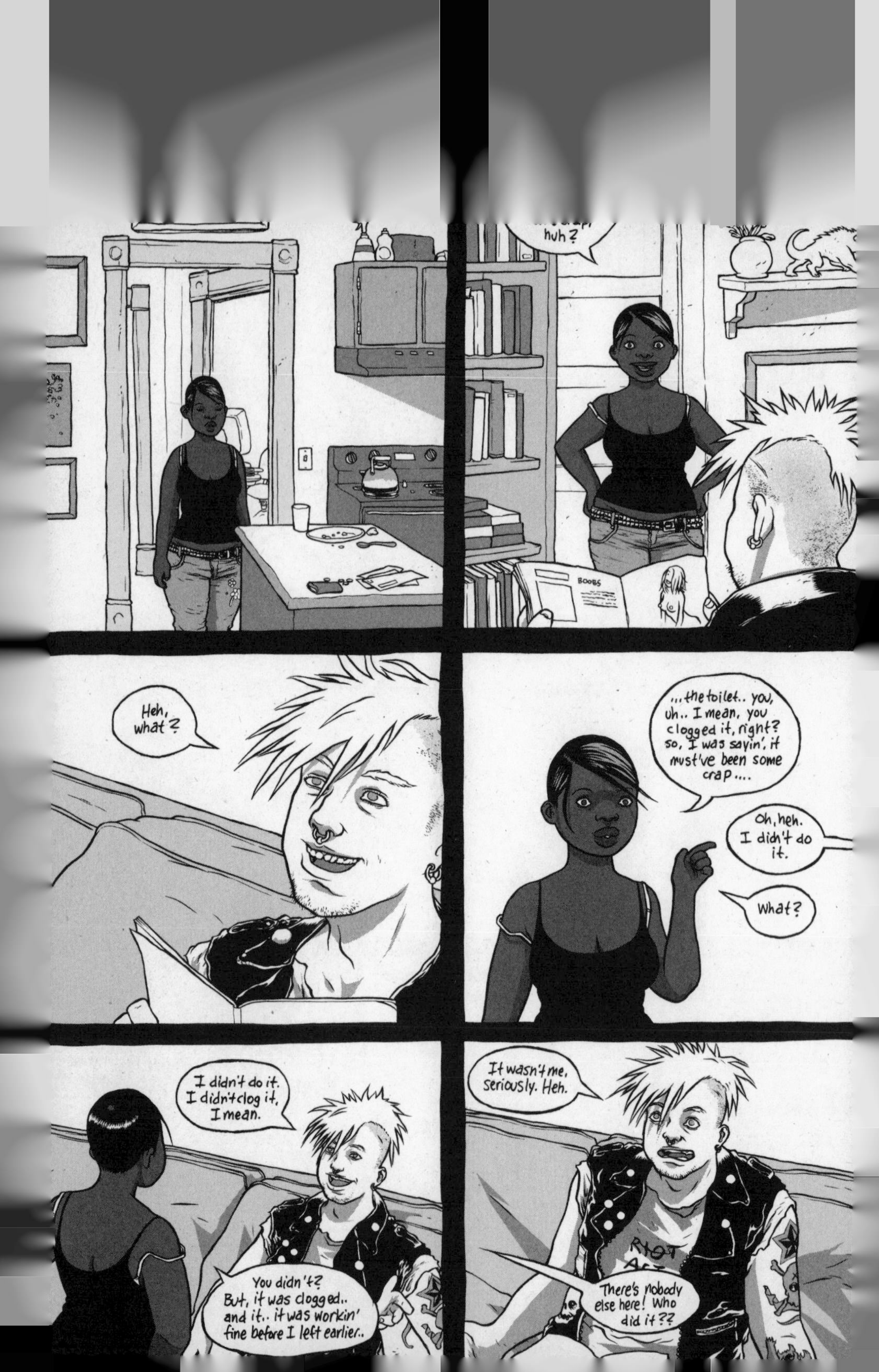
huh?
BOOBS
Heh, what?
...the toilet.. you, uh.. I mean, you clogged it, right? so, I was sayin', it must've been some crap....
Oh, heh. I didn't do it.
What?
I didn't do it. I didn't clog it, I mean.
You didn't? But, it was clogged.. and it.. it was workin' fine before I left earlier..
It wasn't me, seriously. Heh.
There's nobody else here! Who did it??

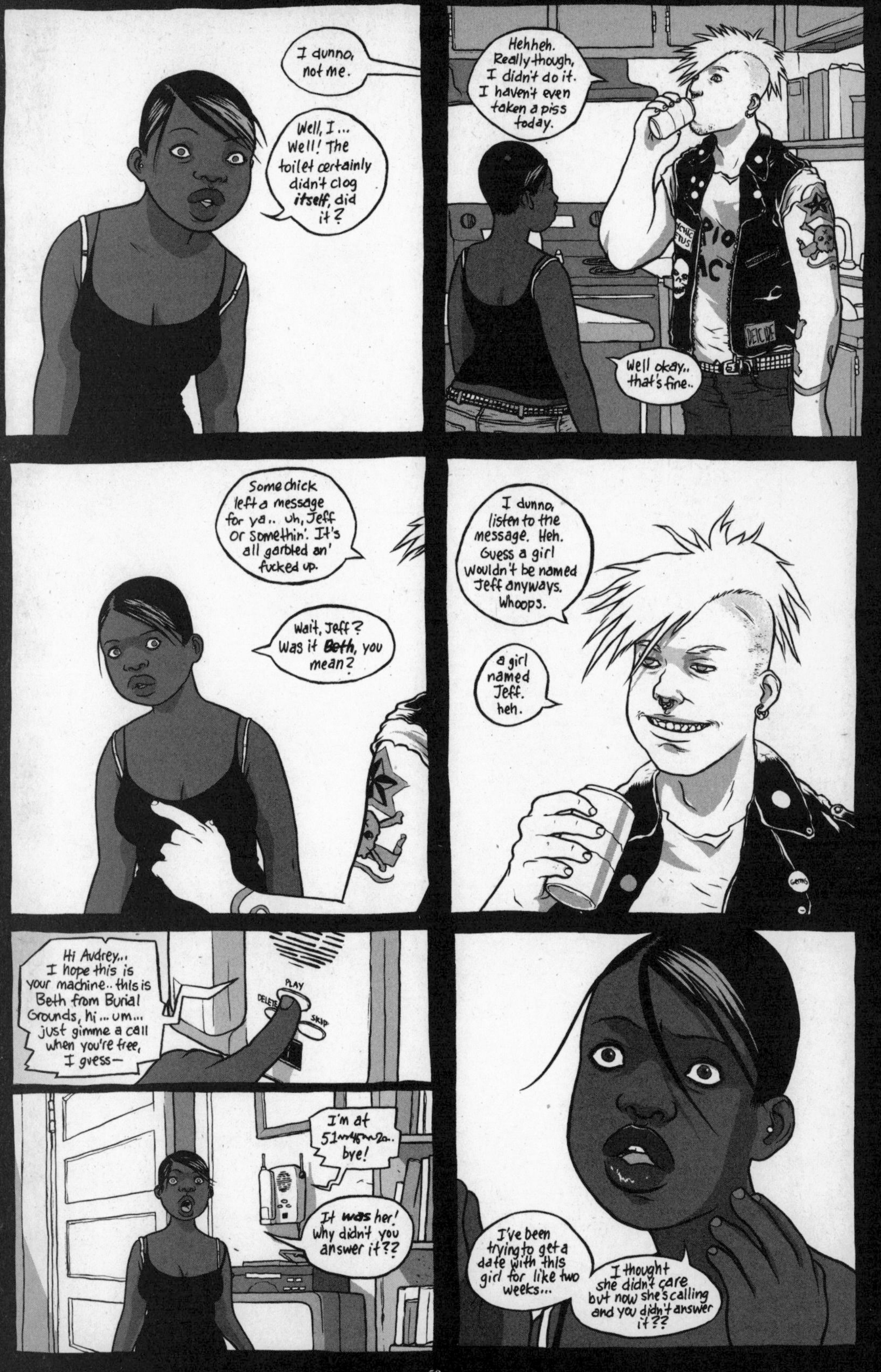
I dunno, not me.
Well, I... Well! The toilet certainly didn't clog itself, did it?
Hehheh. Really though, I didn't do it. I haven't even taken a piss today.
Well okay.. that's fine..
Some chick left a message for ya.. uh, Jeff or somethin'. It's all garbled an' fucked up.
Wait, Jeff? Was it Beth, you mean?
I dunno, listen to the message. Heh. Guess a girl wouldn't be named Jeff anyways. Whoops.
a girl named Jeff. heh.
Hi Audrey.. I hope this is your machine.. this is Beth from Burial Grounds, hi... um... just gimme a call when you're free, I guess—
PLAY
DELETE
SKIP
I'm at 51 bye!
It was her! Why didn't you answer it??
I've been trying to get a date with this girl for like two weeks...
I thought she didn't care but now she's calling and you didn't answer it??

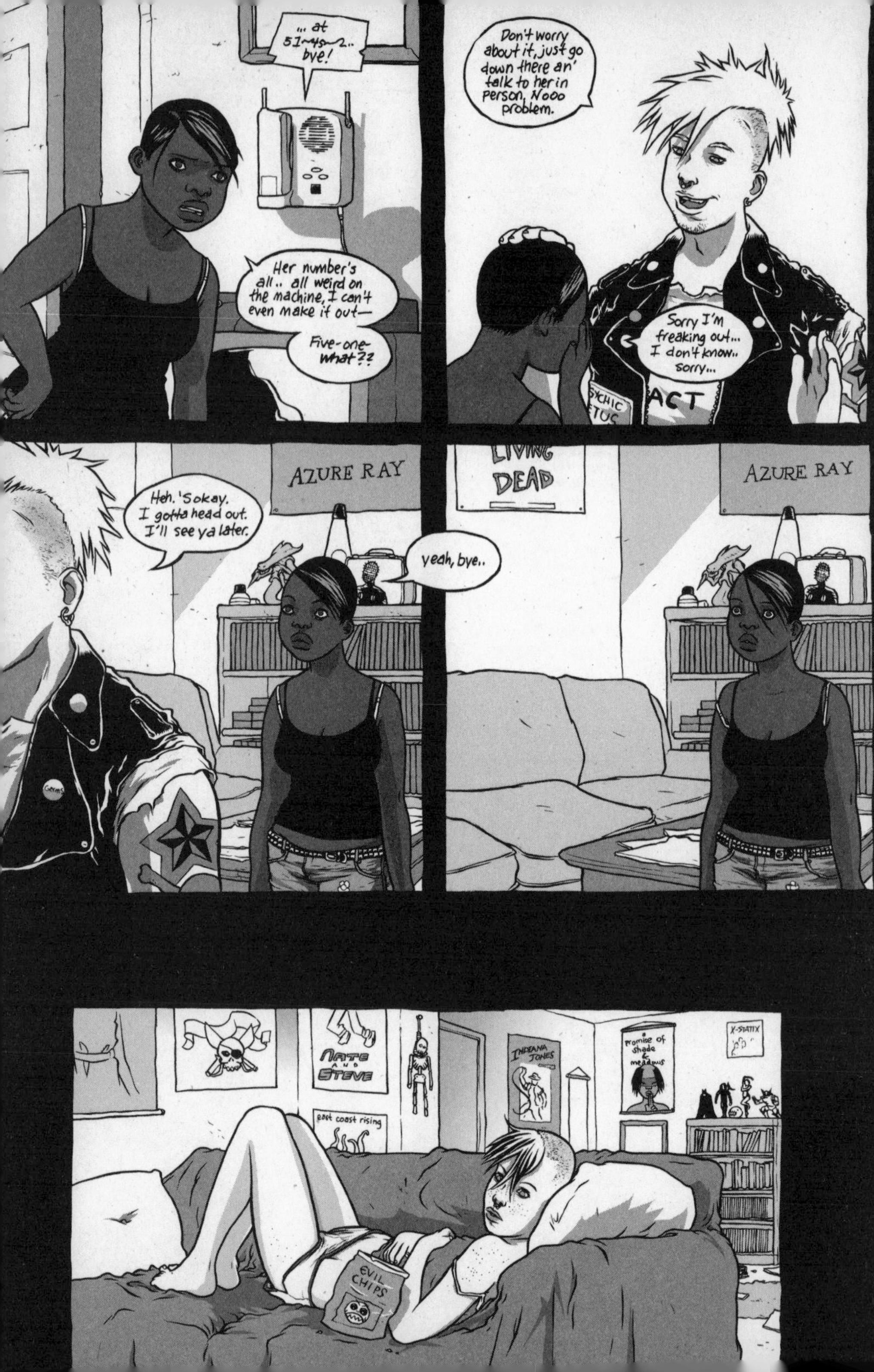
... at 51~45~2.. bye!
Her number's all.. all weird on the machine, I can't even make it out—
Five-one-what??
Don't worry about it, just go down there an' talk to her in person. Nooo problem.
Sorry I'm freaking out... I don't know.. sorry...
SYCHIC ETUS
ACT
AZURE RAY
Heh. 'Sokay. I gotta head out. I'll see ya later.
yeah, bye..
LIVING DEAD
AZURE RAY
NATE AND STEVE
east coast rising
INDIANA JONES
a promise of shade & meadows
X-STATIX
EVIL CHIPS

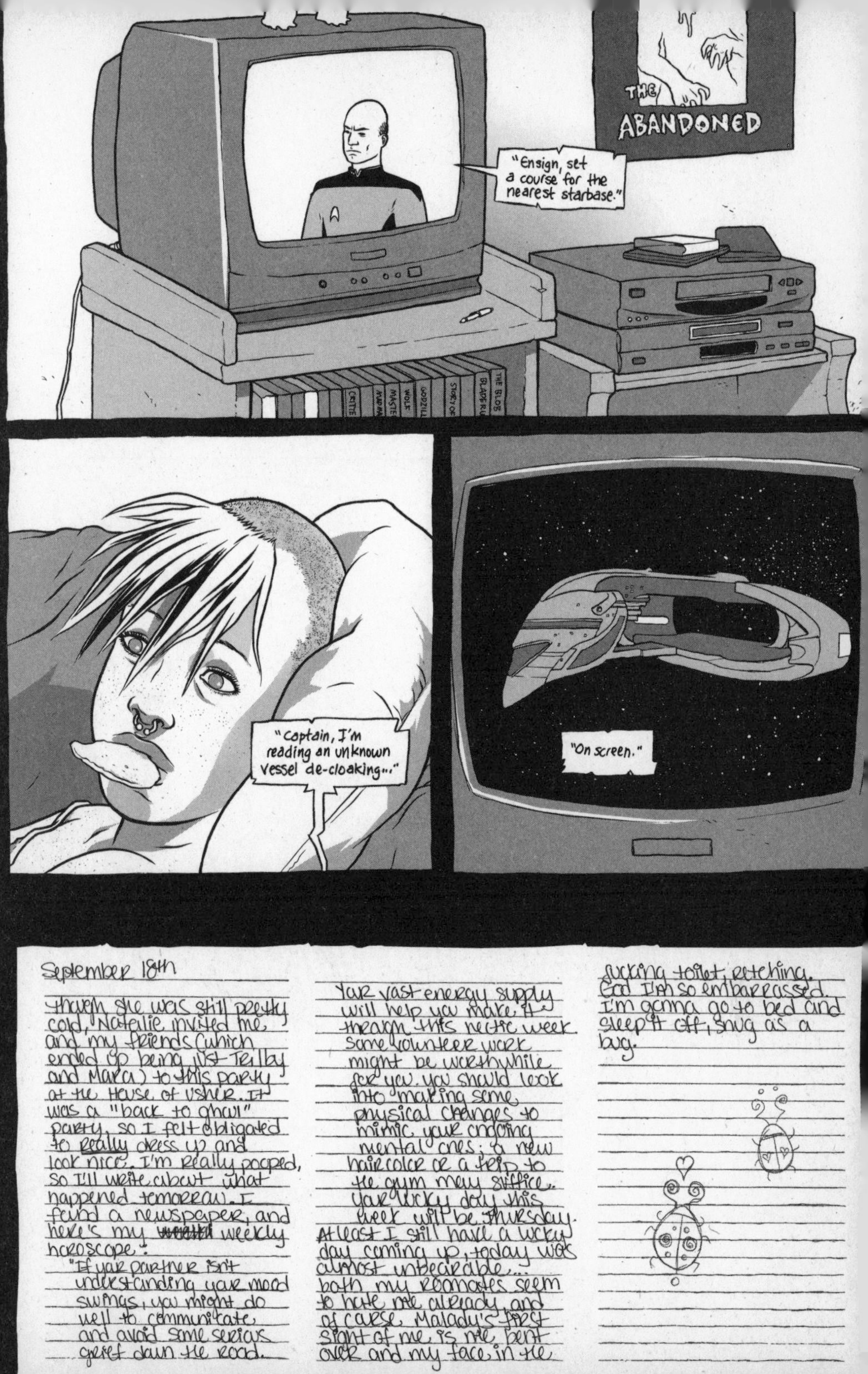
THE ABANDONED
"Ensign, set a course for the nearest starbase."
THE BLOB
BLADE RU
STORY OF
GODZILLA
WOLF
MASTE
CRITTE
"Captain, I'm reading an unknown vessel de-cloaking..."
"On screen."
September 18th
though she was still pretty cold, Natalie invited me and my friends (which ended up being just Trilby and Mara) to this party at the House of Usher. It was a "back to ghoul" party, so I felt obligated to really dress up and look nice. I'm really pooped, so I'll write about what happened tomorrow. I found a newspaper, and here's my weekly horoscope:
"If your partner isn't understanding your mood swings, you might do well to communicate and avoid some serious grief down the road. Your vast energy supply will help you make it through this hectic week. Some volunteer work might be worthwhile for you. You should look into making some physical changes to mimic your ongoing mental ones; a new haircolor or a trip to the gym may suffice. Your lucky day this week will be Thursday.
At least I still have a lucky day coming up, today was almost unbearable... both my roomates seem to hate me already, and of course, Malady's first sight of me is me, bent over and my face in the fucking toilet, retching. God I'm so embarrassed. I'm gonna go to bed and sleep it off, snug as a bug.

KNOCK
shit—
HOLD ON!
EVIL
CHIPS
eject,
ejeectt
...
KNOCK
KNOCK
HOLD
OONNN!!

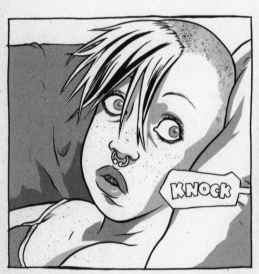

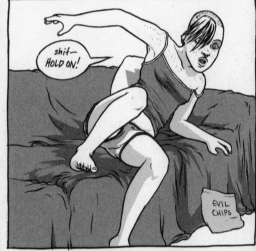

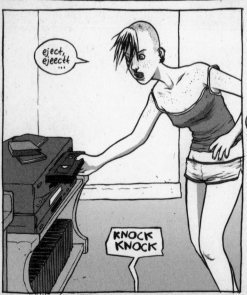

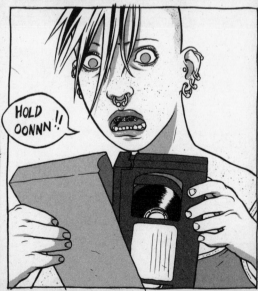

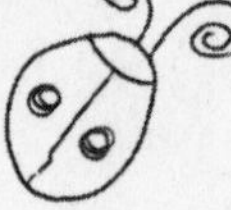

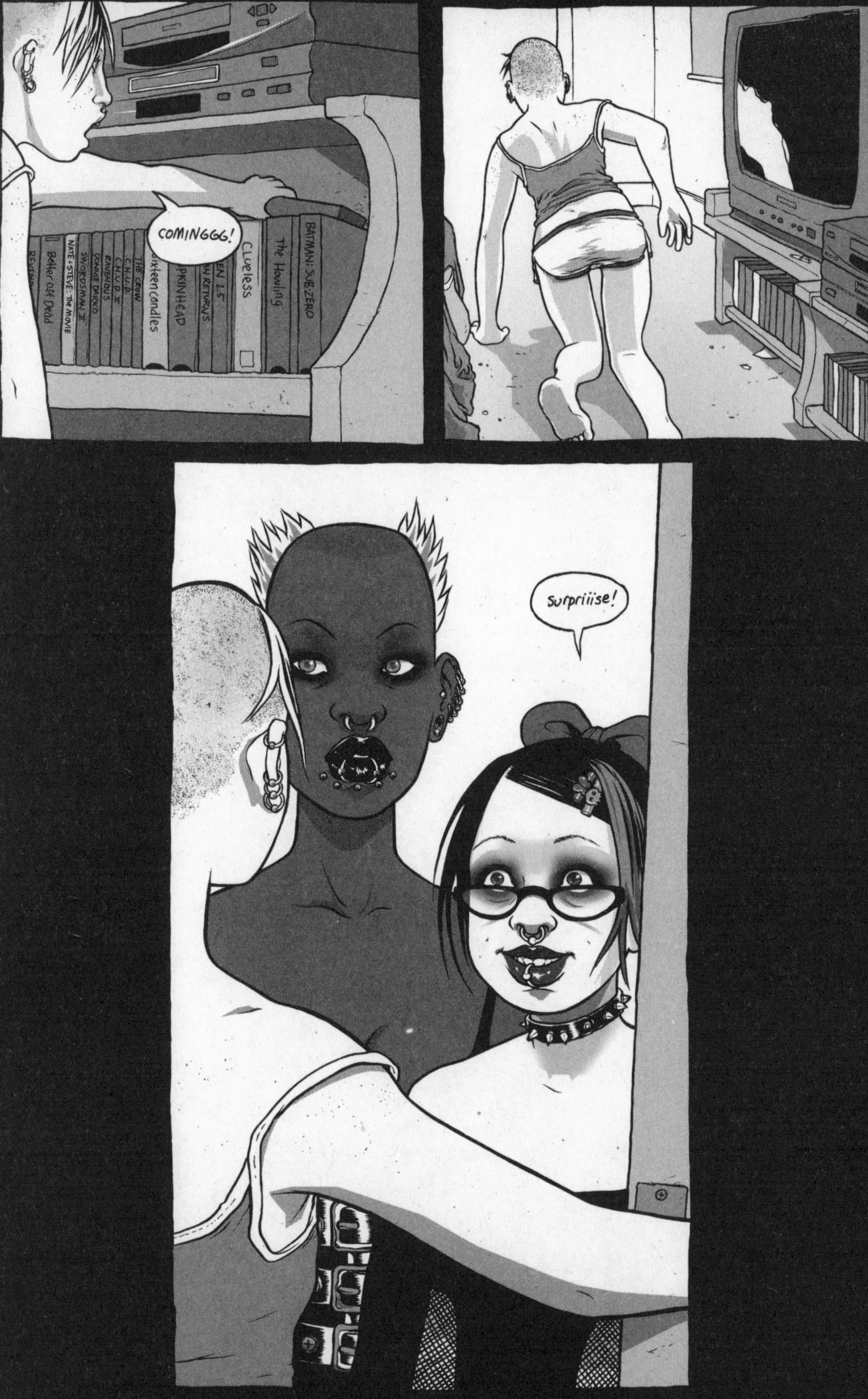
COMINGGG!
Better off Dead
NATE + STEVE: THE MOVIE
SWORDSMAN II
DONNIE DARKO
RAVENOUS
C.H.U.D.
C.H.U.D. II
THE CROW
Clueless
The Howling
BATMAN: SUB-ZERO
surpriiise!

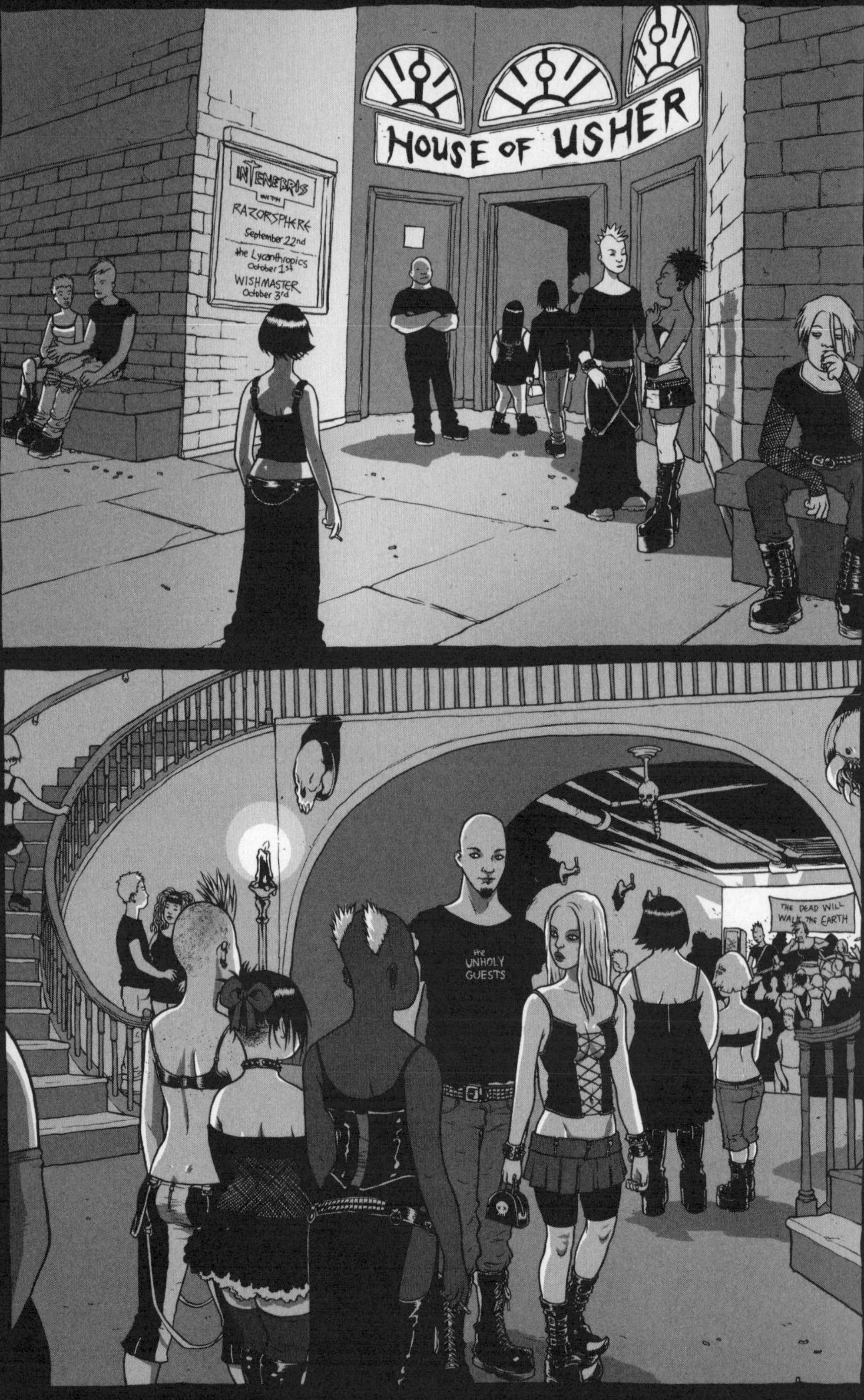
HOUSE OF USHER
IN TENEBRIS
WITH
RAZORSPHERE
September 22nd
the Lycanthropics
October 1st
WISHMASTER
October 3rd
the UNHOLY GUESTS
THE DEAD WILL WALK THE EARTH

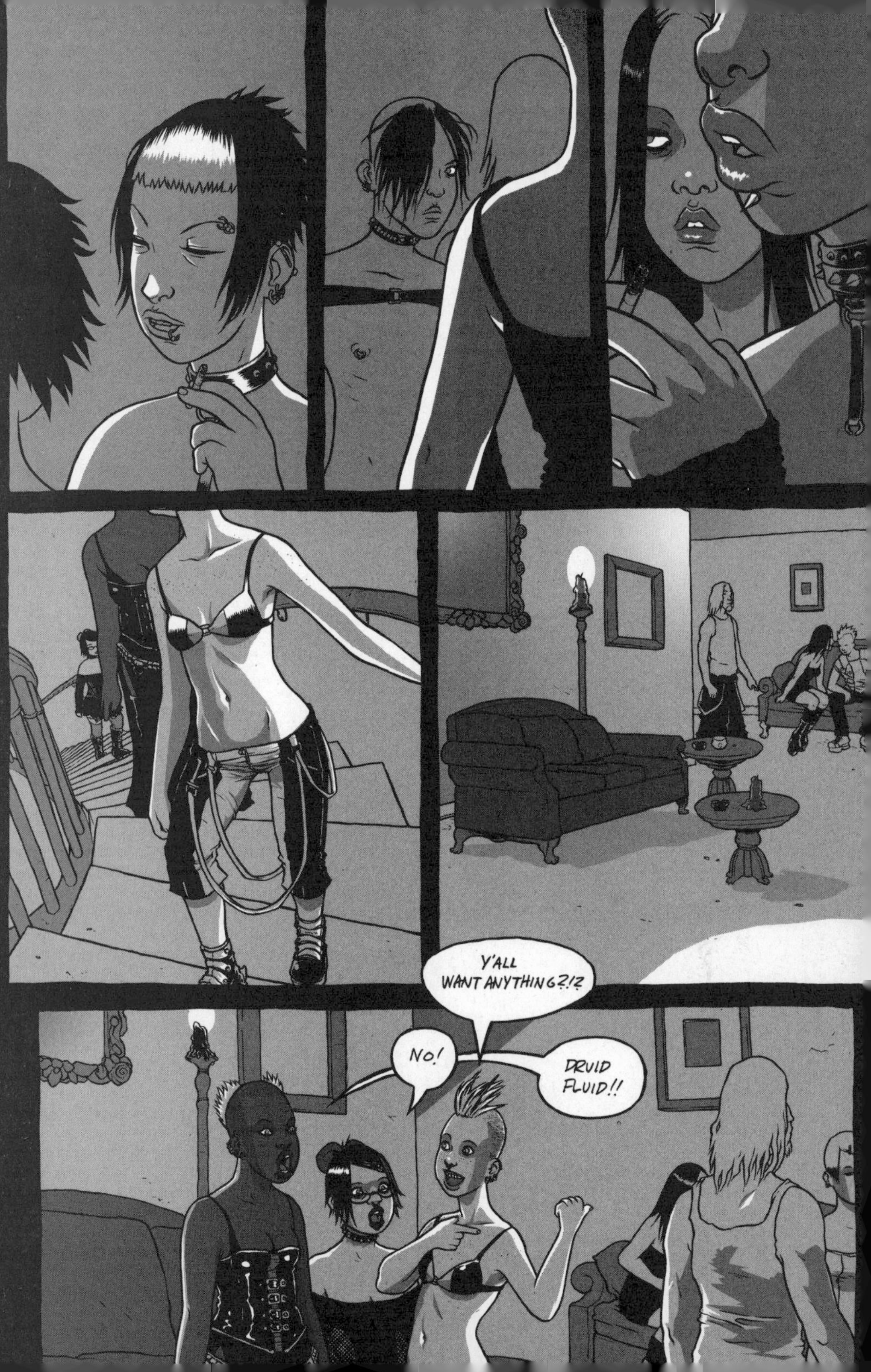
Y'ALL WANT ANYTHING?!?
NO!
DRUID FLUID!!

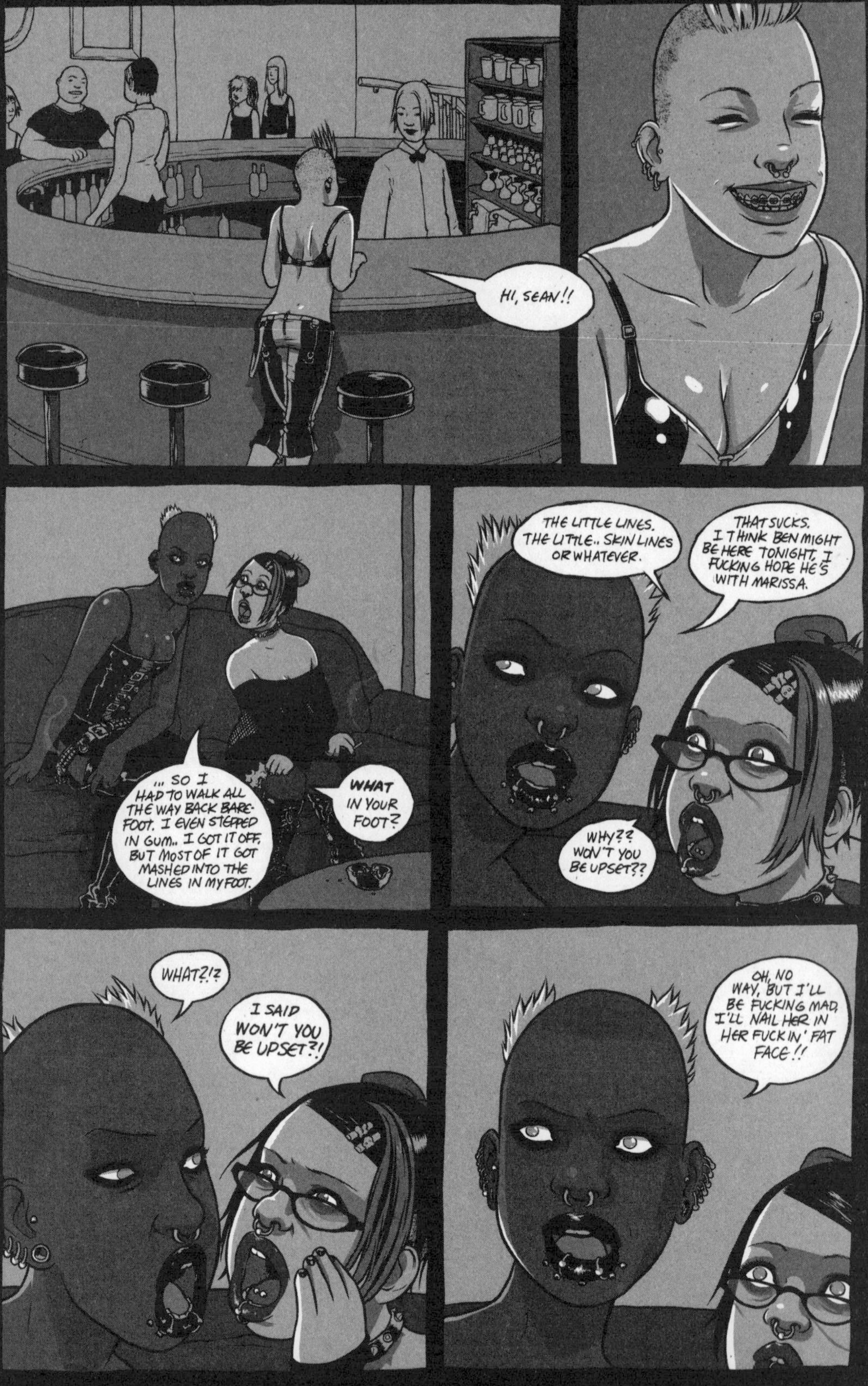
HI, SEAN!!
... SO I HAD TO WALK ALL THE WAY BACK BARE-FOOT. I EVEN STEPPED IN GUM.. I GOT IT OFF, BUT MOST OF IT GOT MASHED INTO THE LINES IN MY FOOT.
WHAT IN YOUR FOOT?
THE LITTLE LINES. THE LITTLE.. SKIN LINES OR WHATEVER.
THAT SUCKS. I THINK BEN MIGHT BE HERE TONIGHT, I FUCKING HOPE HE'S WITH MARISSA.
WHY?? WON'T YOU BE UPSET??
WHAT?!?
I SAID WON'T YOU BE UPSET?!
OH, NO WAY, BUT I'LL BE FUCKING MAD, I'LL NAIL HER IN HER FUCKIN' FAT FACE!!

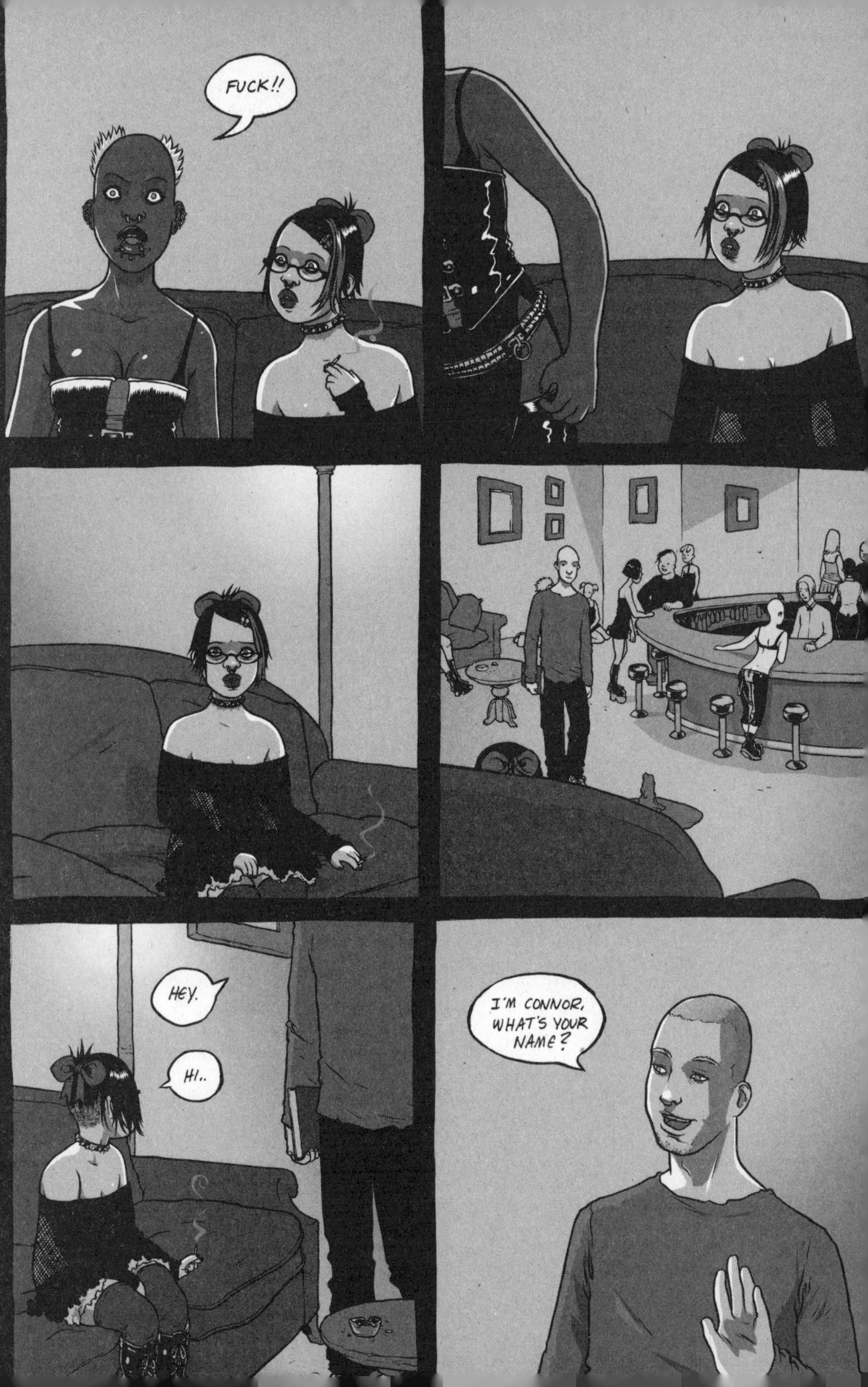
FUCK!!
HEY.
HI..
I'M CONNOR, WHAT'S YOUR NAME?

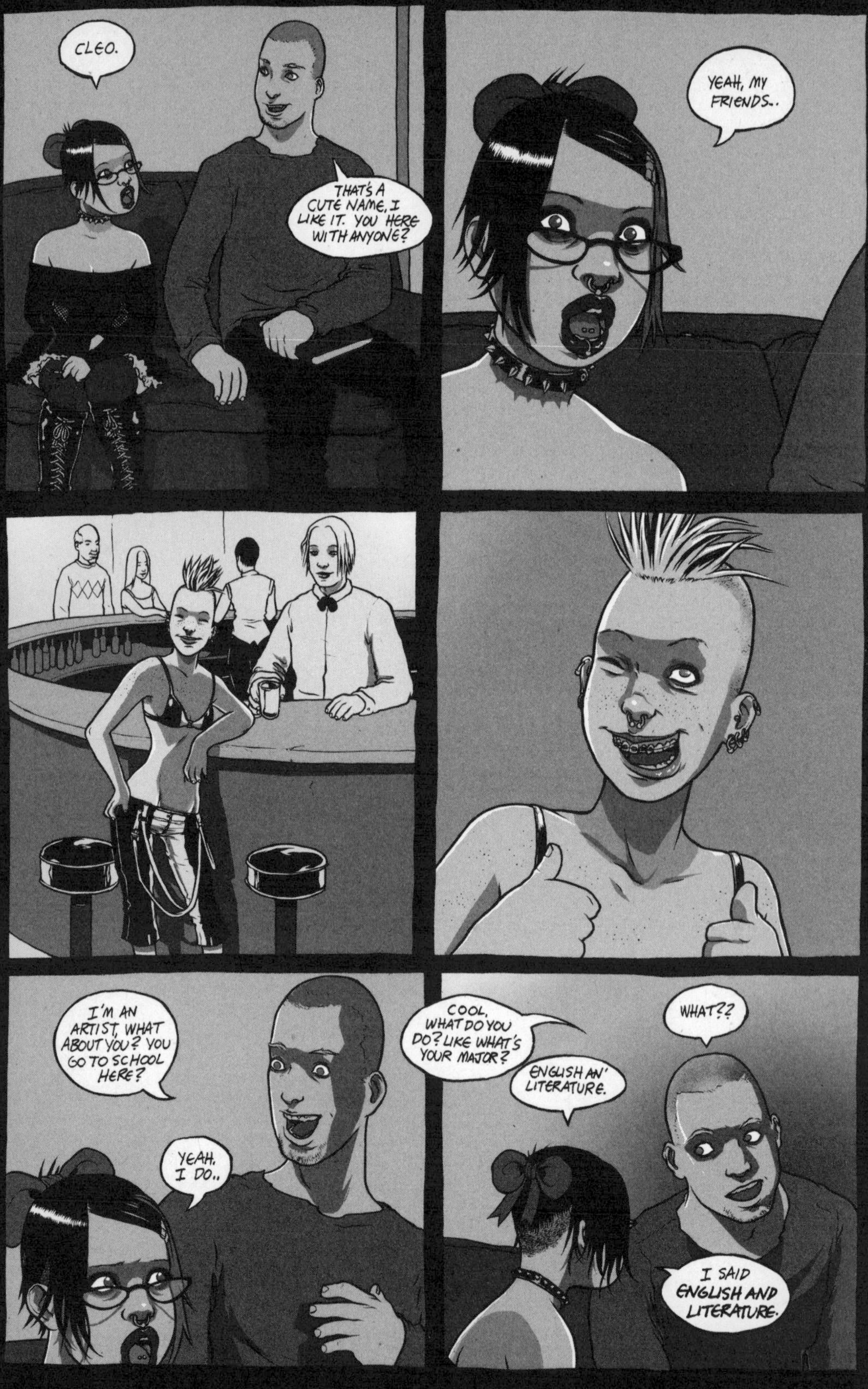
CLEO.
THAT'S A CUTE NAME, I LIKE IT. YOU HERE WITH ANYONE?
YEAH, MY FRIENDS..
I'M AN ARTIST, WHAT ABOUT YOU? YOU GO TO SCHOOL HERE?
YEAH. I DO..
COOL, WHAT DO YOU DO? LIKE WHAT'S YOUR MAJOR?
WHAT??
ENGLISH AN' LITERATURE.
I SAID ENGLISH AND LITERATURE.

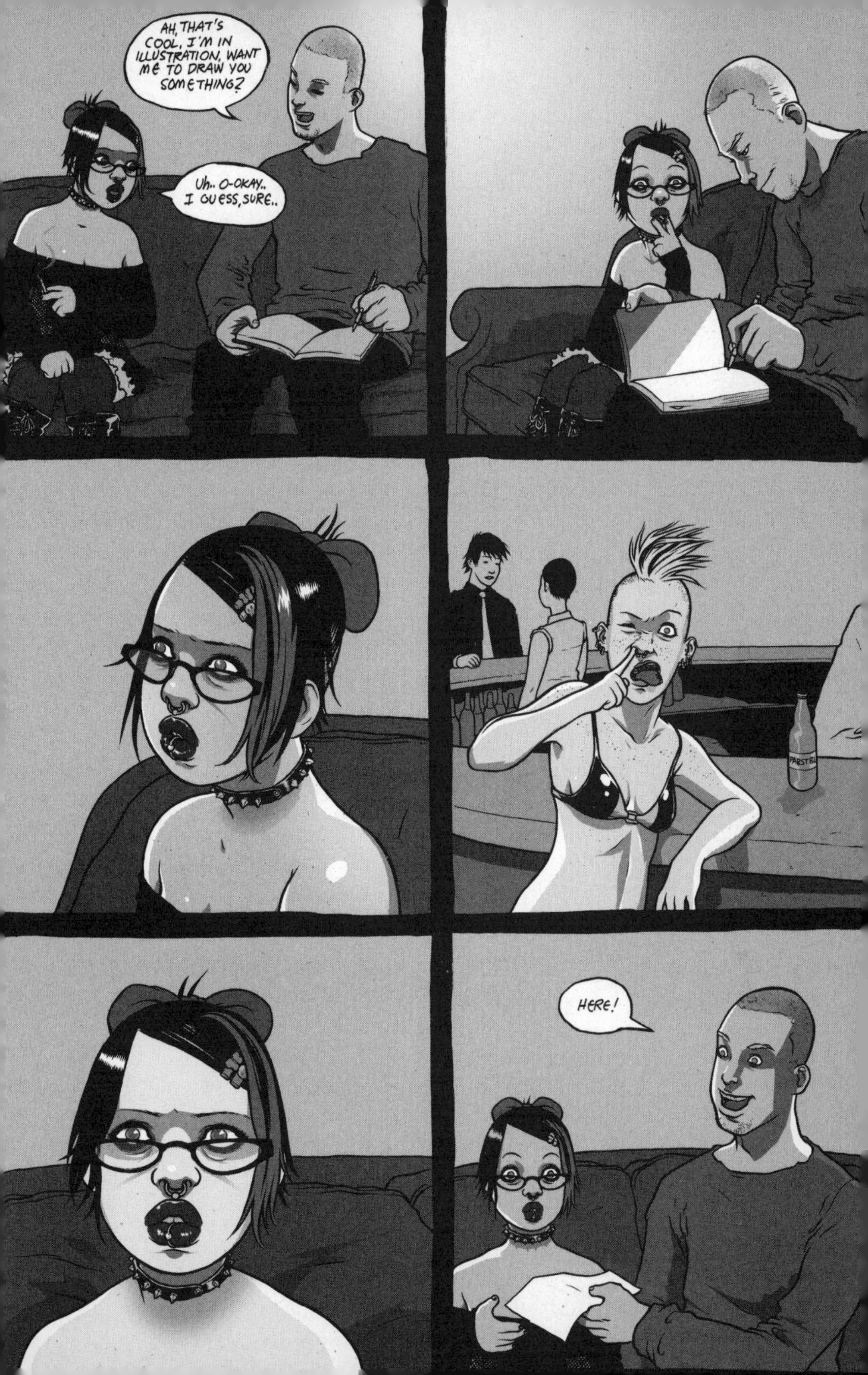
AH, THAT'S COOL, I'M IN ILLUSTRATION, WANT ME TO DRAW YOU SOMETHING?
Uh.. O-OKAY.. I GUESS, SURE..
HERE!

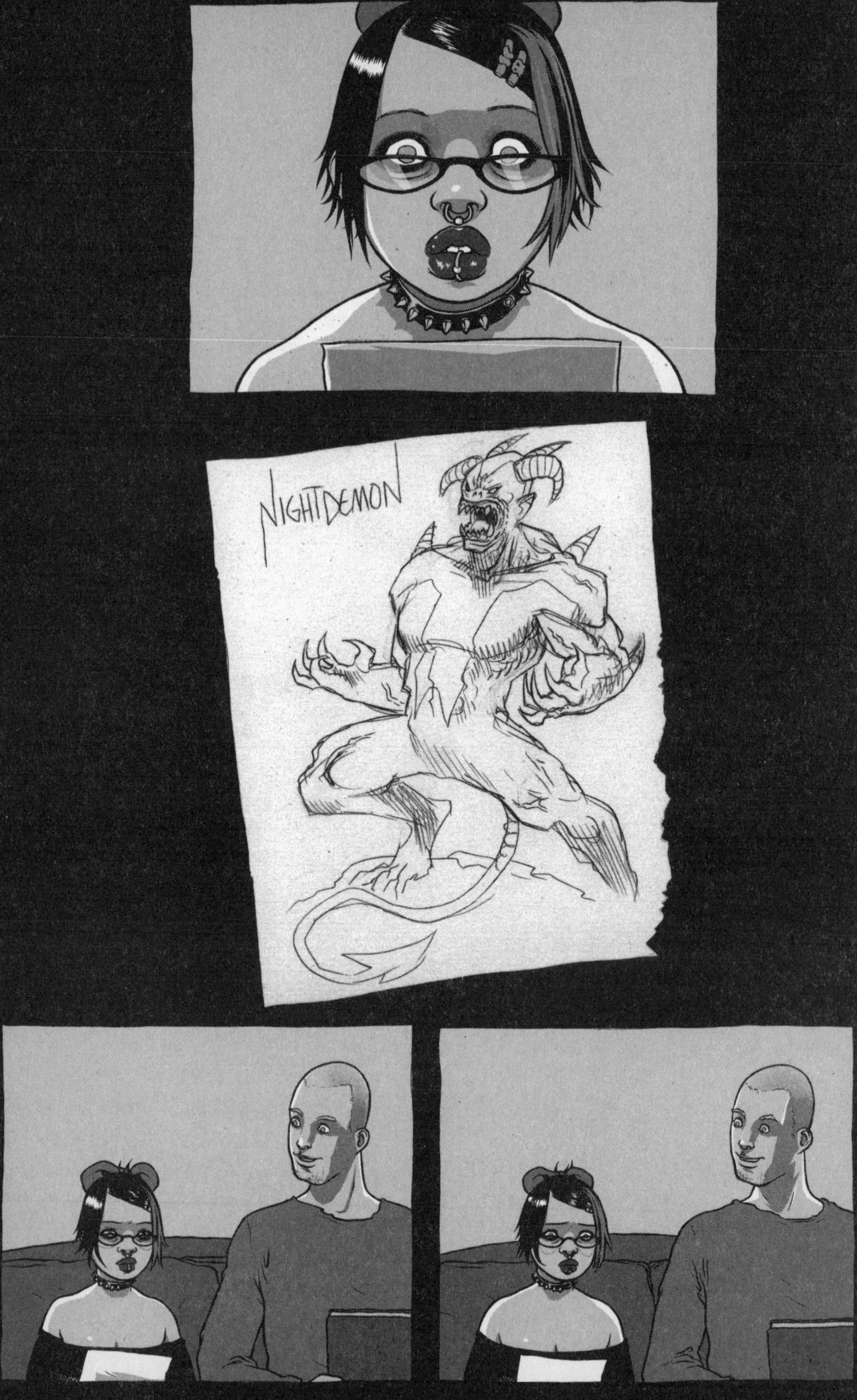
NIGHTDEMON

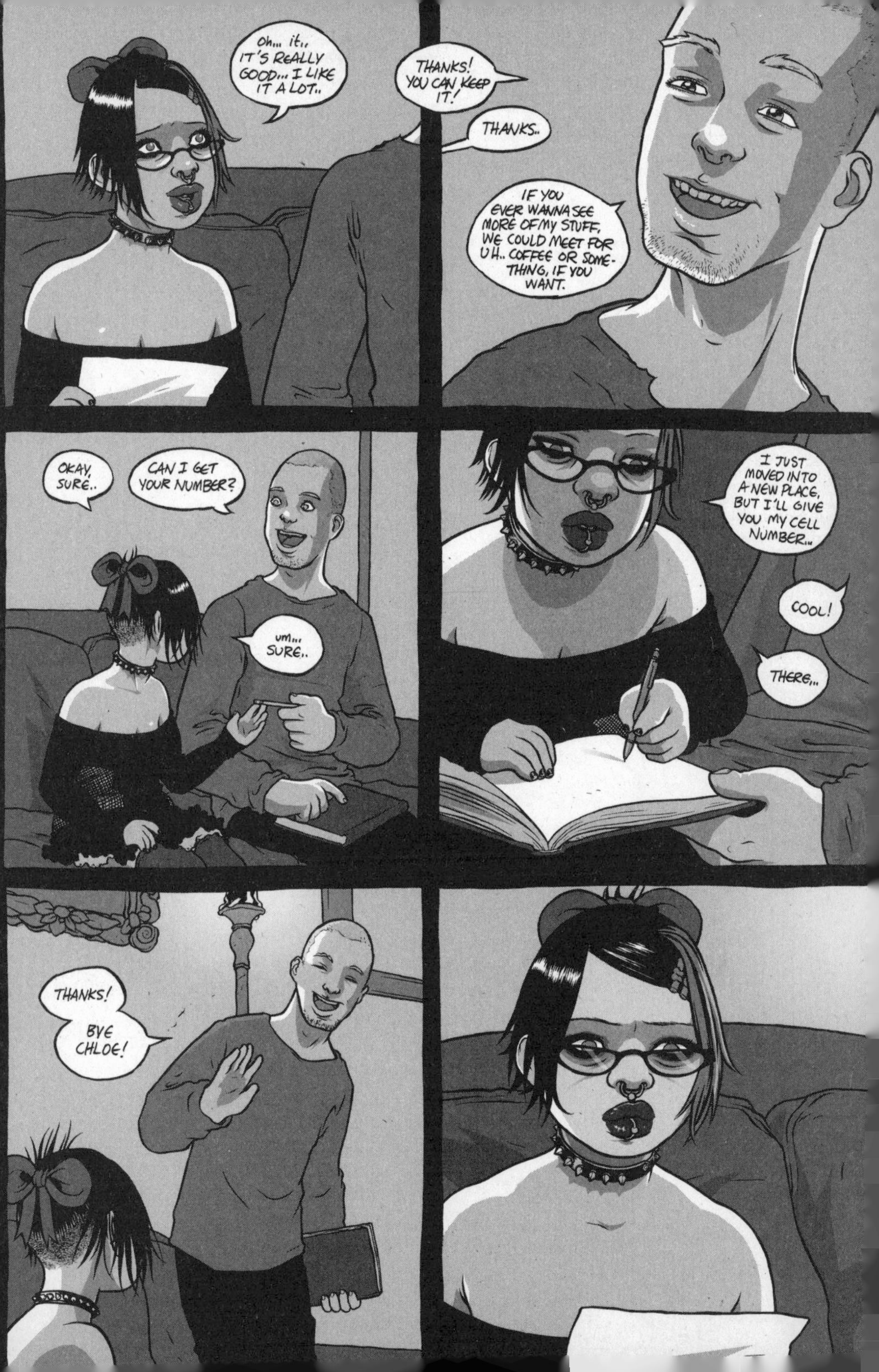
Oh... it.. IT'S REALLY GOOD... I LIKE IT A LOT..
THANKS! YOU CAN KEEP IT!
THANKS..
IF YOU EVER WANNA SEE MORE OF MY STUFF, WE COULD MEET FOR UH.. COFFEE OR SOME-THING, IF YOU WANT.
OKAY, SURE..
CAN I GET YOUR NUMBER?
um... SURE..
I JUST MOVED INTO A NEW PLACE, BUT I'LL GIVE YOU MY CELL NUMBER...
COOL!
THERE...
THANKS!
BYE CHLOE!

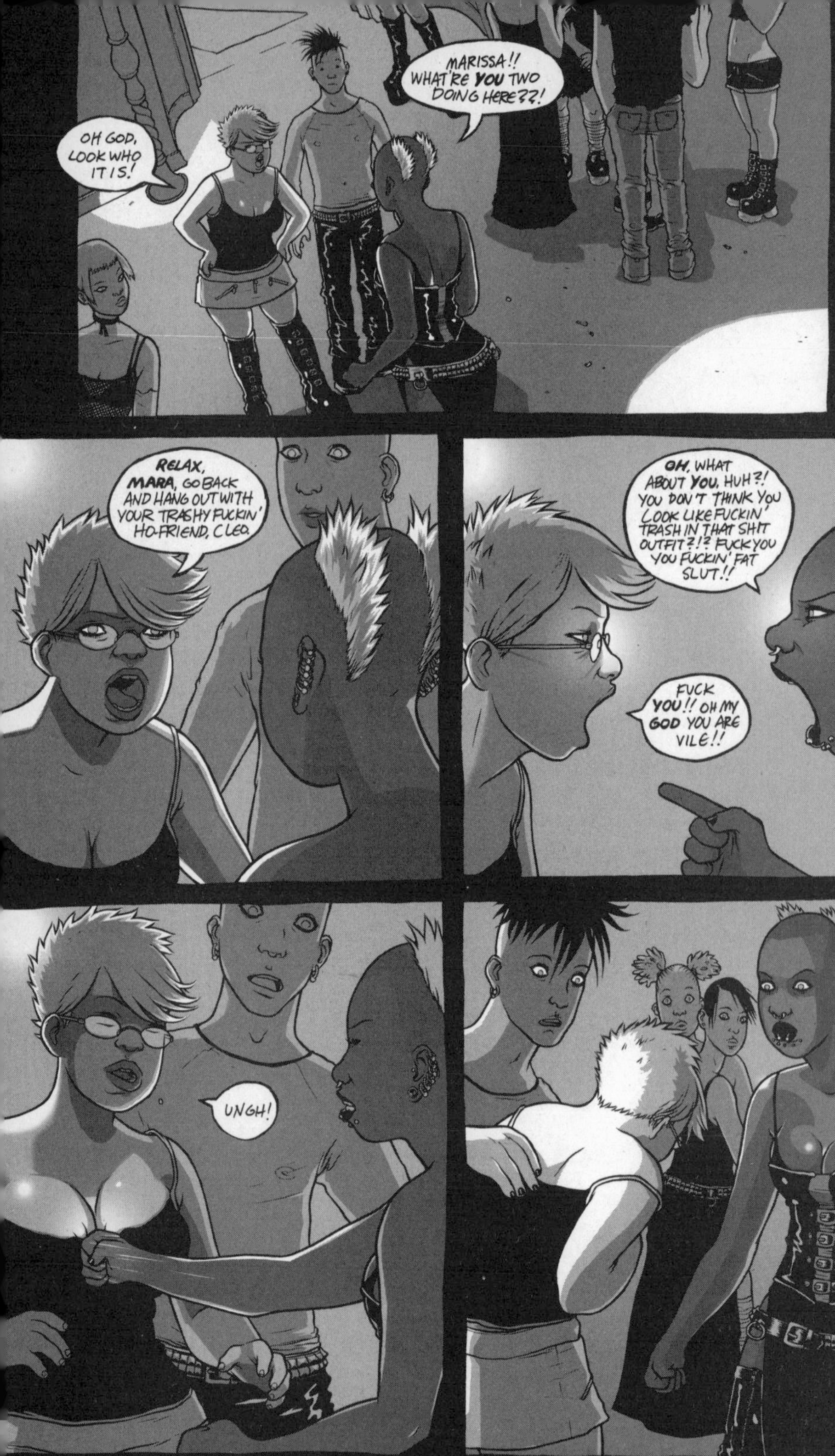
MARISSA!! WHAT'RE YOU TWO DOING HERE??!
OH GOD, LOOK WHO IT IS!
RELAX, MARA, GO BACK AND HANG OUT WITH YOUR TRASHY FUCKIN' HO-FRIEND, CLEO.
OH, WHAT ABOUT YOU, HUH?! YOU DON'T THINK YOU LOOK LIKE FUCKIN' TRASH IN THAT SHIT OUTFIT?!? FUCK YOU YOU FUCKIN' FAT SLUT!!
FUCK YOU!! OH MY GOD YOU ARE VILE!!
UNGH!

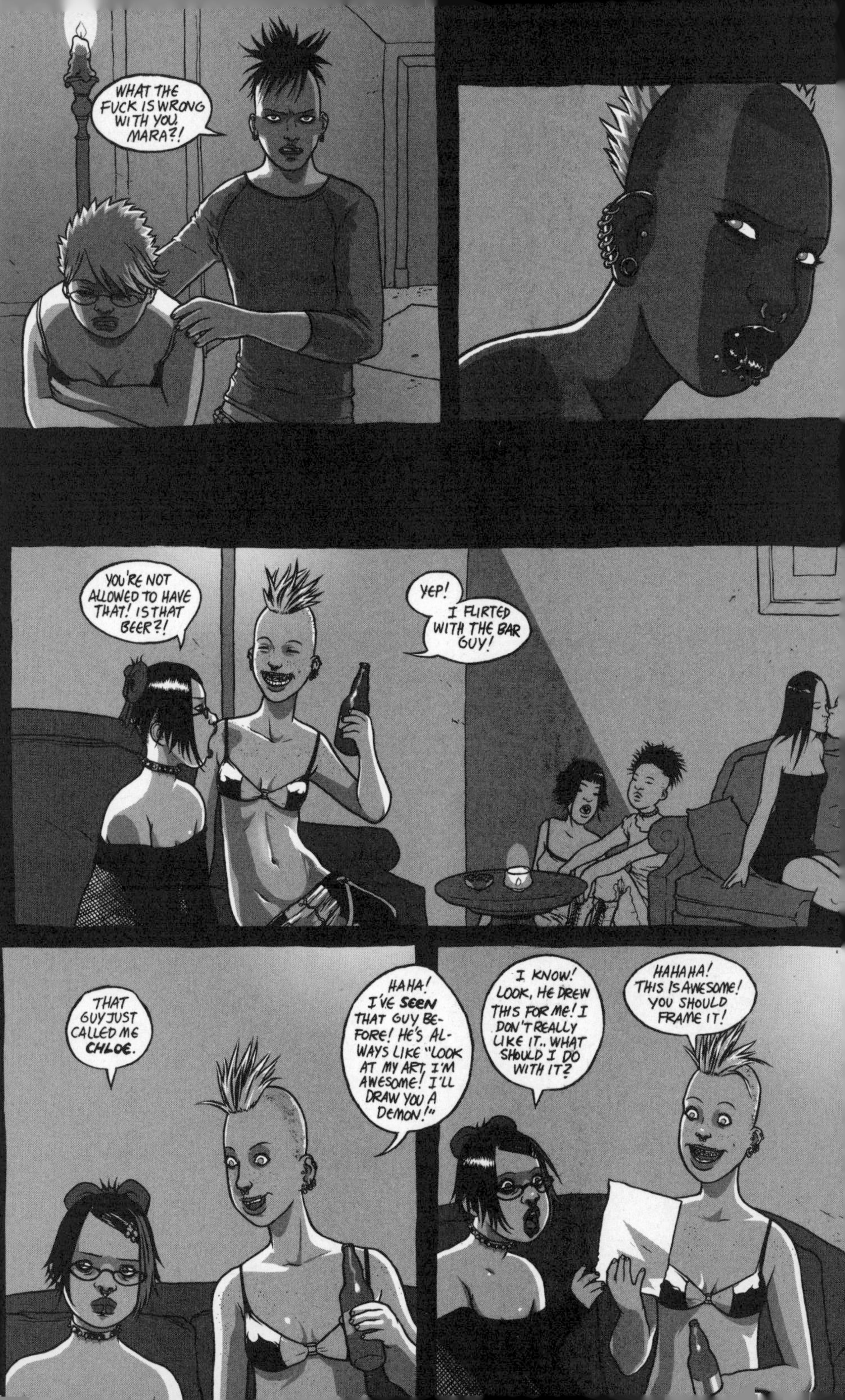
WHAT THE FUCK IS WRONG WITH YOU, MARA?!
YOU'RE NOT ALLOWED TO HAVE THAT! IS THAT BEER?!
YEP! I FLIRTED WITH THE BAR GUY!
THAT GUY JUST CALLED ME CHLOE.
HAHA! I'VE SEEN THAT GUY BEFORE! HE'S ALWAYS LIKE "LOOK AT MY ART, I'M AWESOME! I'LL DRAW YOU A DEMON!"
I KNOW! LOOK, HE DREW THIS FOR ME! I DON'T REALLY LIKE IT.. WHAT SHOULD I DO WITH IT?
HAHAHA! THIS IS AWESOME! YOU SHOULD FRAME IT!

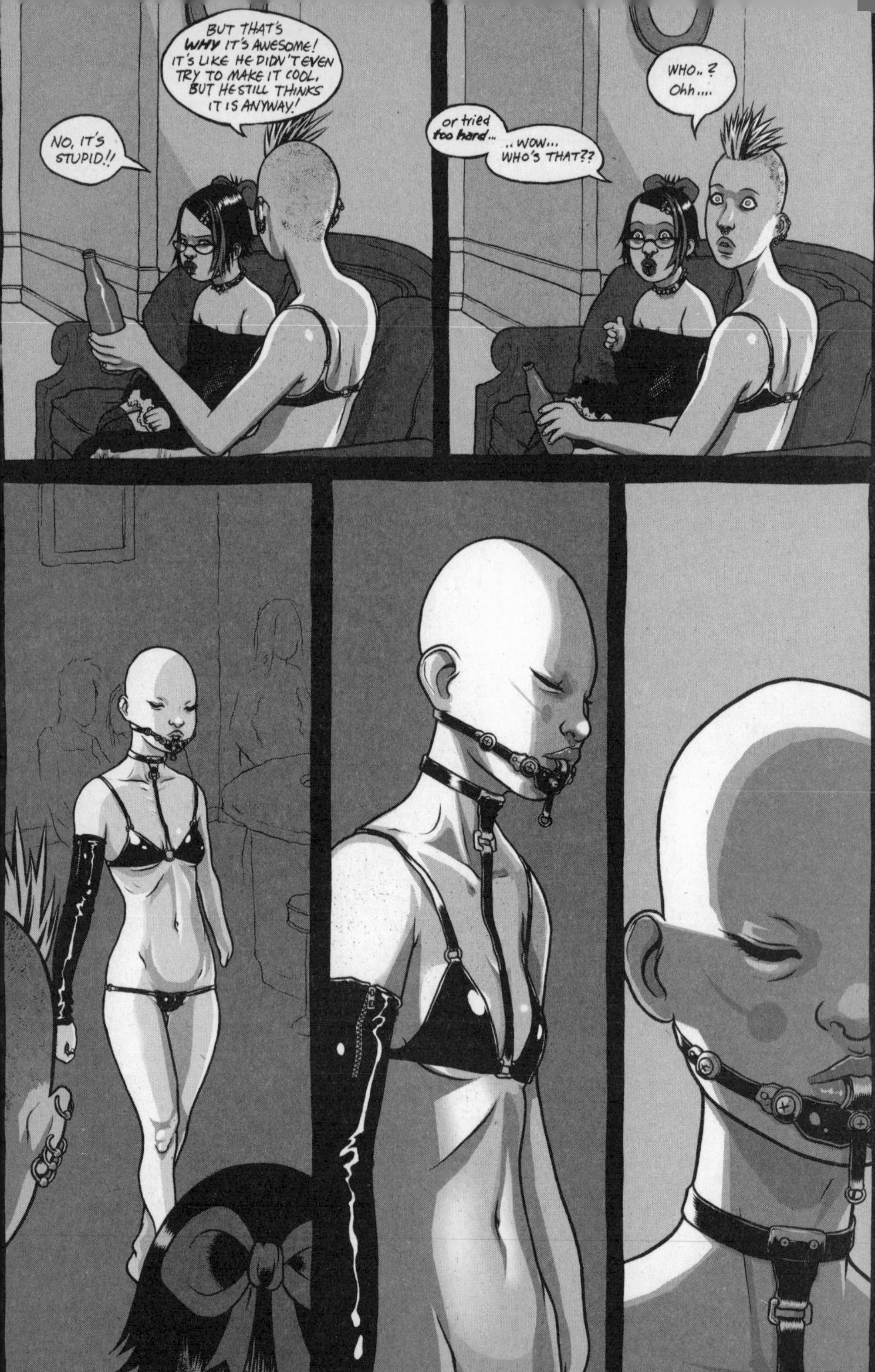
BUT THAT'S **WHY** IT'S AWESOME! IT'S LIKE HE DIDN'T EVEN TRY TO MAKE IT COOL, BUT HE STILL THINKS IT IS ANYWAY!
NO, IT'S STUPID!!
or tried *too hard*...
..WOW... WHO'S THAT??
WHO.. ? Ohh....

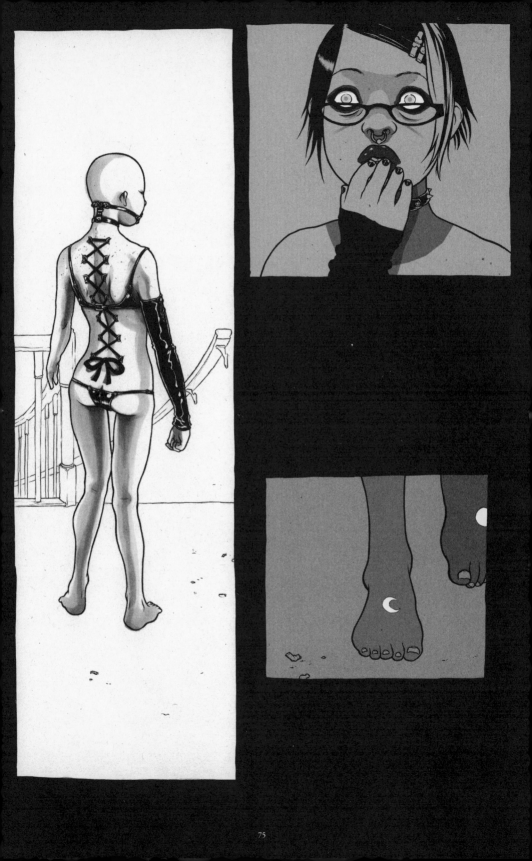

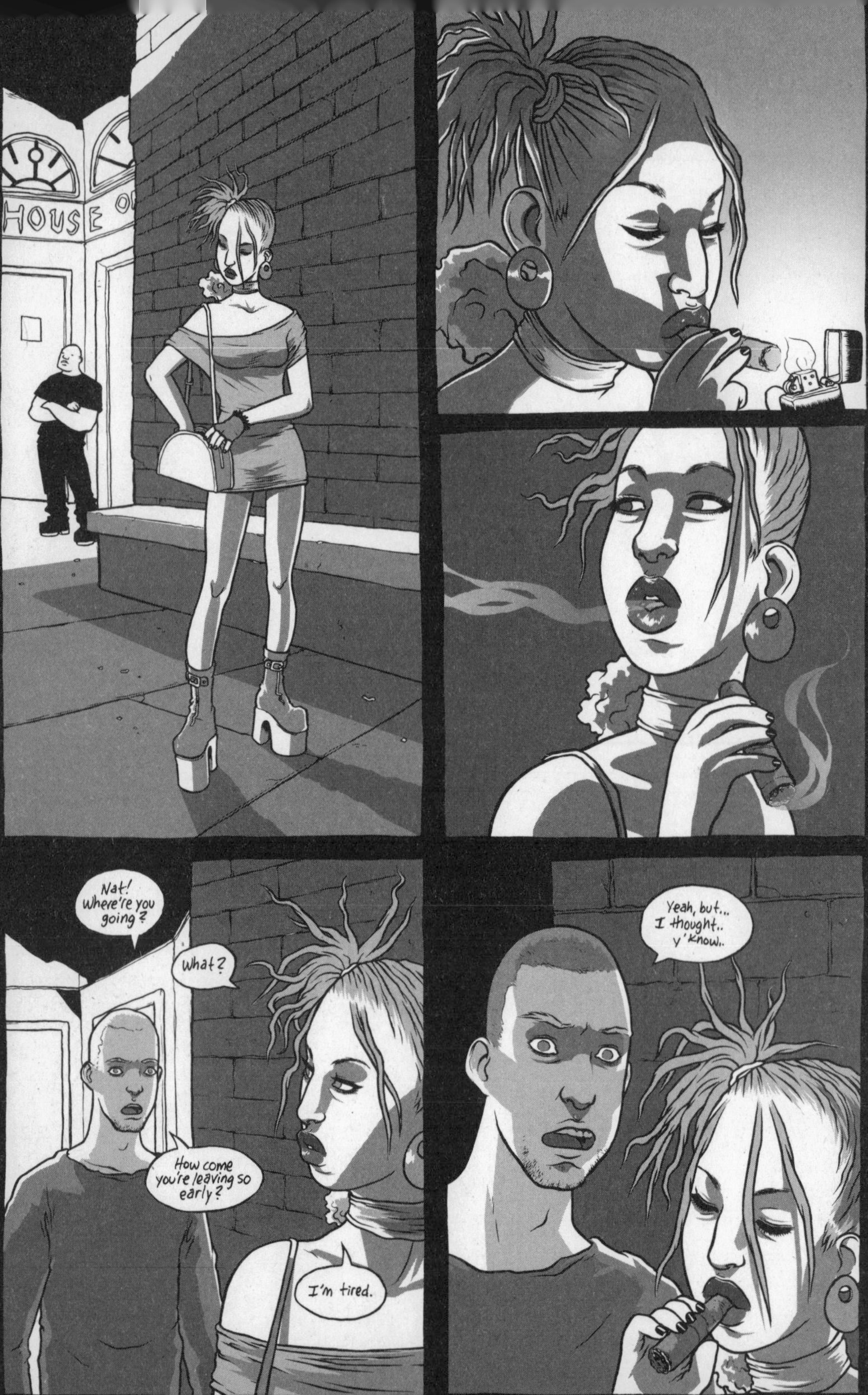
HOUSE OF
Nat! where're you going?
What?
How come you're leaving so early?
I'm tired.
Yeah, but... I thought.. y'know..

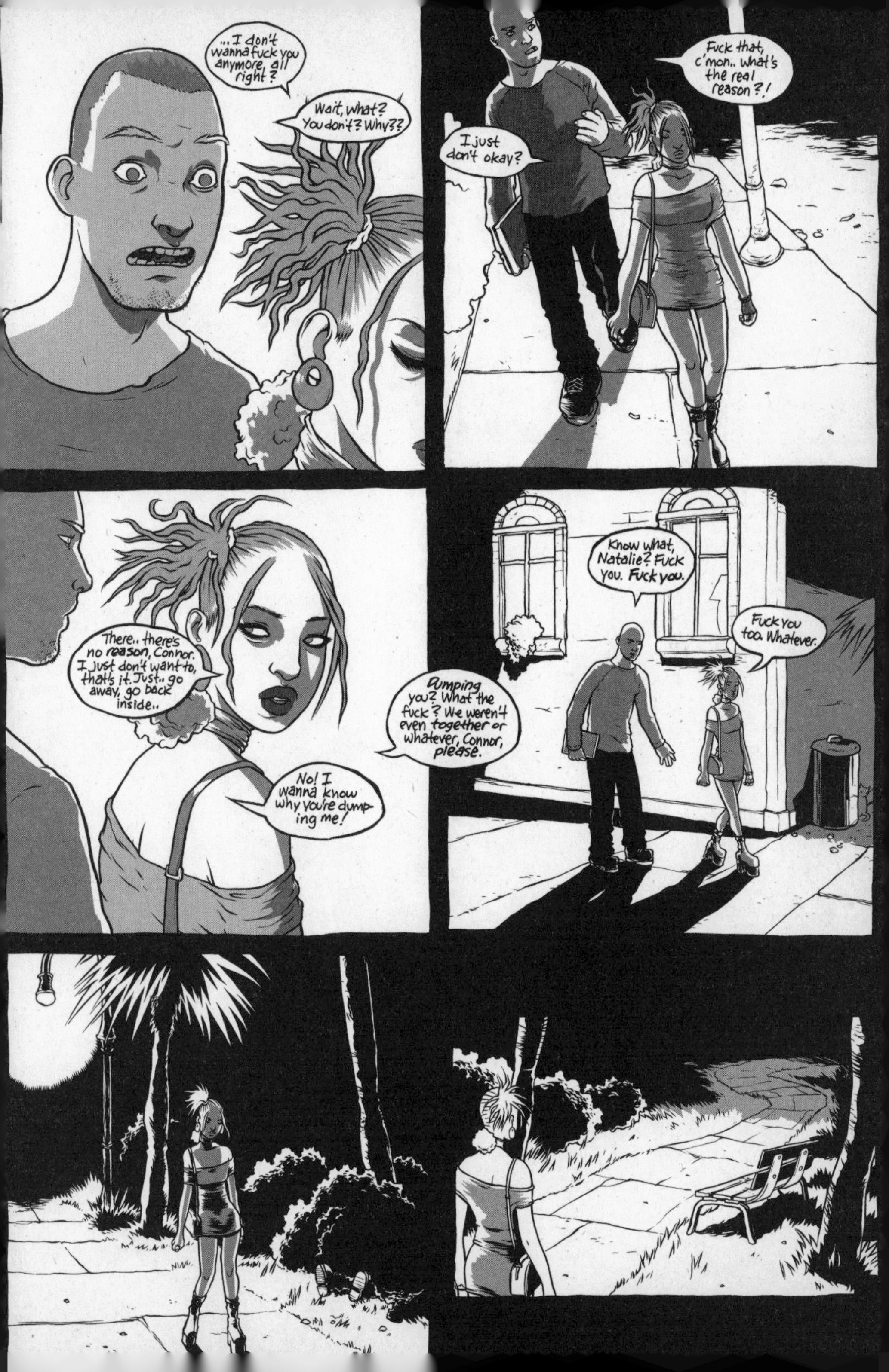
...I don't wanna fuck you anymore, all right?
Wait, what? You don't? Why??
Fuck that, c'mon.. what's the real reason?!
I just don't okay?
There.. there's no reason, Connor. I just don't want to, that's it. Just.. go away, go back inside..
No! I wanna know why you're dump-ing me!
Dumping you? What the fuck? We weren't even together or whatever, Connor, please.
Know what, Natalie? Fuck you. Fuck you.
Fuck you too. Whatever.

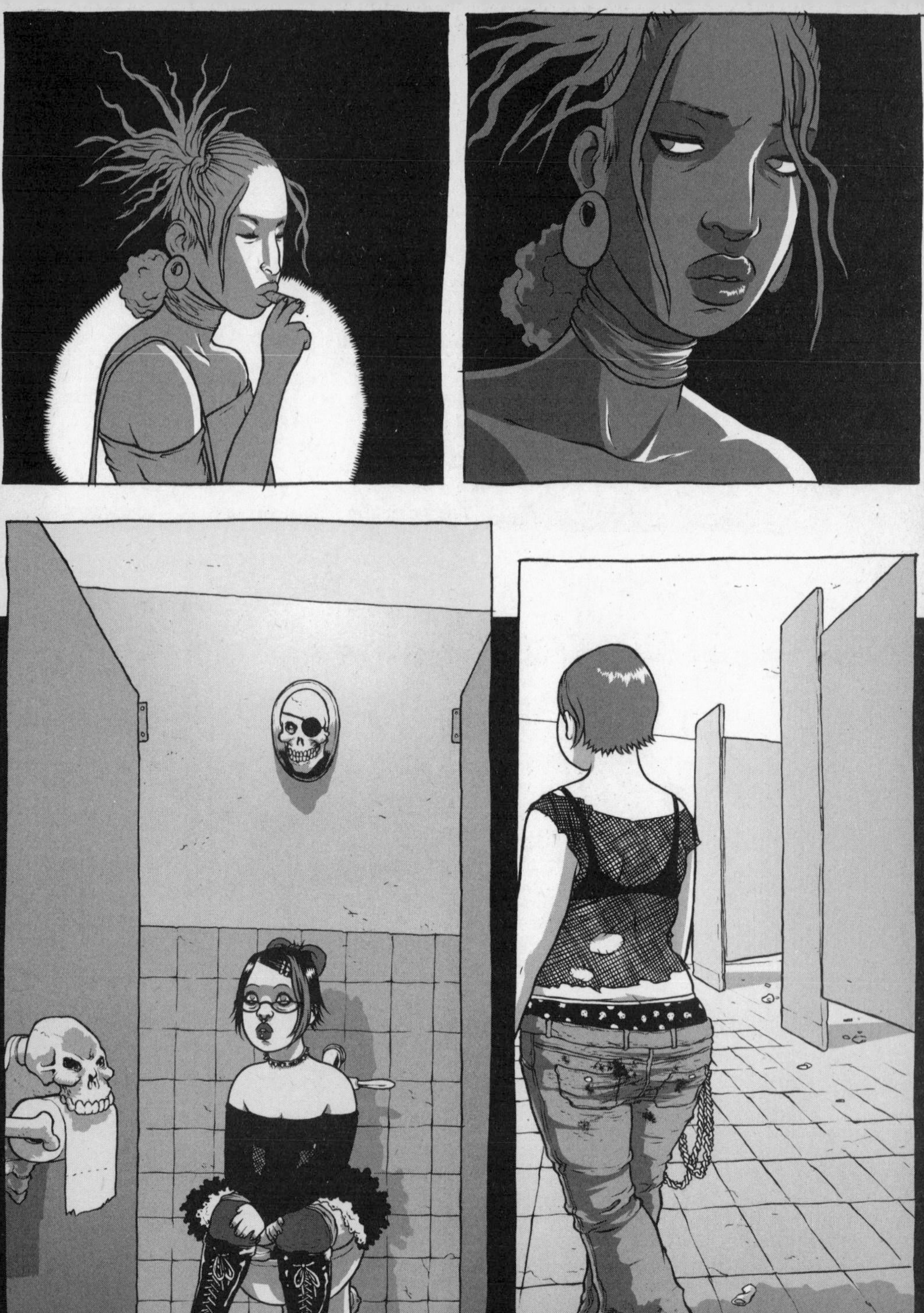

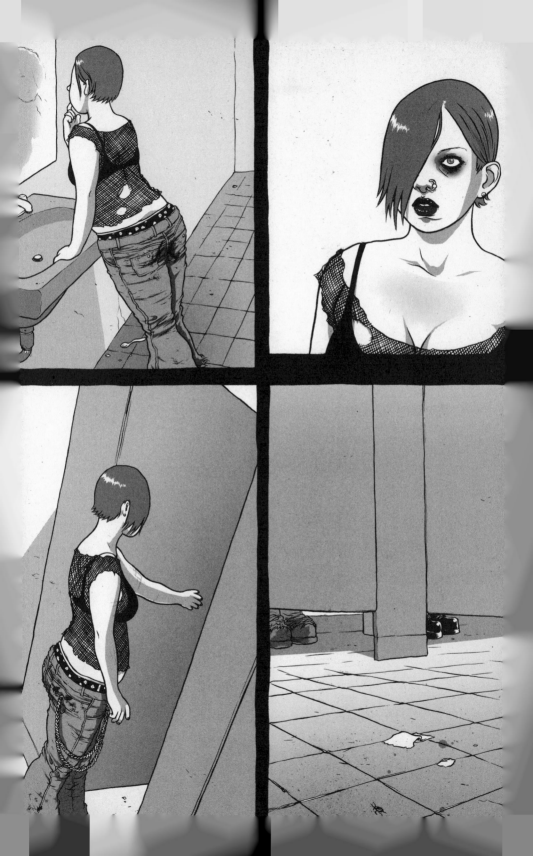

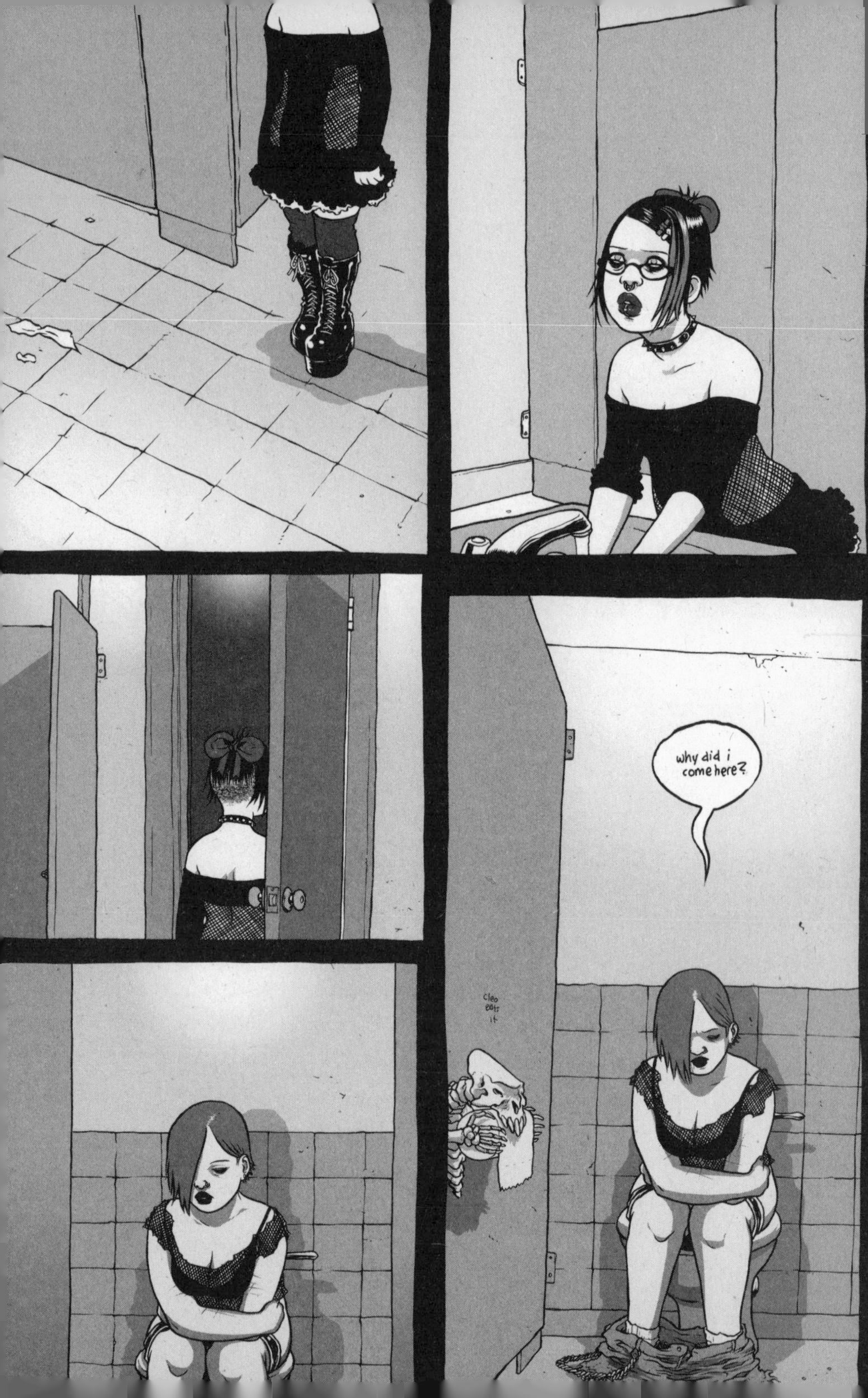
why did i come here?
cleo eats it

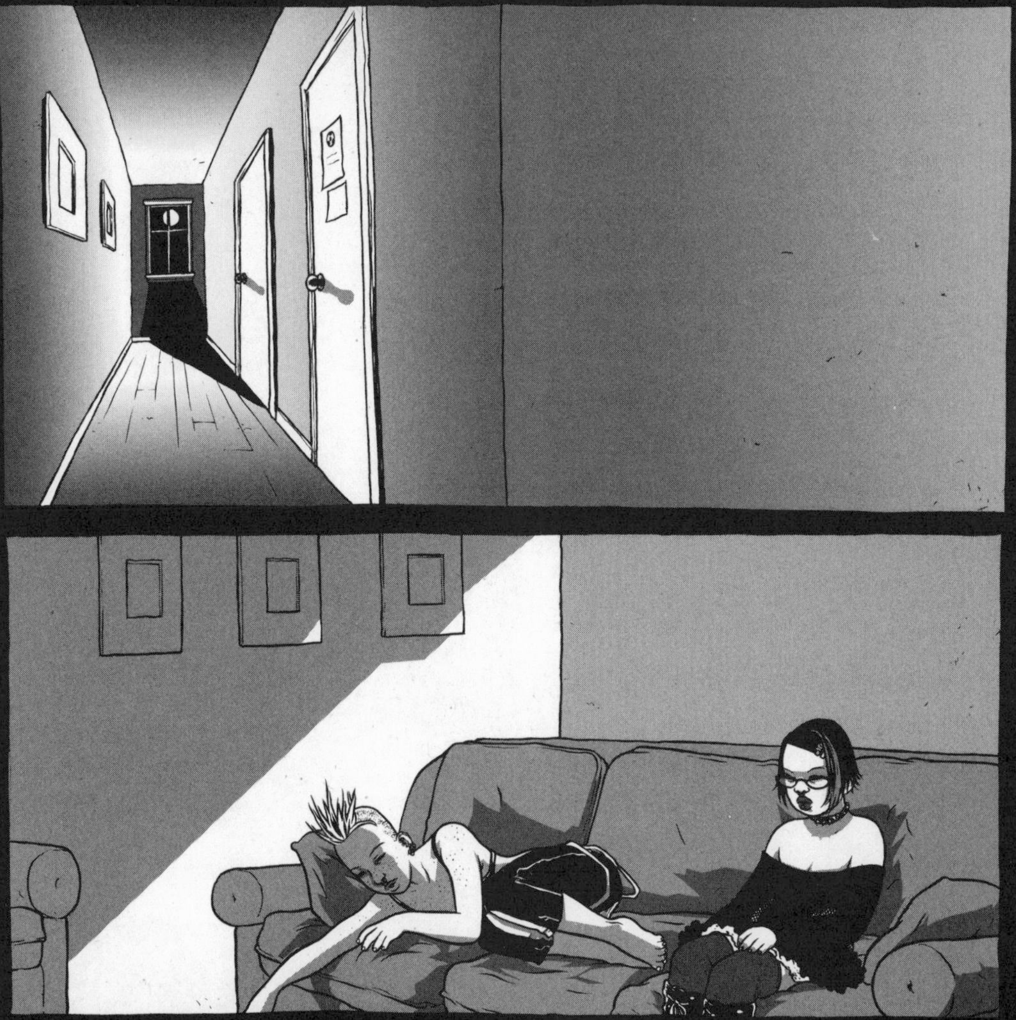

"i didn't even see Natalie there at all. she invited us, and then doesn't talk to us... maybe she really does hate me. maybe this sofa is her great-grandmother's sofa from world war II that she passed down after her husband was killed in the pacific by a kamikaze raid, and now i sat on it... i wonder if there could be a ghost, like her grandmother's ghost, living inside the sofa, like she's hanging on to the last memories of her husband's life. and when i sat on it, her ghost or part of it went into my butt, and now i have an old woman's ghost living in my butt. i guess it's big enough to hold probably at least four ghosts. i feel bad for Natalie now... i should apologize..."

"now i'm sitting here with a rather drunk Trilby; she only had a couple drinks, too. i don't know what her problem is..."

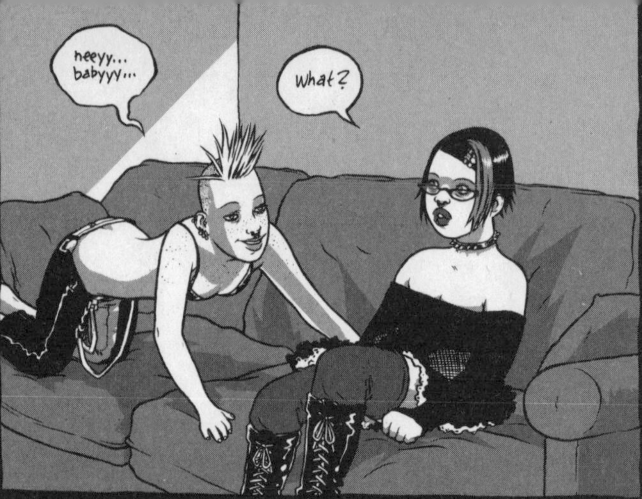
neeyy... babyyy...
what?

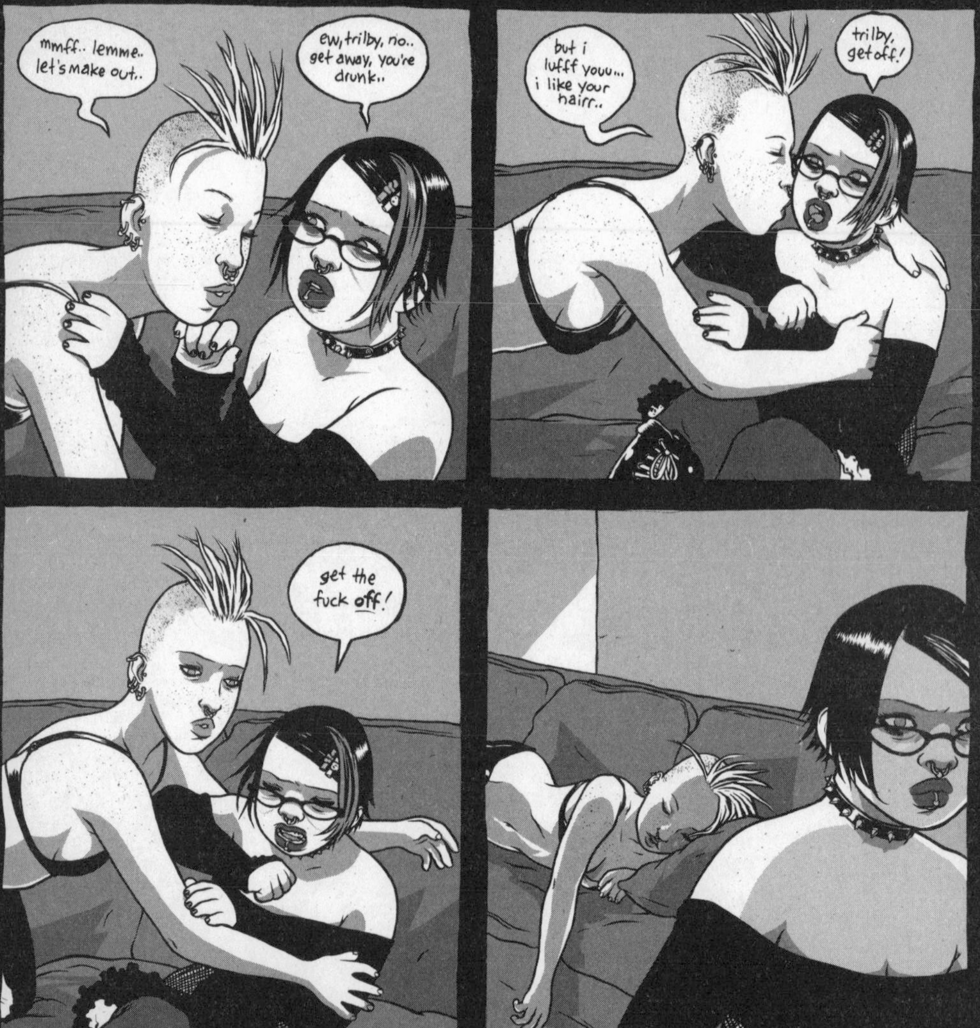
mmff.. lemme.. let's make out..
ew, trilby, no.. get away, you're drunk..
but i lufff youu... i like your hairr..
trilby, get off!
get the fuck off!

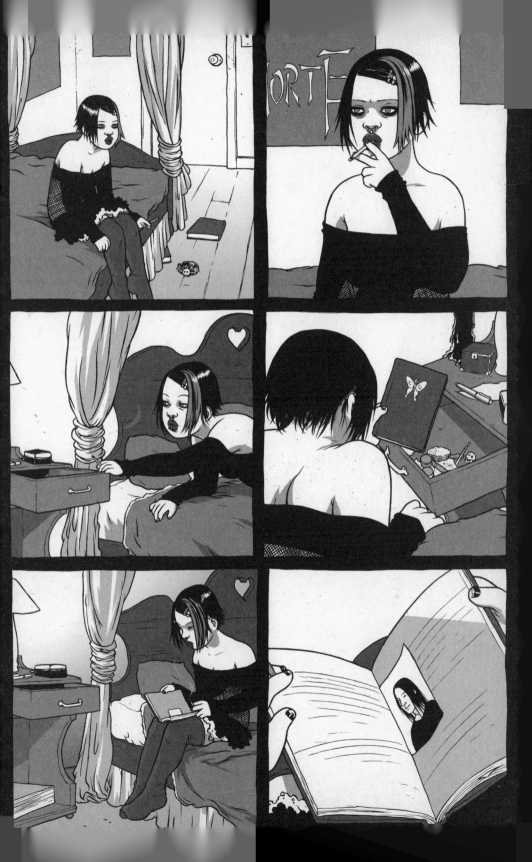

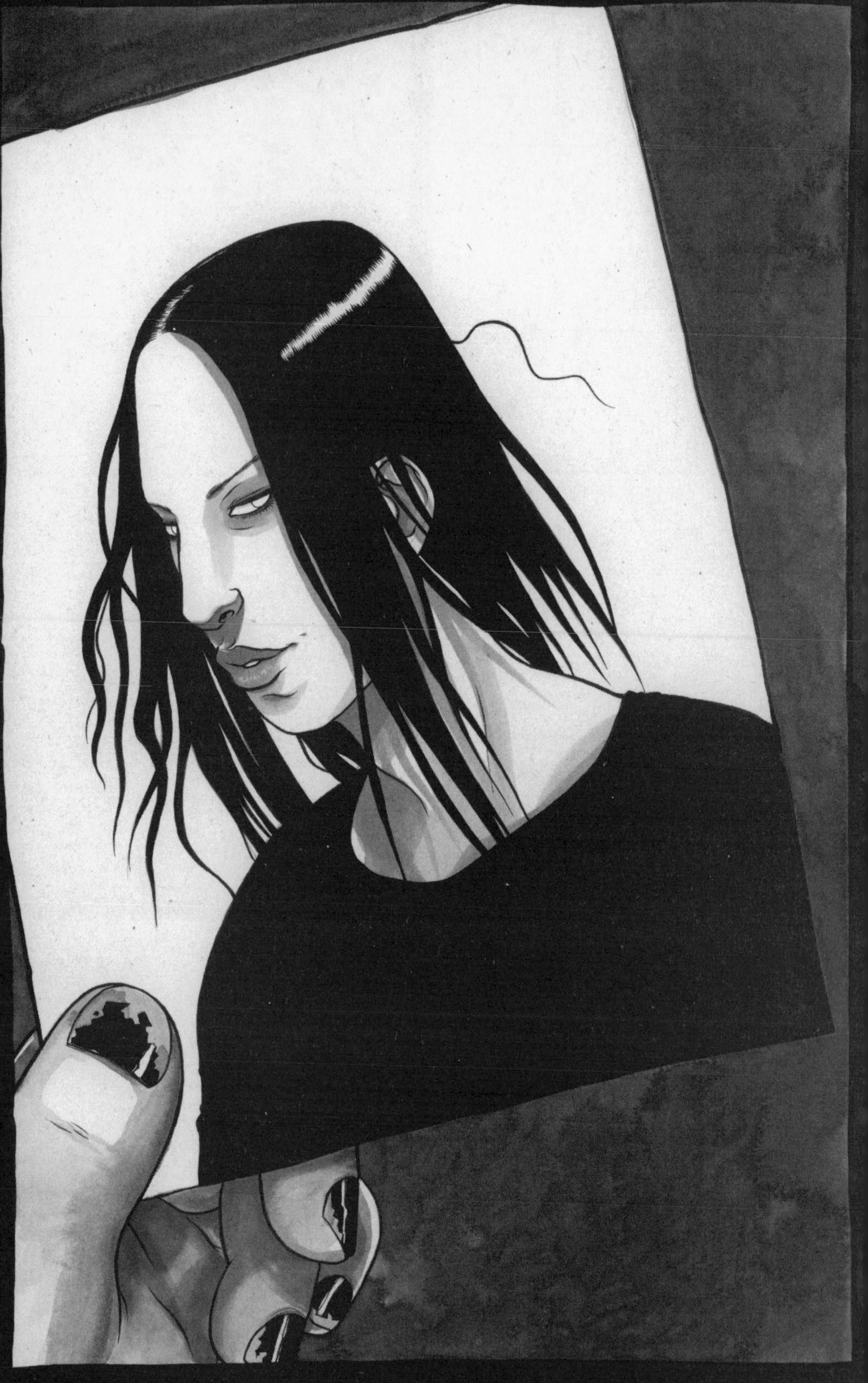

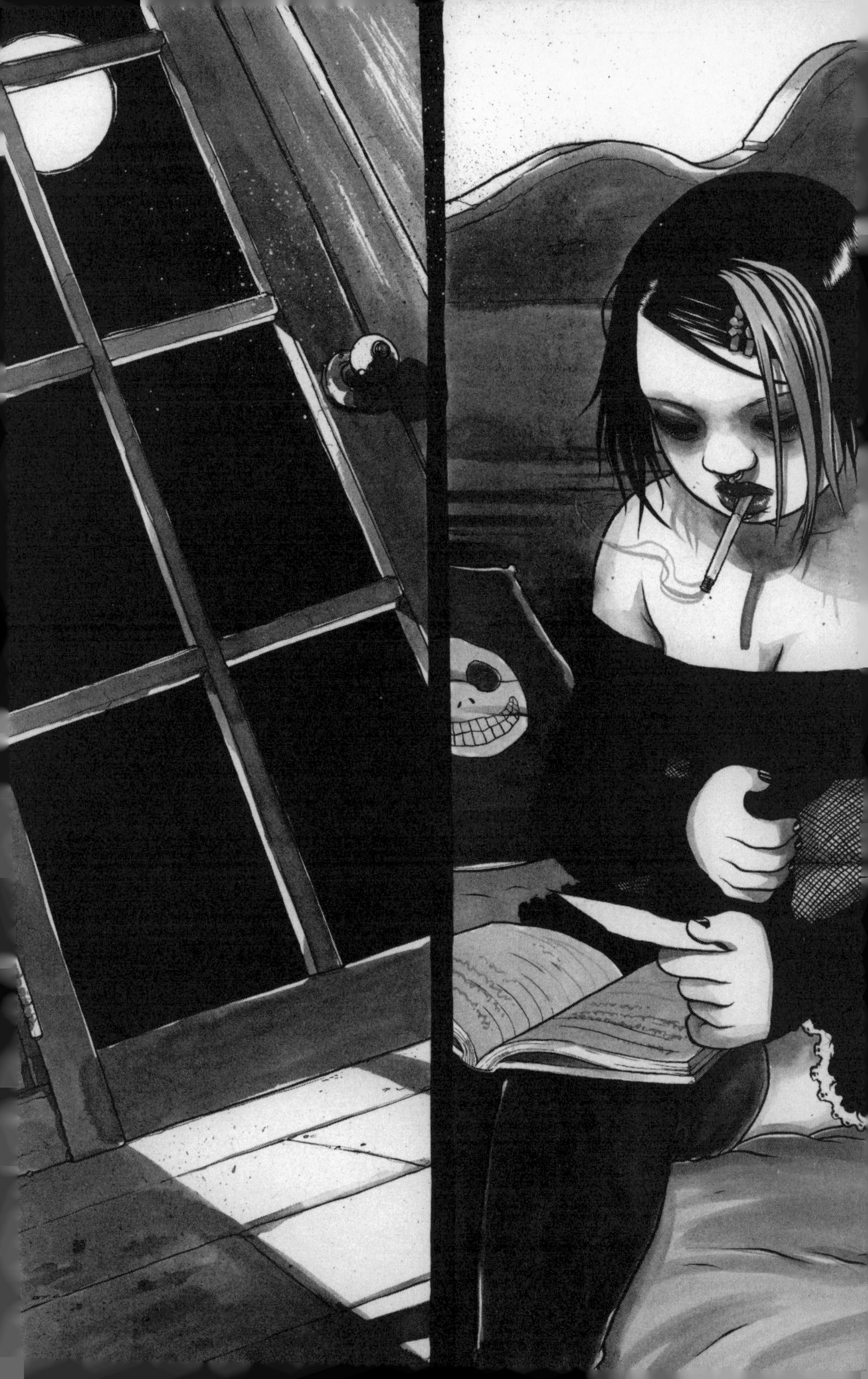

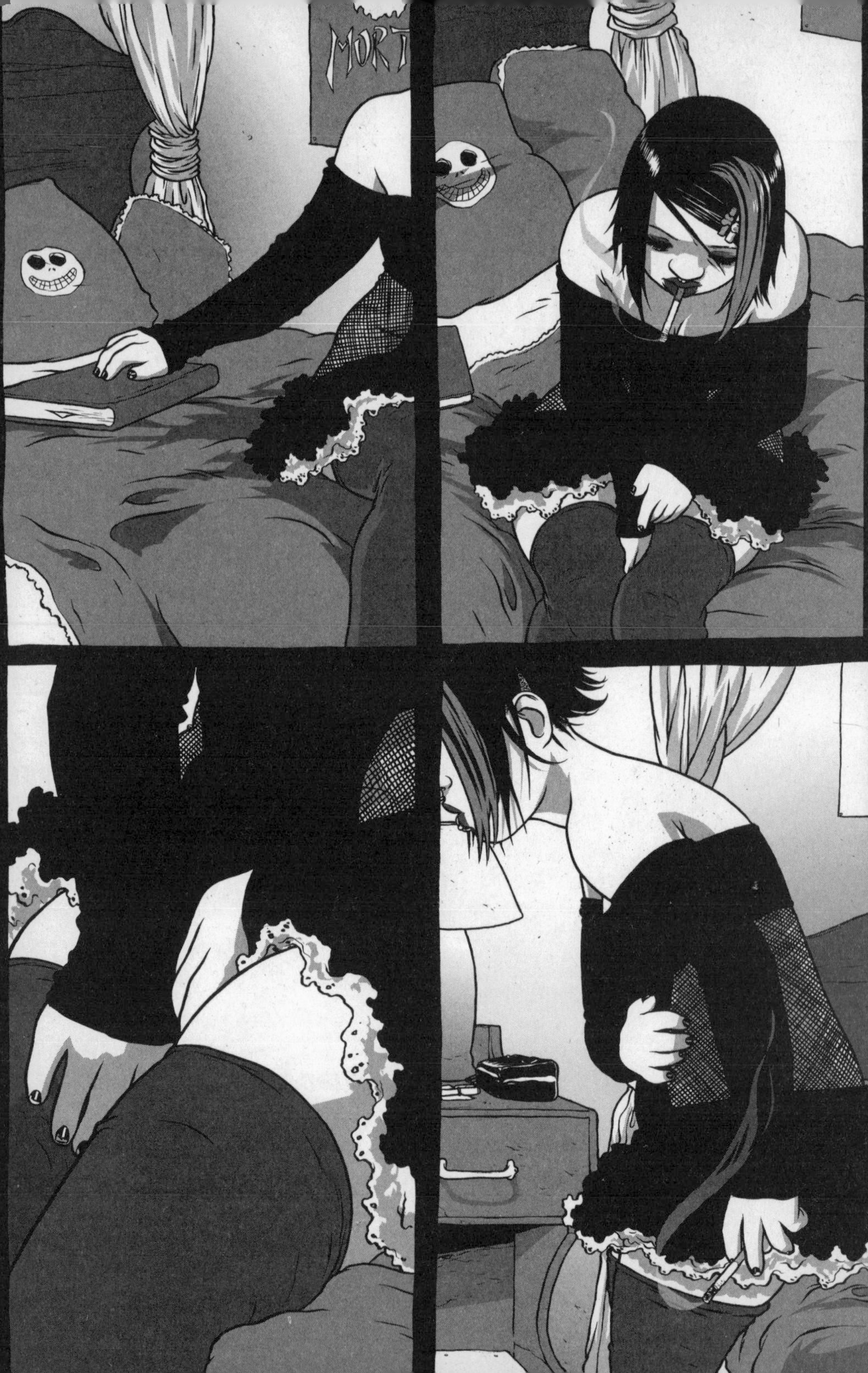
MORT

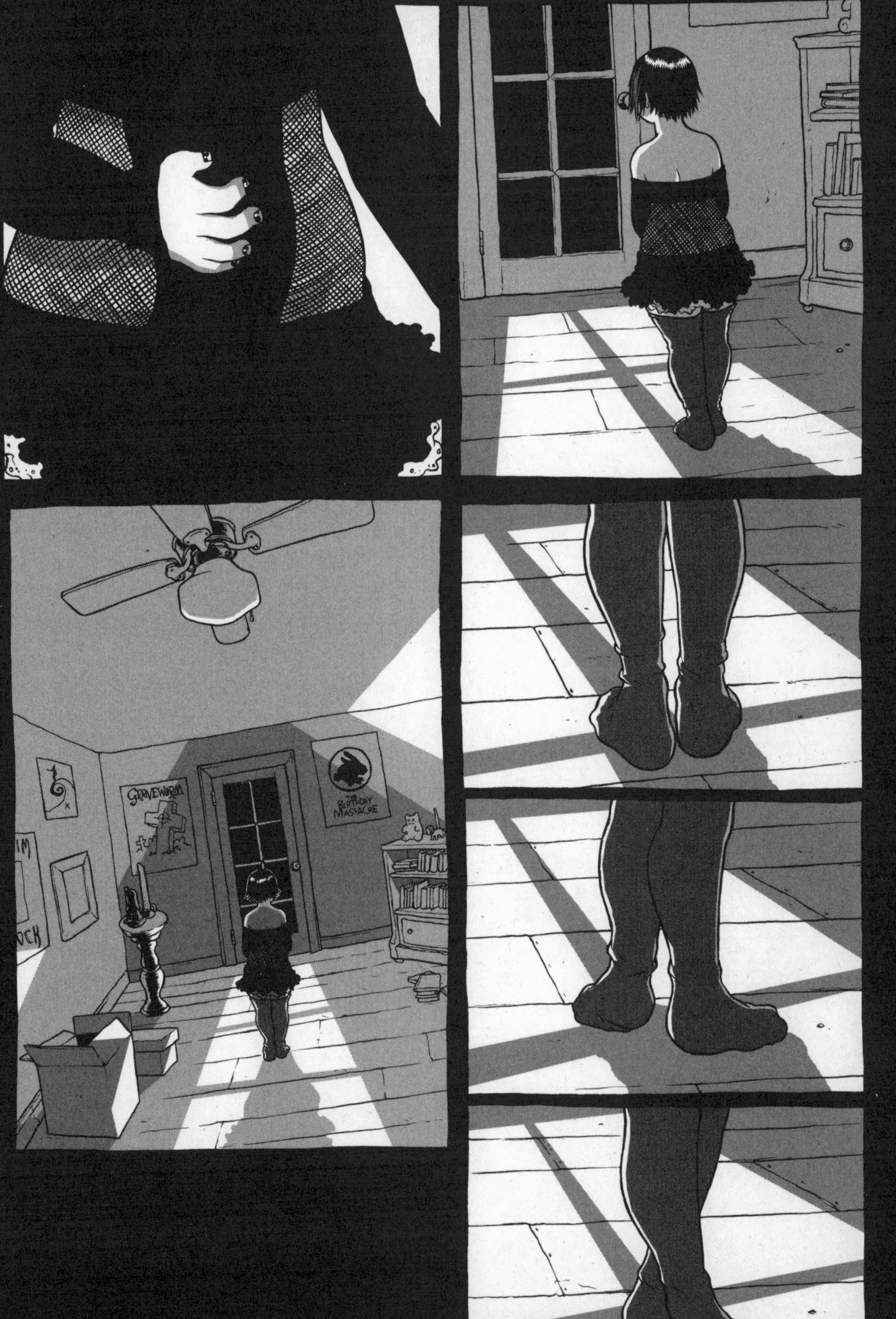
GRAVEWORM
THE BIRTHDAY MASSACRE

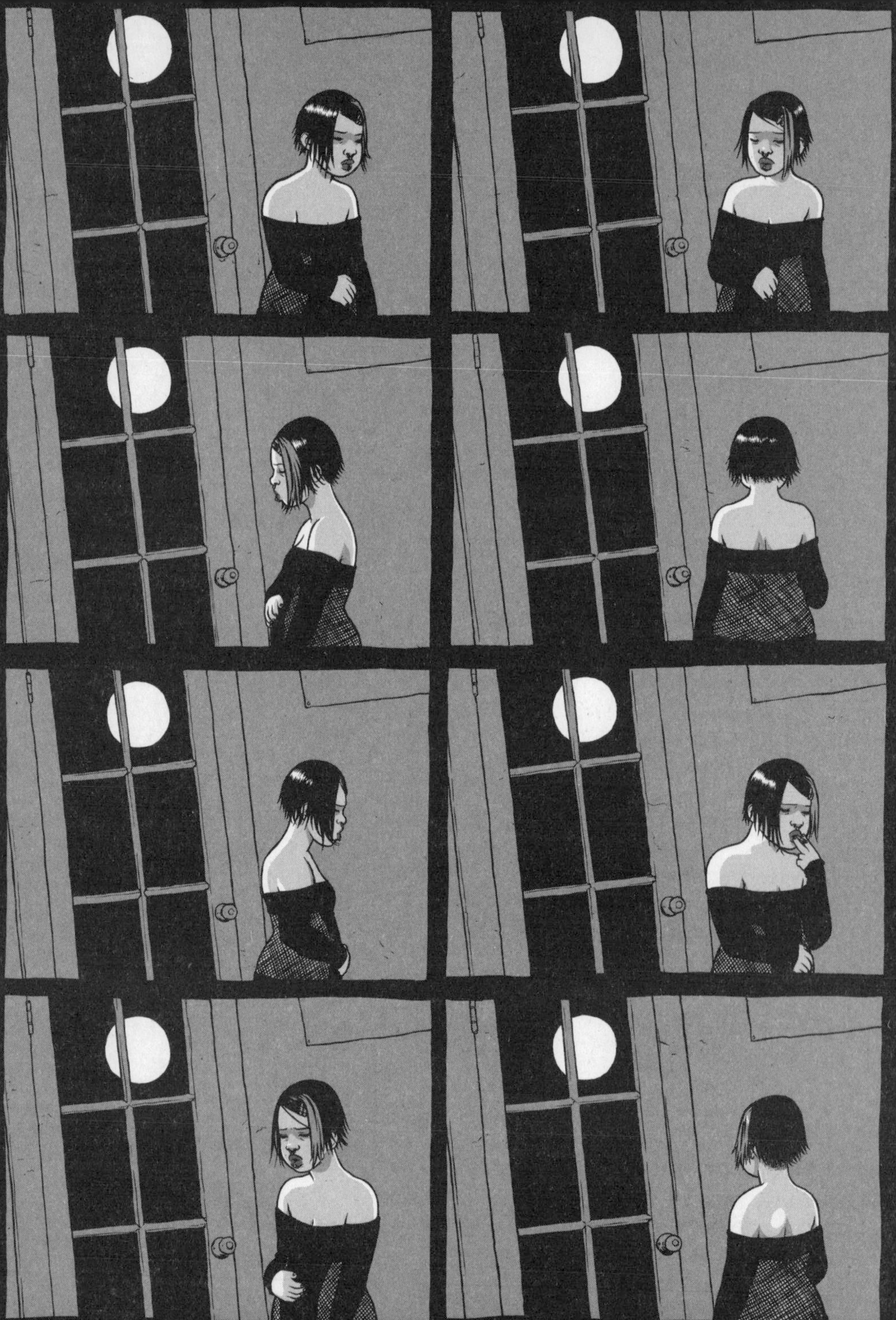

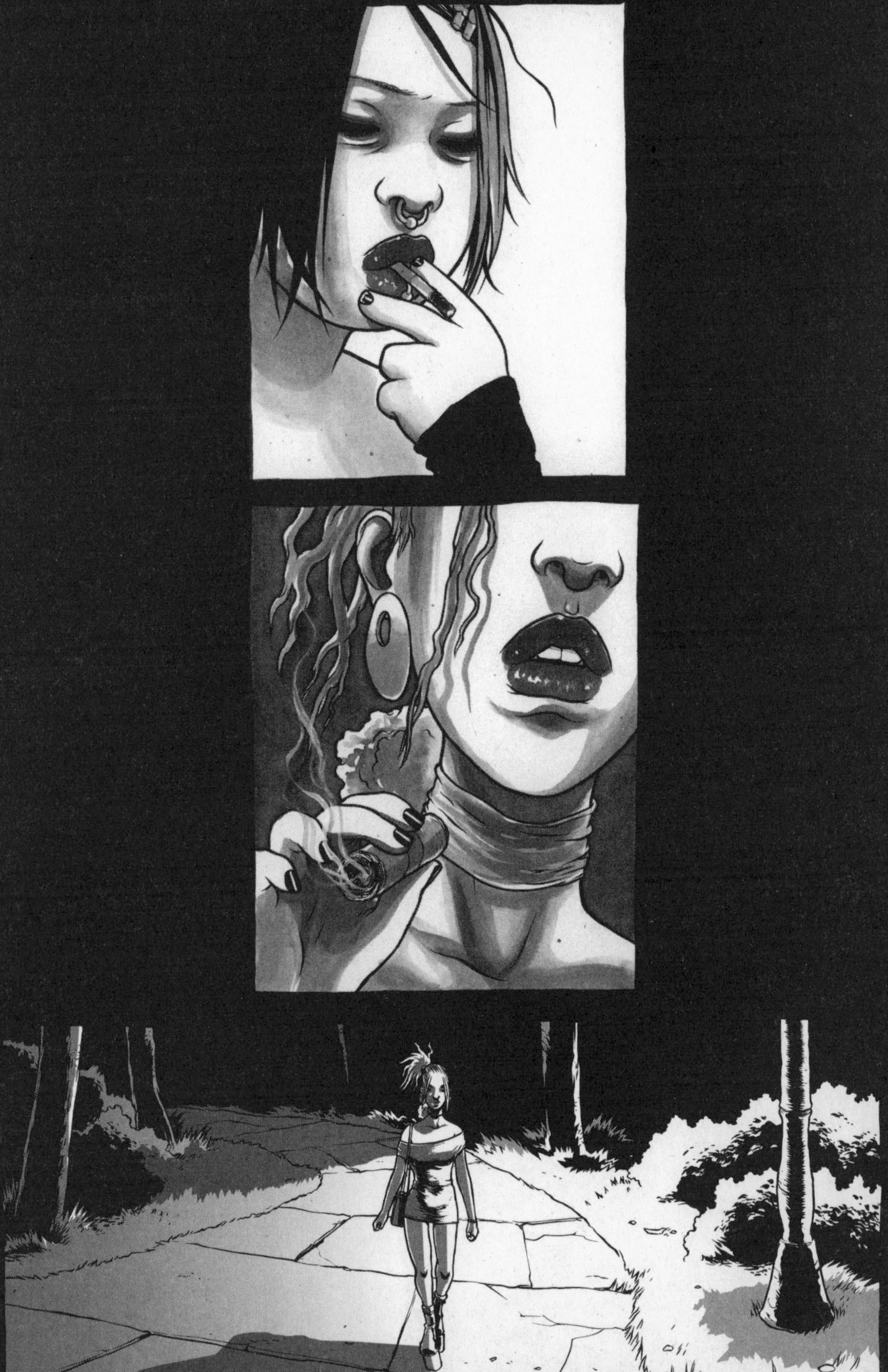

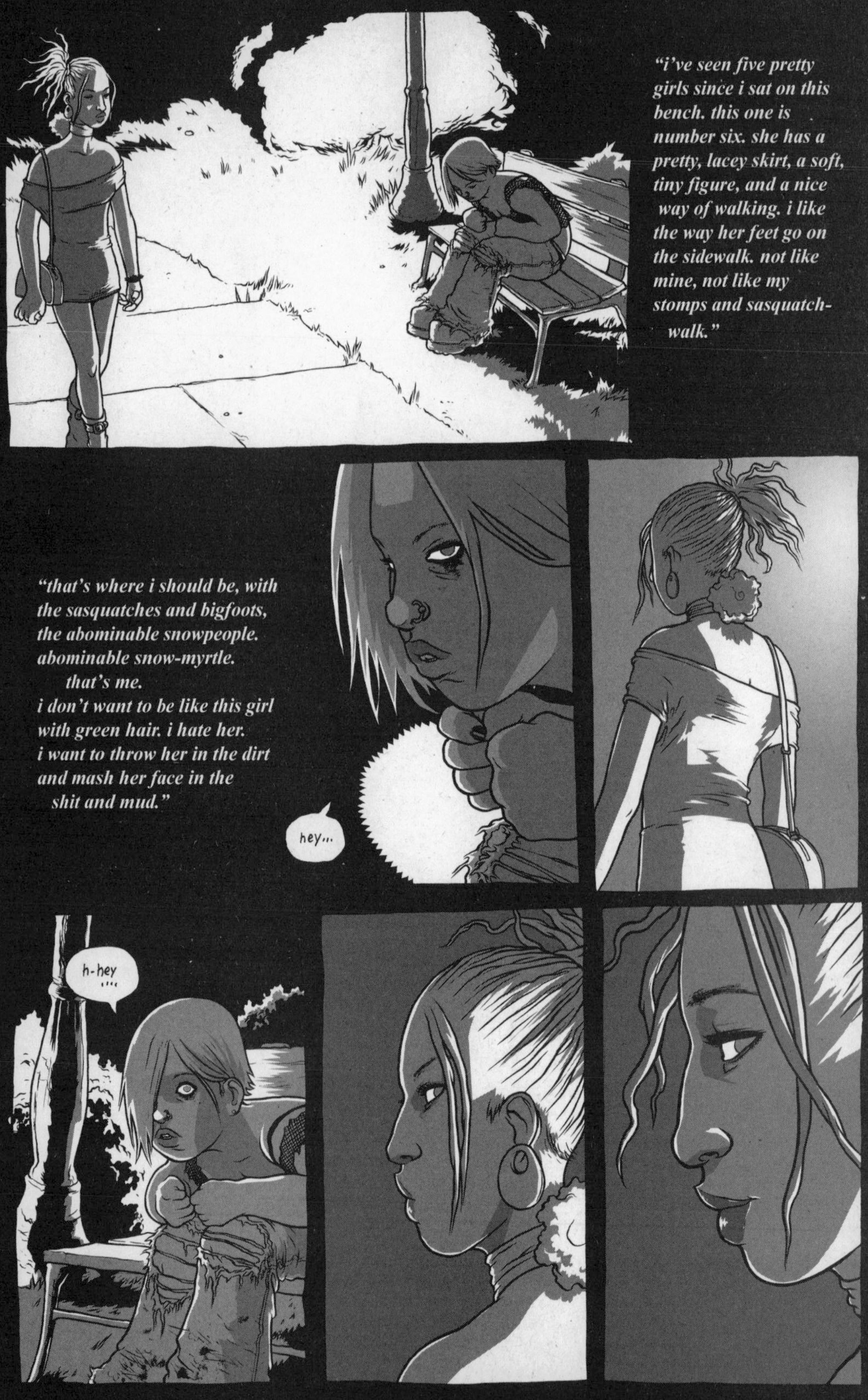
"i've seen five pretty girls since i sat on this bench. this one is number six. she has a pretty, lacey skirt, a soft, tiny figure, and a nice way of walking. i like the way her feet go on the sidewalk. not like mine, not like my stomps and sasquatch-walk."
"that's where i should be, with the sasquatches and bigfoots, the abominable snowpeople. abominable snow-myrtle. that's me. i don't want to be like this girl with green hair. i hate her. i want to throw her in the dirt and mash her face in the shit and mud."
hey...
h-hey ....

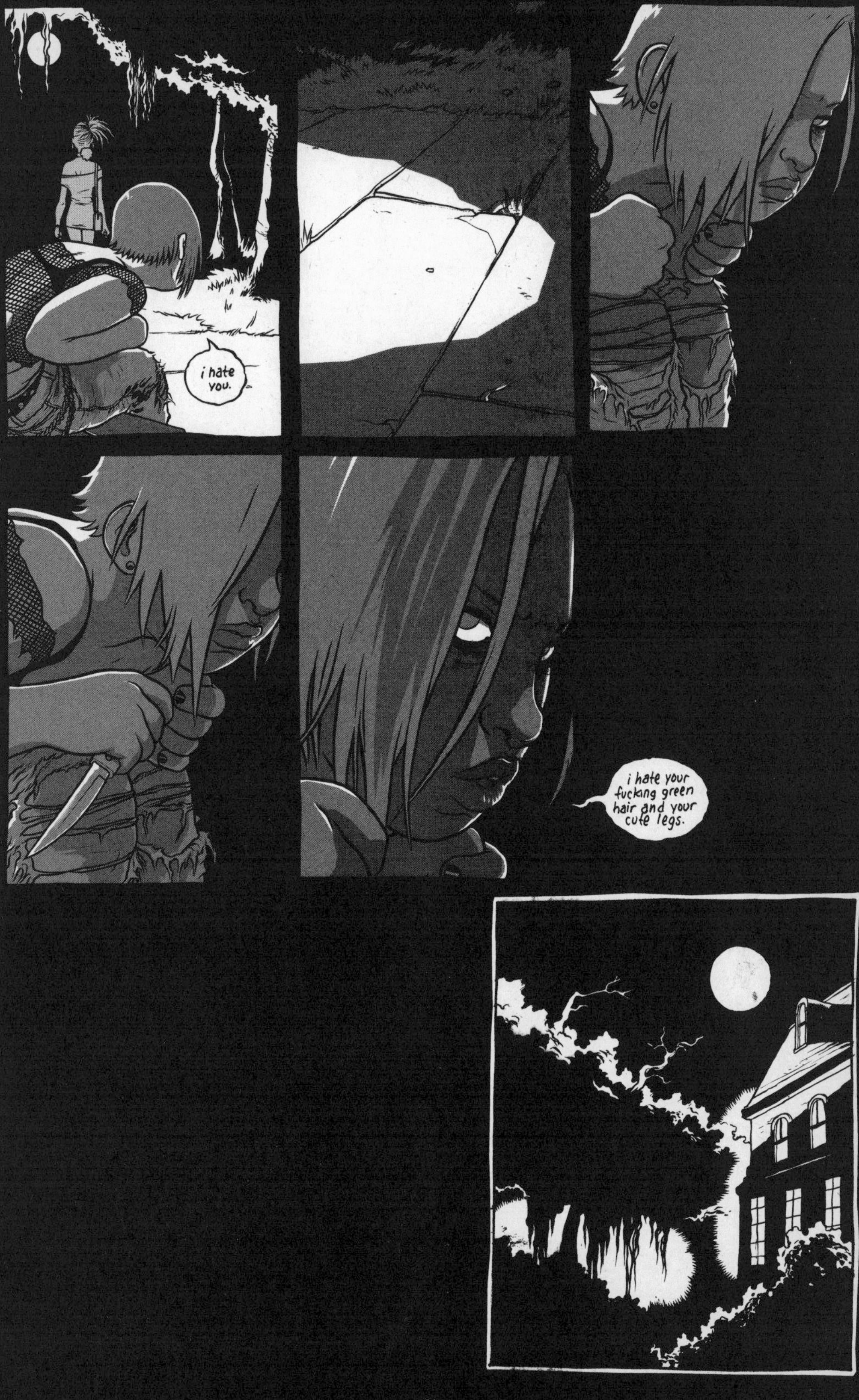
i hate you.
i hate your fucking green hair and your cute legs.

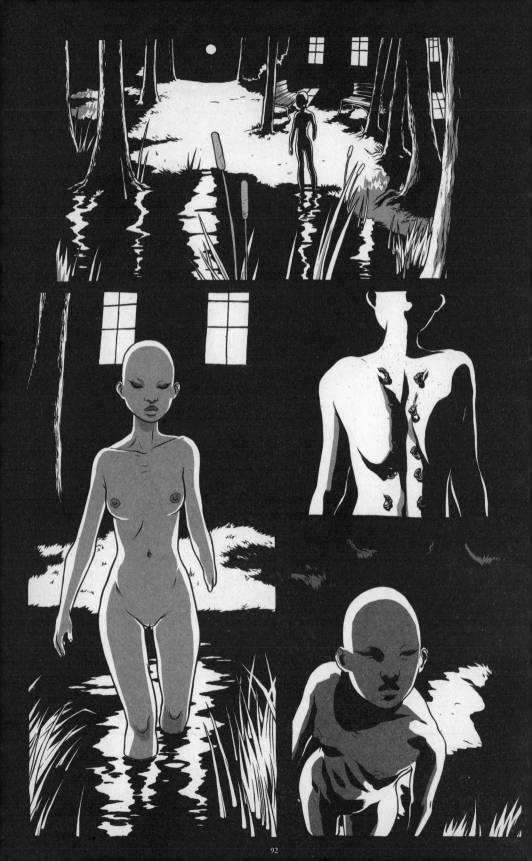

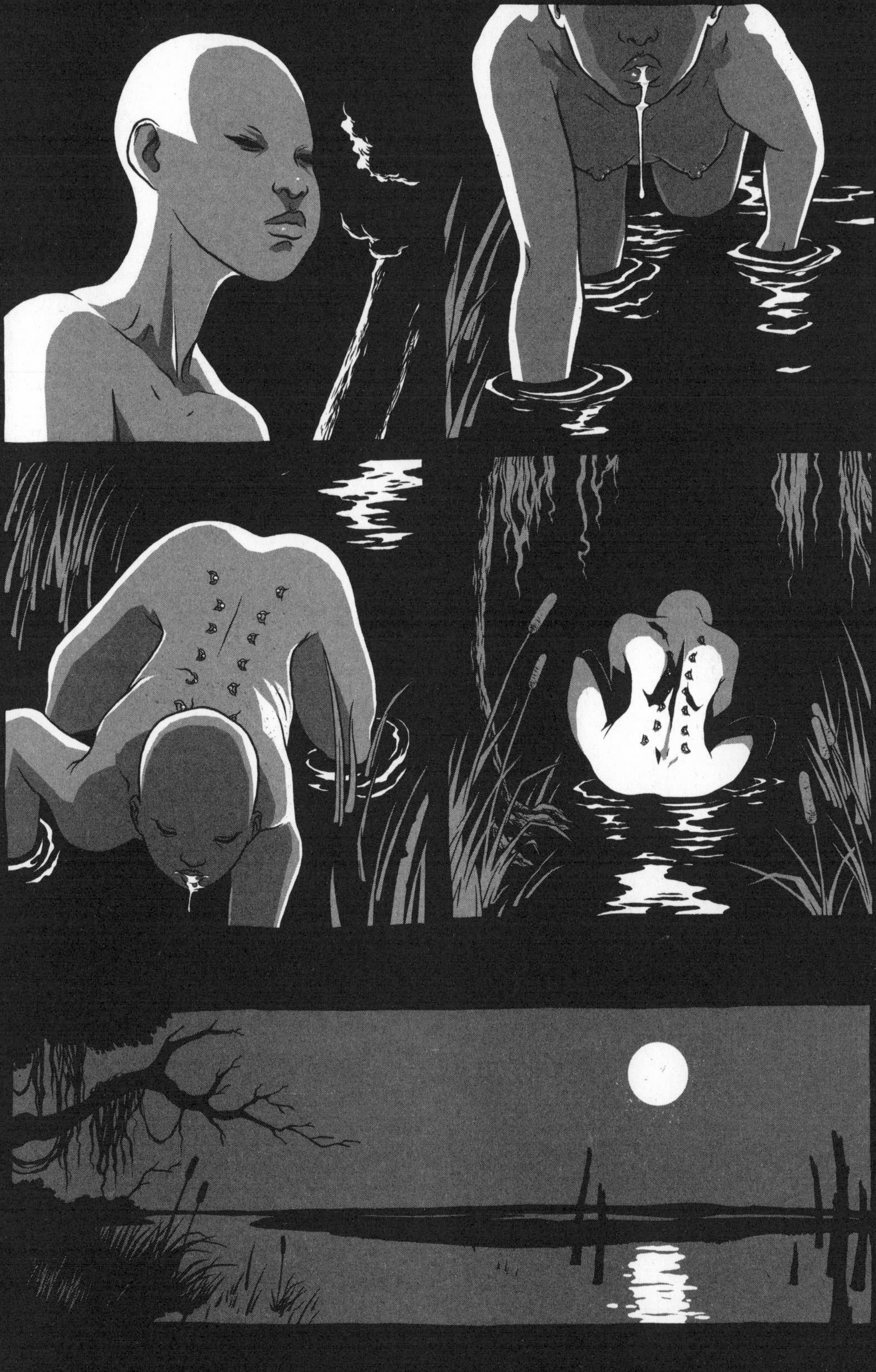

"I never expected you to love me
The way I loved you
To have you near
Was all I wanted
Just to have you near."

-Azure Ray

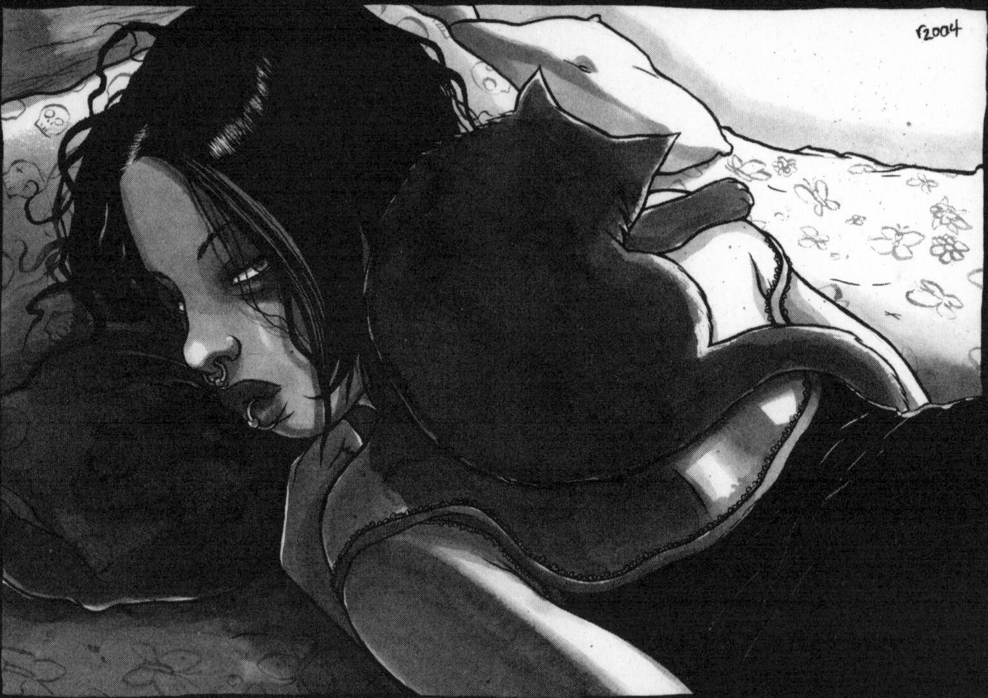
r2004

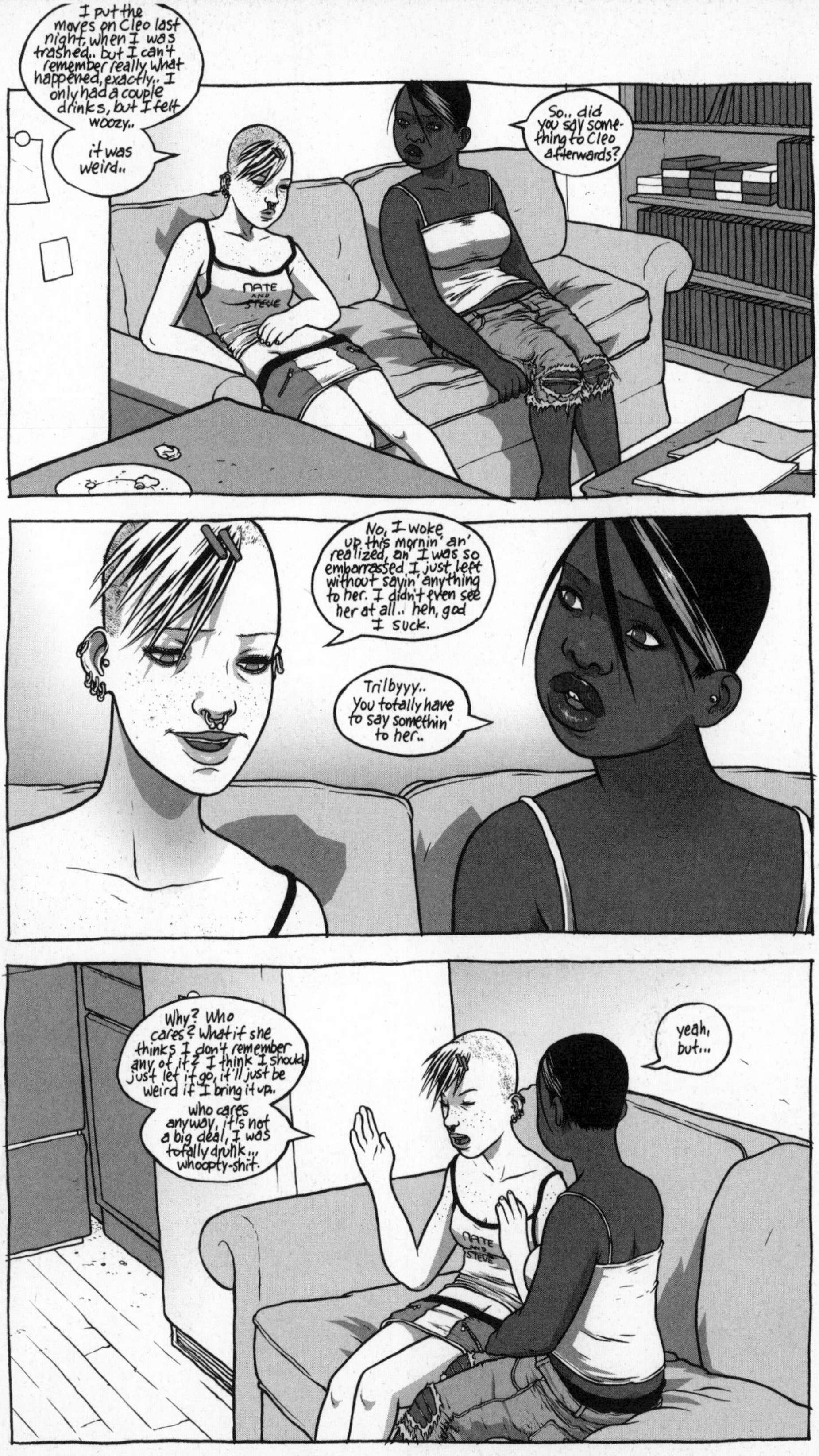
I put the moves on Cleo last night, when I was trashed.. but I can't remember really what happened, exactly.. I only had a couple drinks, but I felt woozy..
it was weird..
So.. did you say something to Cleo afterwards?
No, I woke up this mornin' an' realized, an' I was so embarrassed I just left without sayin' anything to her. I didn't even see her at all.. heh, god I suck.
Trilbyyy.. You totally have to say somethin' to her..
Why? Who cares? What if she thinks I don't remember any of it? I think I should just let it go, it'll just be weird if I bring it up.
Who cares anyway, it's not a big deal, I was totally drunk... whoopty-shit.
yeah, but...

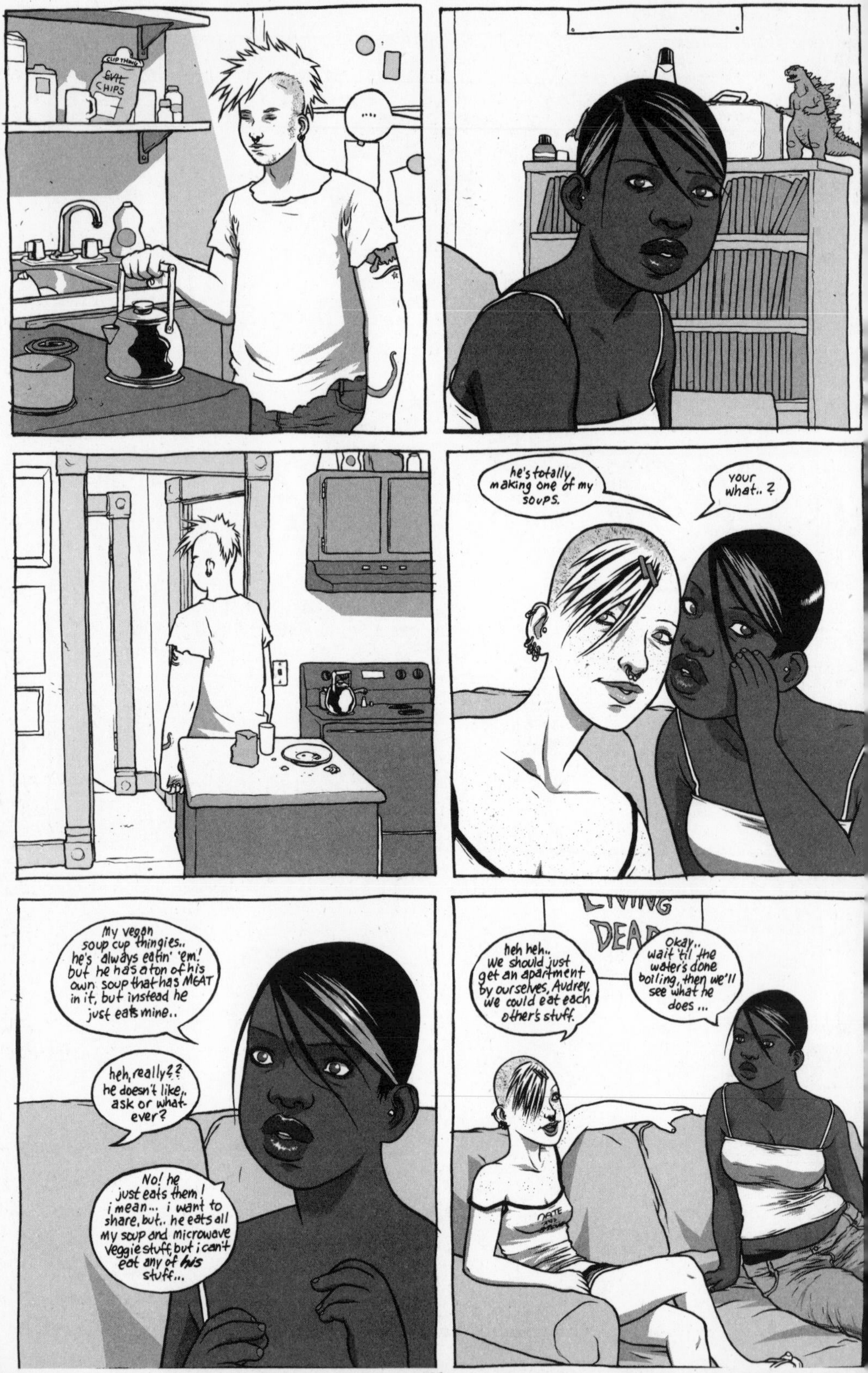

he's totally making one of my soups.
your what.. ?
My vegan soup cup thingies.. he's always eatin' 'em! but he has a ton of his own soup that has MEAT in it, but instead he just eats mine..
heh, really?? he doesn't like,, ask or what-ever?
No! he just eats them! i mean... i want to share, but.. he eats all my soup and microwave veggie stuff, but i can't eat any of his stuff...
heh heh.. We should just get an apartment by ourselves, Audrey. we could eat each other's stuff.
Okay.. wait 'til the water's done boiling, then we'll see what he does...

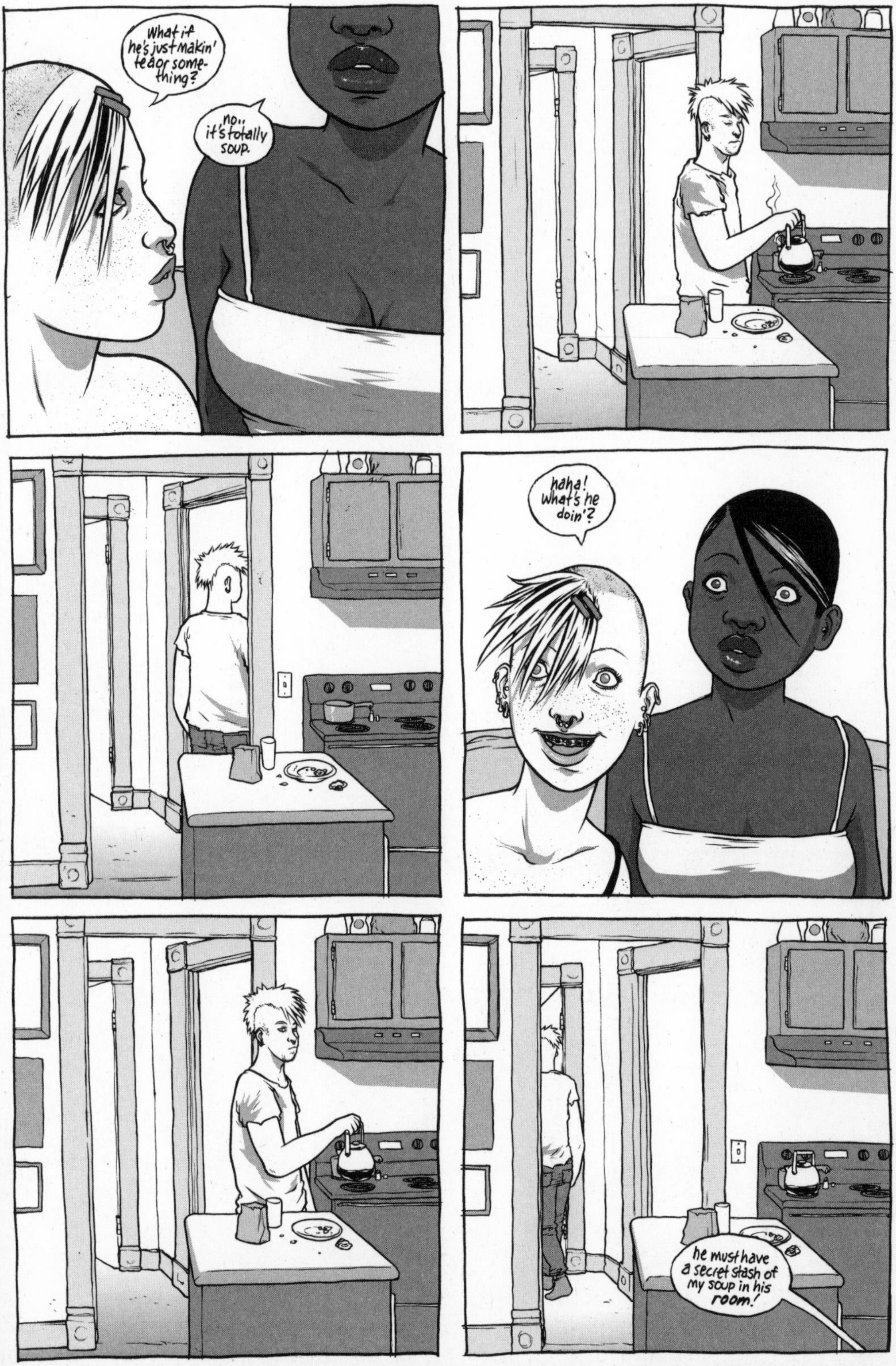
What if he's just makin' tea or something?
no.. it's totally soup.
haha! What's he doin'?
he must have a secret stash of my soup in his room!

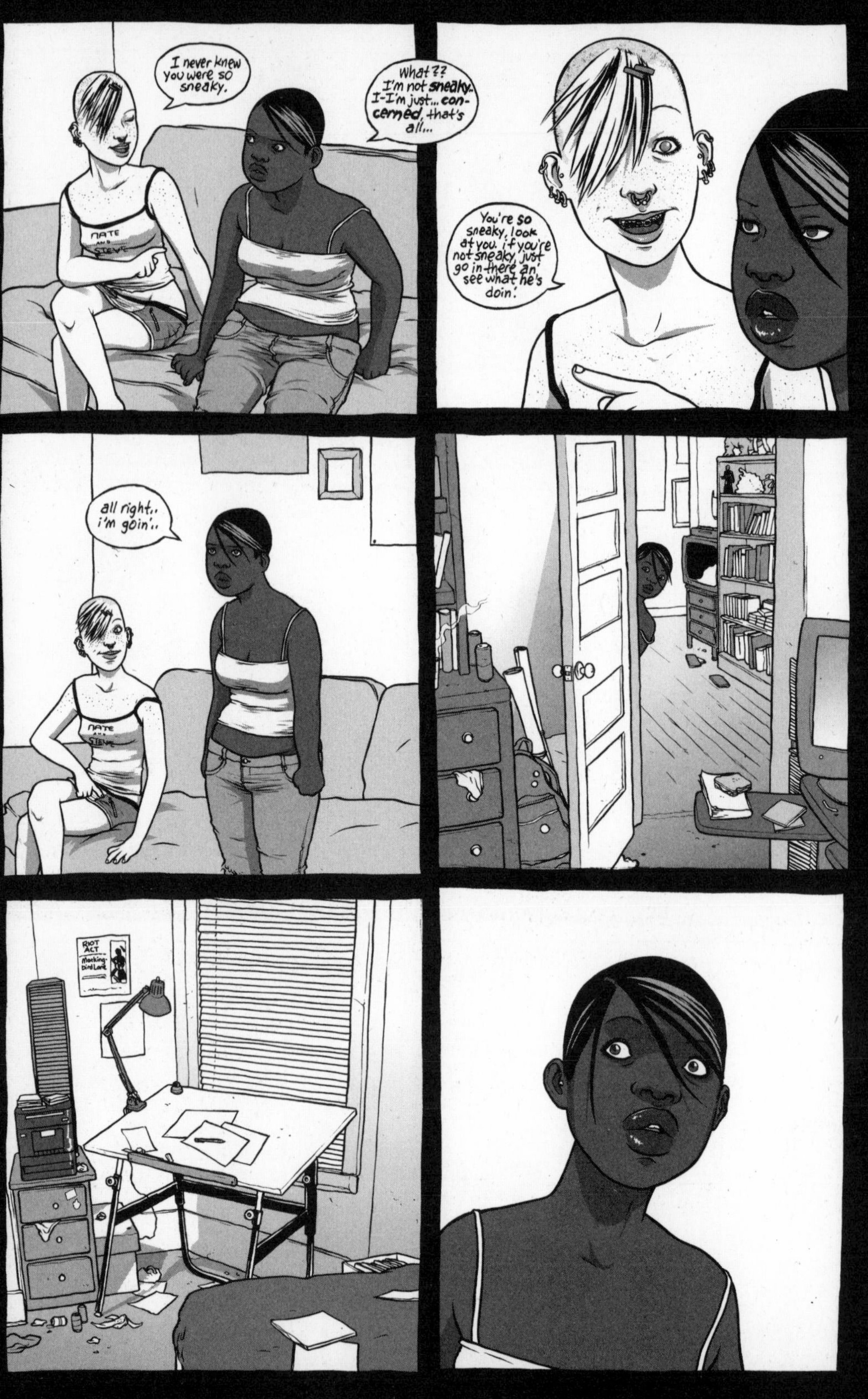

I never knew you were so sneaky.
what?? I'm not **sneaky**.. I-I'm just... **concerned**, that's all...
You're **so** sneaky, look at you. if you're not sneaky, just go in there an' see what he's doin'.
NATE AND STEVE
all right,, i'm goin',,
RIOT ACT Mocking-bird Lane

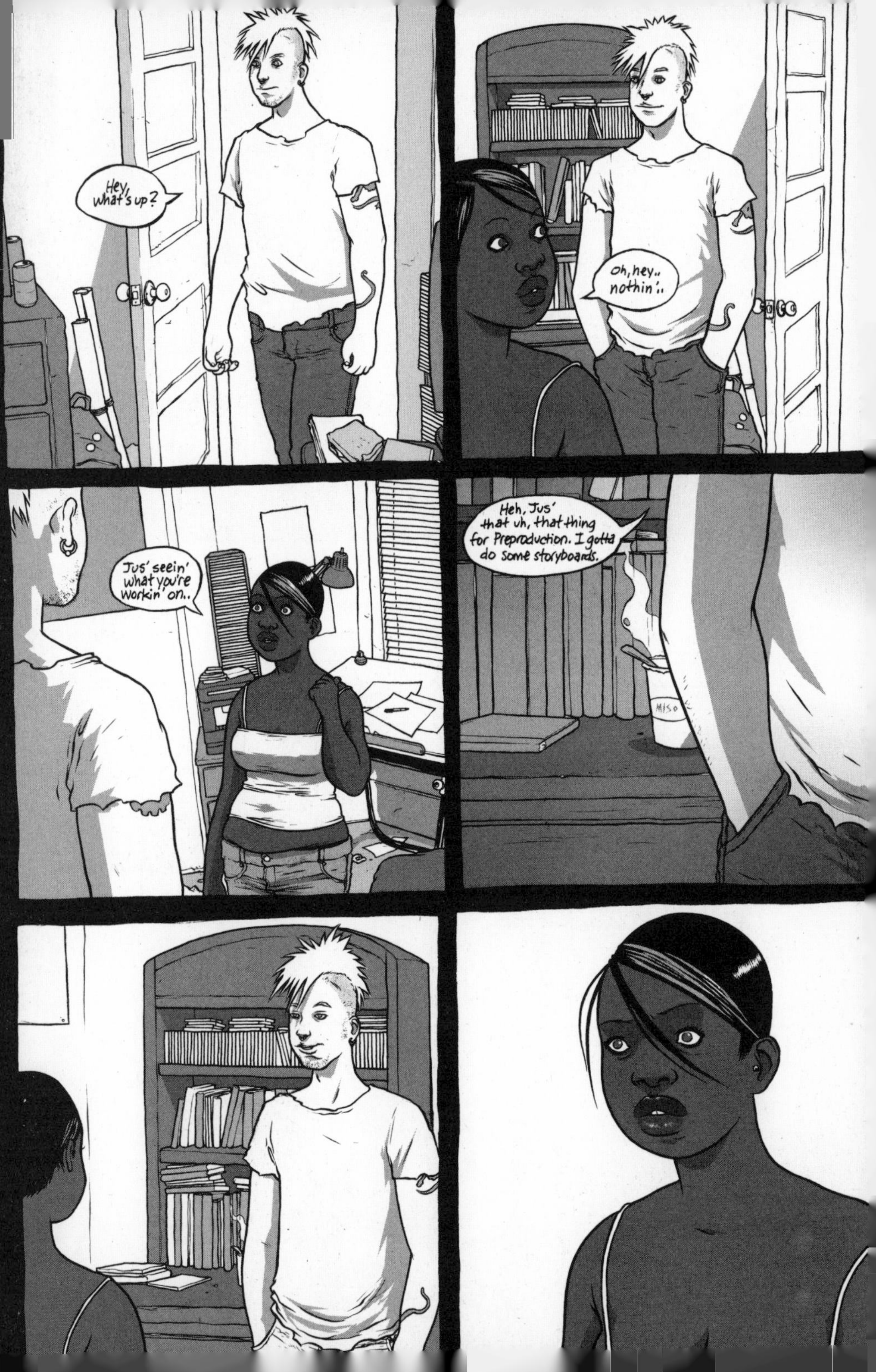
Hey, what's up?
Oh, hey.. nothin'..
Jus' seein' what you're workin' on..
Heh, Jus' that uh, that thing for Preproduction. I gotta do some storyboards.
MISO

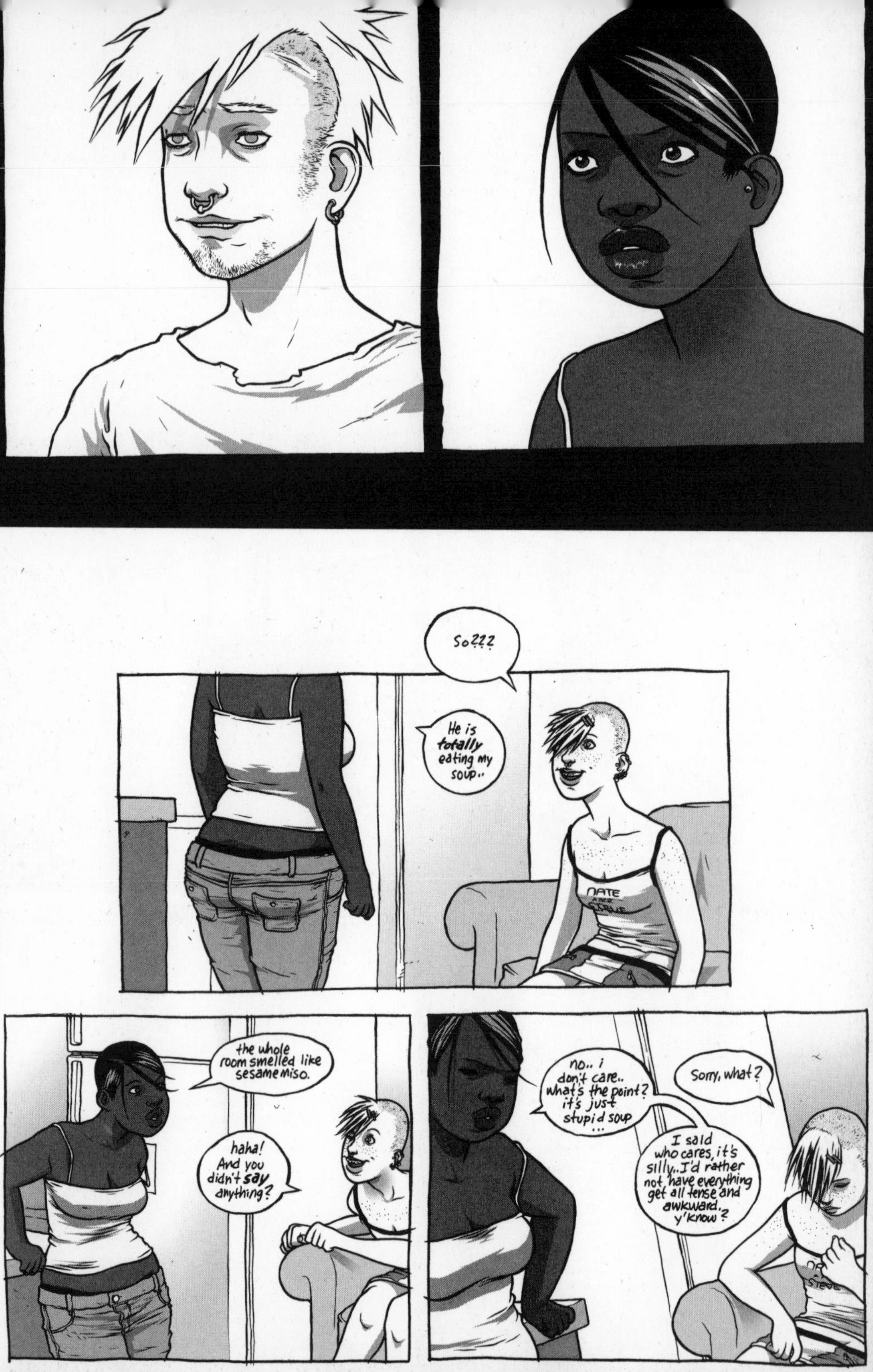
So???
He is totally eating my soup..
the whole room smelled like sesame miso.
haha! And you didn't say anything?
no.. i don't care.. what's the point? it's just stupid soup ...
Sorry, what?
I said who cares, it's silly.. I'd rather not have everything get all tense and awkward, y'know?

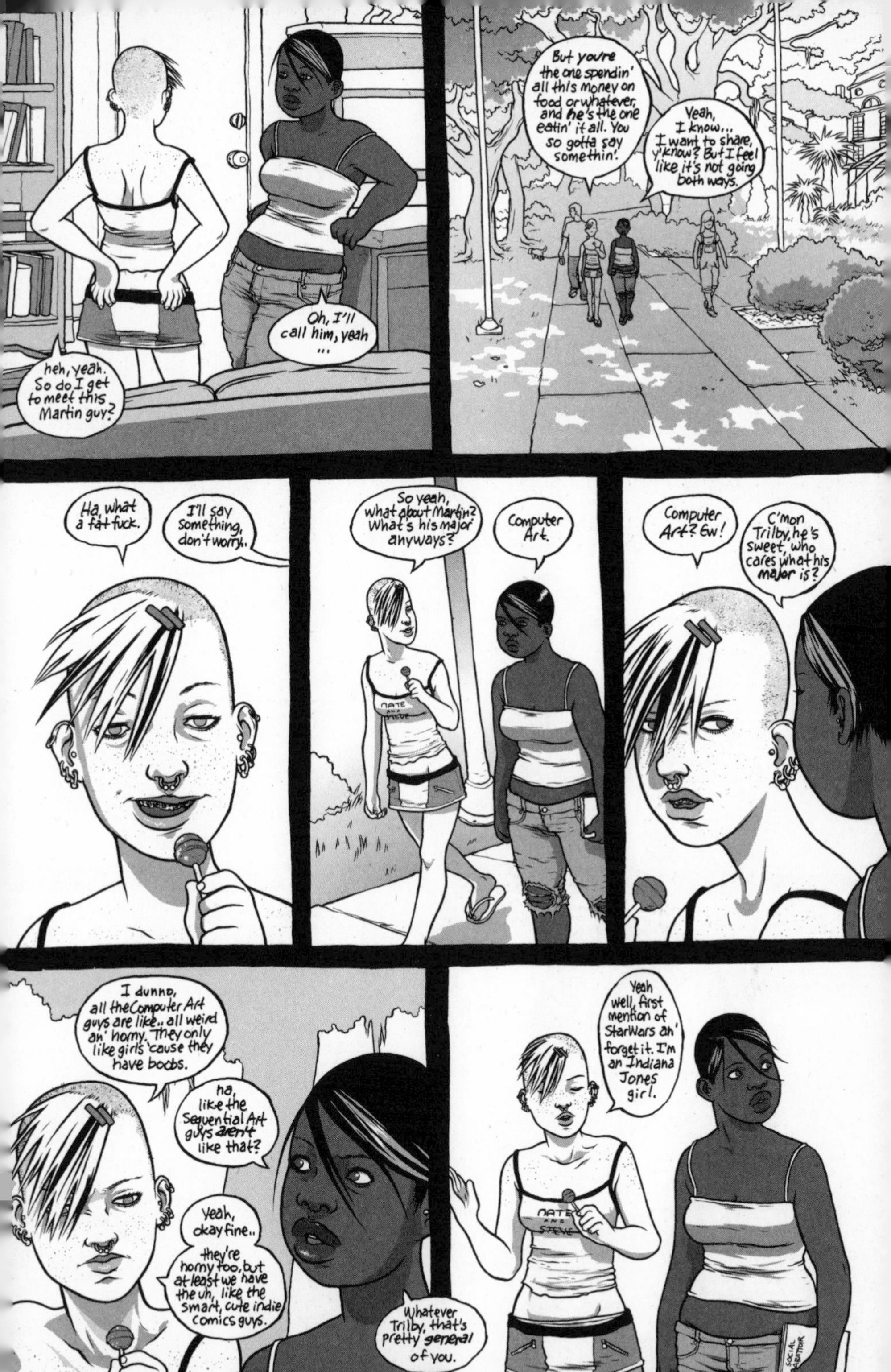
heh, yeah. So do I get to meet this Martin guy?
Oh, I'll call him, yeah ...
But you're the one spendin' all this money on food or whatever, and he's the one eatin' it all. You so gotta say somethin'.
Yeah, I know... I want to share, y'know? But I feel like it's not going both ways.
Ha, what a fat fuck.
I'll say something, don't worry.
So yeah, what about Martin? What's his major anyways?
Computer Art.
Computer Art? Ew!
C'mon Trilby, he's sweet, who cares what his major is?
I dunno, all the Computer Art guys are like.. all weird an' horny. They only like girls 'cause they have boobs.
ha, like the Sequential Art guys aren't like that?
Yeah, okay fine.. they're horny too, but at least we have the uh, like the smart, cute indie comics guys.
Whatever Trilby, that's pretty general of you.
Yeah well, first mention of StarWars an' forget it. I'm an Indiana Jones girl.

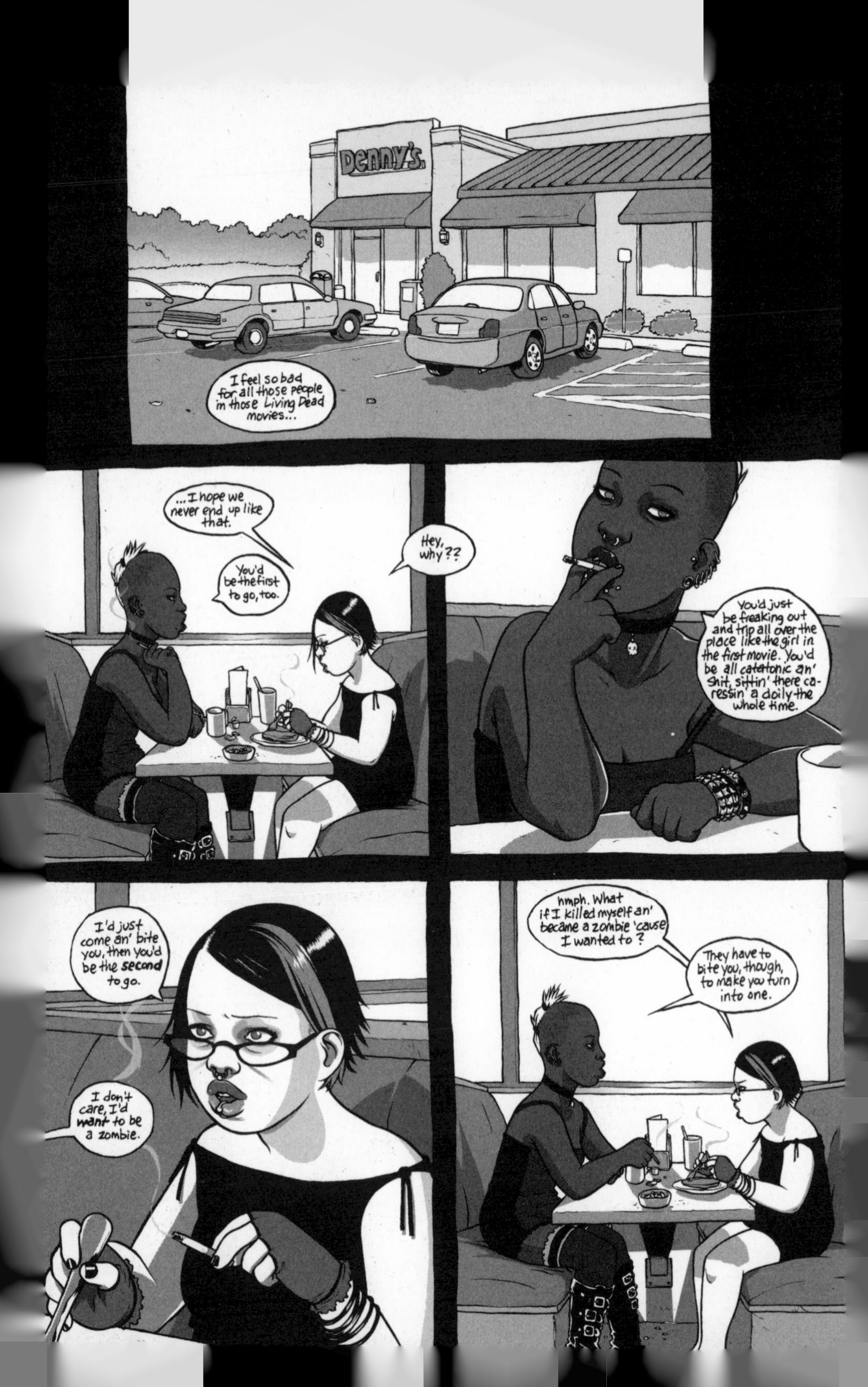
Denny's
I feel so bad for all those people in those Living Dead movies...
...I hope we never end up like that.
You'd be the first to go, too.
Hey, why??
You'd just be freaking out and trip all over the place like the girl in the first movie. You'd be all catatonic an' shit, sittin' there caressin' a doily the whole time.
I'd just come an' bite you, then you'd be the **second** to go.
I don't care, I'd ***want*** to be a zombie.
hmph. What if I killed myself an' became a zombie 'cause I wanted to?
They have to bite you, though, to make you turn into one.

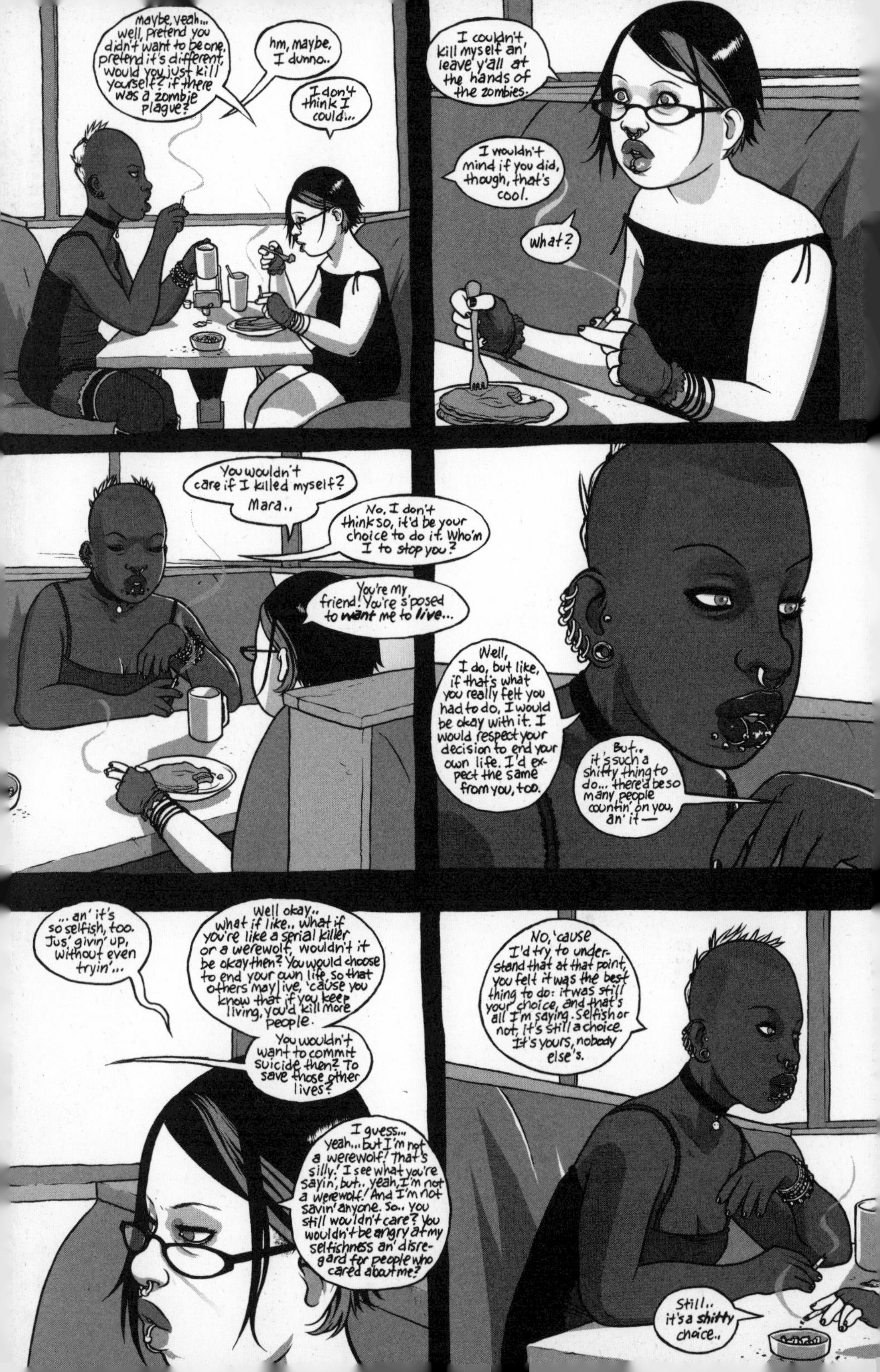
maybe, yeah... well, pretend you didn't want to be one, pretend it's different, would you just kill yourself? if there was a zombie plague?
hm, maybe, I dunno..
I don't think I could...
I couldn't kill myself an' leave y'all at the hands of the zombies.
I wouldn't mind if you did, though, that's cool.
what?
You wouldn't care if I killed myself? Mara..
No, I don't think so, it'd be your choice to do it. Who'm I to stop you?
You're my friend! You're s'posed to want me to live...
Well, I do, but like, if that's what you really felt you had to do, I would be okay with it. I would respect your decision to end your own life. I'd expect the same from you, too.
But.. it's such a shitty thing to do... there'd be so many people countin' on you, an' it—
...an' it's so selfish, too. Jus' givin' up, without even tryin'...
Well okay.. what if like.. what if you're like a serial killer or a werewolf, wouldn't it be okay then? You would choose to end your own life, so that others may live, 'cause you know that if you keep living, you'd kill more people.
You wouldn't want to commit suicide then? To save those other lives?
I guess... yeah... But I'm not a werewolf! That's silly! I see what you're sayin', but.. yeah, I'm not a werewolf! And I'm not savin' anyone. So.. you still wouldn't care? You wouldn't be angry at my selfishness an' disregard for people who cared about me?
No, 'cause I'd try to understand that at that point, you felt it was the best thing to do: it was still your choice, and that's all I'm saying. Selfish or not, it's still a choice. It's yours, nobody else's.
Still.. it's a shitty choice..

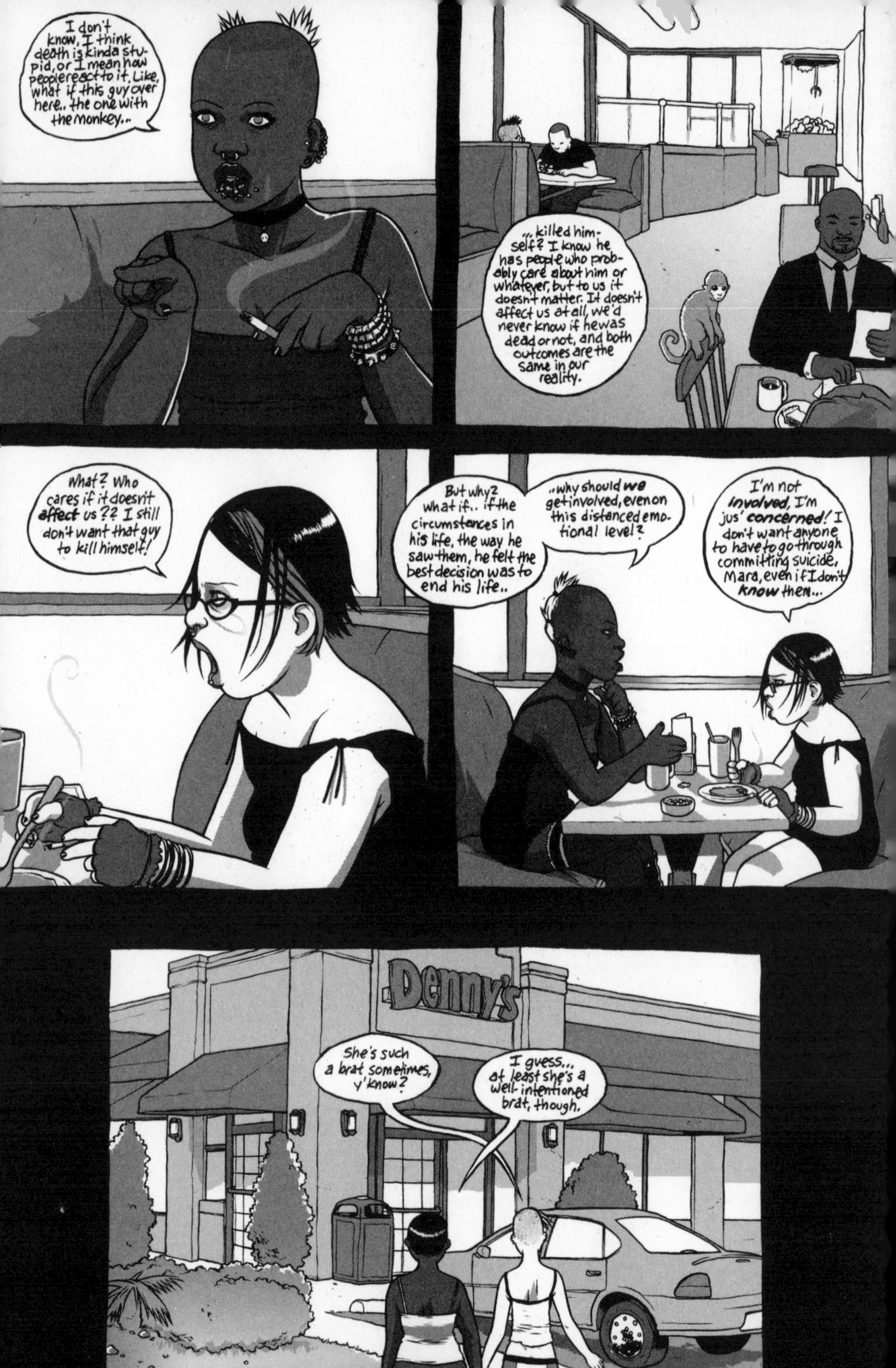
I don't know, I think death is kinda stupid, or I mean how people react to it. Like, what if this guy over here.. the one with the monkey..
..killed himself? I know he has people who probably care about him or whatever, but to us it doesn't matter. It doesn't affect us at all, we'd never know if he was dead or not, and both outcomes are the same in our reality.
What? Who cares if it doesn't **affect** us?? I still don't want that guy to kill himself!
But why? what if.. if the circumstances in his life, the way he saw them, he felt the best decision was to end his life..
..why should **we** get involved, even on this distanced emotional level?
I'm not **involved**, I'm jus' **concerned**! I don't want anyone to have to go through committing suicide, Mara, even if I don't **know** them...
Denny's
She's such a brat sometimes, y'know?
I guess... at least she's a well-intentioned brat, though.

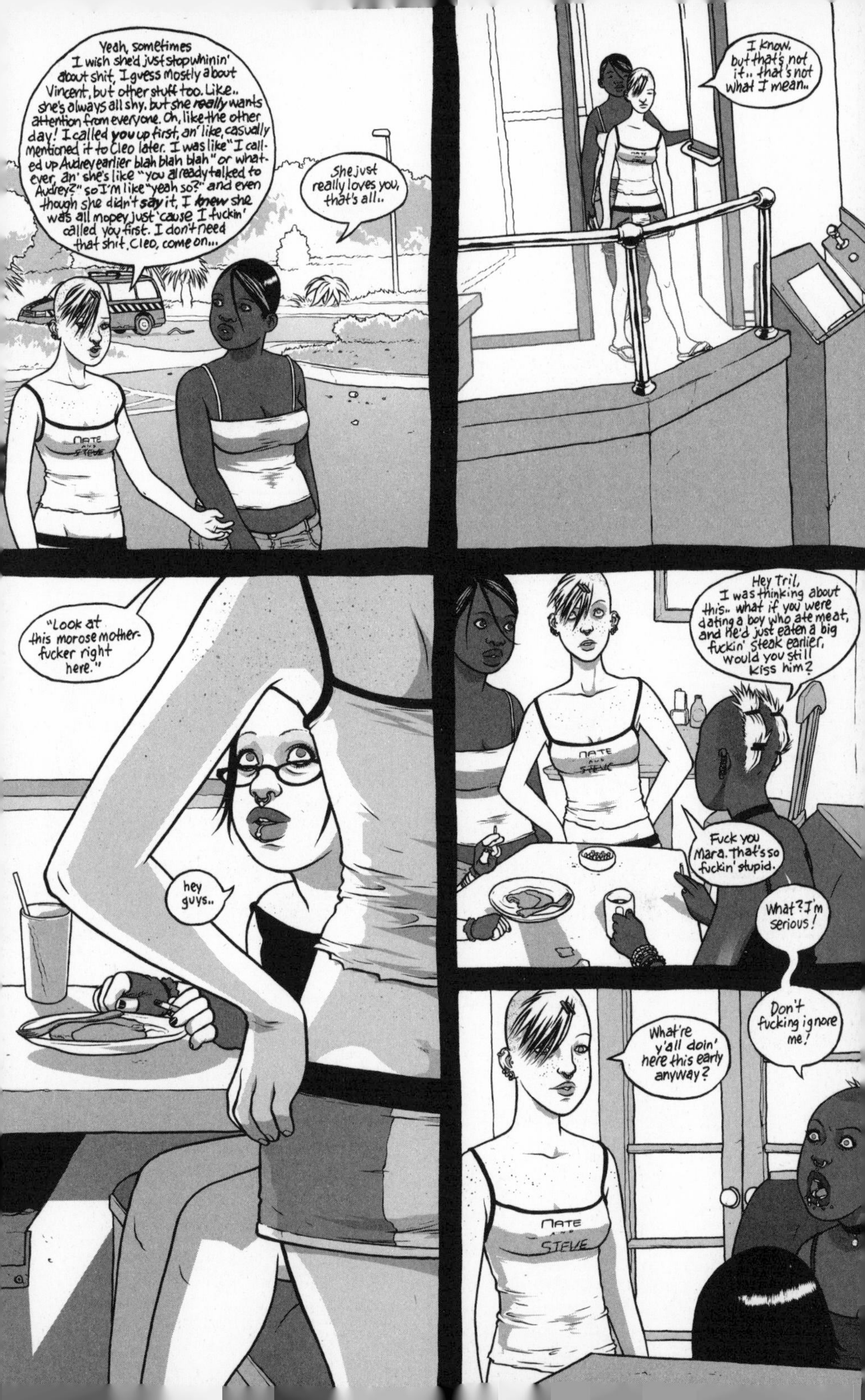
Yeah, sometimes I wish she'd just stop whinin' about shit, I guess mostly about Vincent, but other stuff too. Like.. she's always all shy, but she really wants attention from everyone. Oh, like the other day! I called you up first, an' like, casually mentioned it to Cleo later. I was like "I called up Audrey earlier blah blah blah" or whatever, an' she's like "you already talked to Audrey?" so I'm like "yeah so?" and even though she didn't say it, I knew she was all mopey just 'cause I fuckin' called you first. I don't need that shit. Cleo, come on...
She just really loves you, that's all..
I know, but that's not it.. that's not what I mean..
"Look at this morose motherfucker right here."
hey guys..
Hey Tril, I was thinking about this.. what if you were dating a boy who ate meat, and he'd just eaten a big fuckin' steak earlier, would you still kiss him?
Fuck you Mara. That's so fuckin' stupid.
What? I'm serious!
Don't fucking ignore me!
What're y'all doin' here this early anyway?
NATE AND STEVE

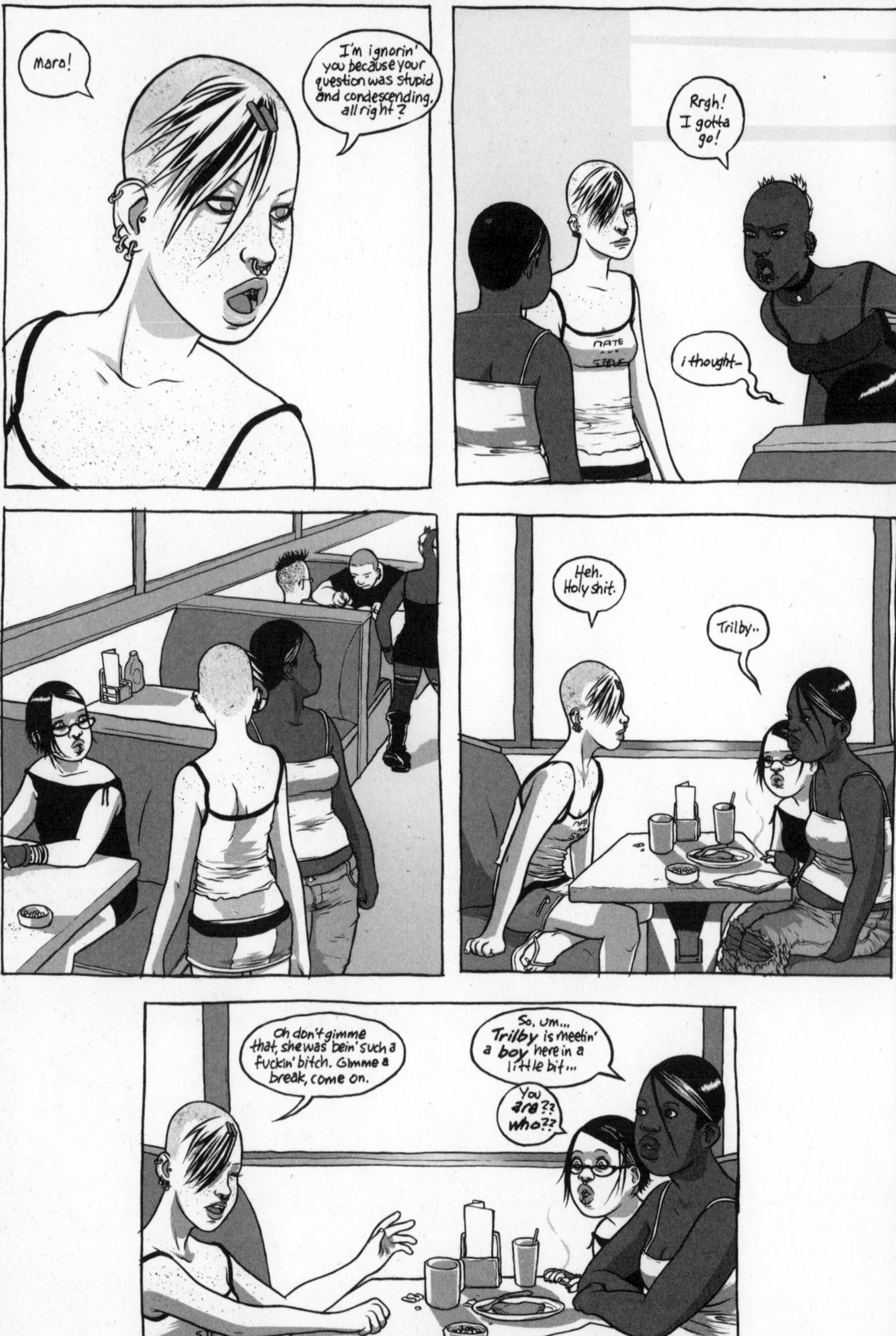

mara!
I'm ignorin' you because your question was stupid and condescending, all right?
Rrgh! I gotta go!
NATE
i thought-
Heh. Holy shit.
Trilby..
Oh don't gimme that, she was bein' such a fuckin' bitch. Gimme a break, come on.
So, um... Trilby is meetin' a boy here in a little bit...
You are?? who??

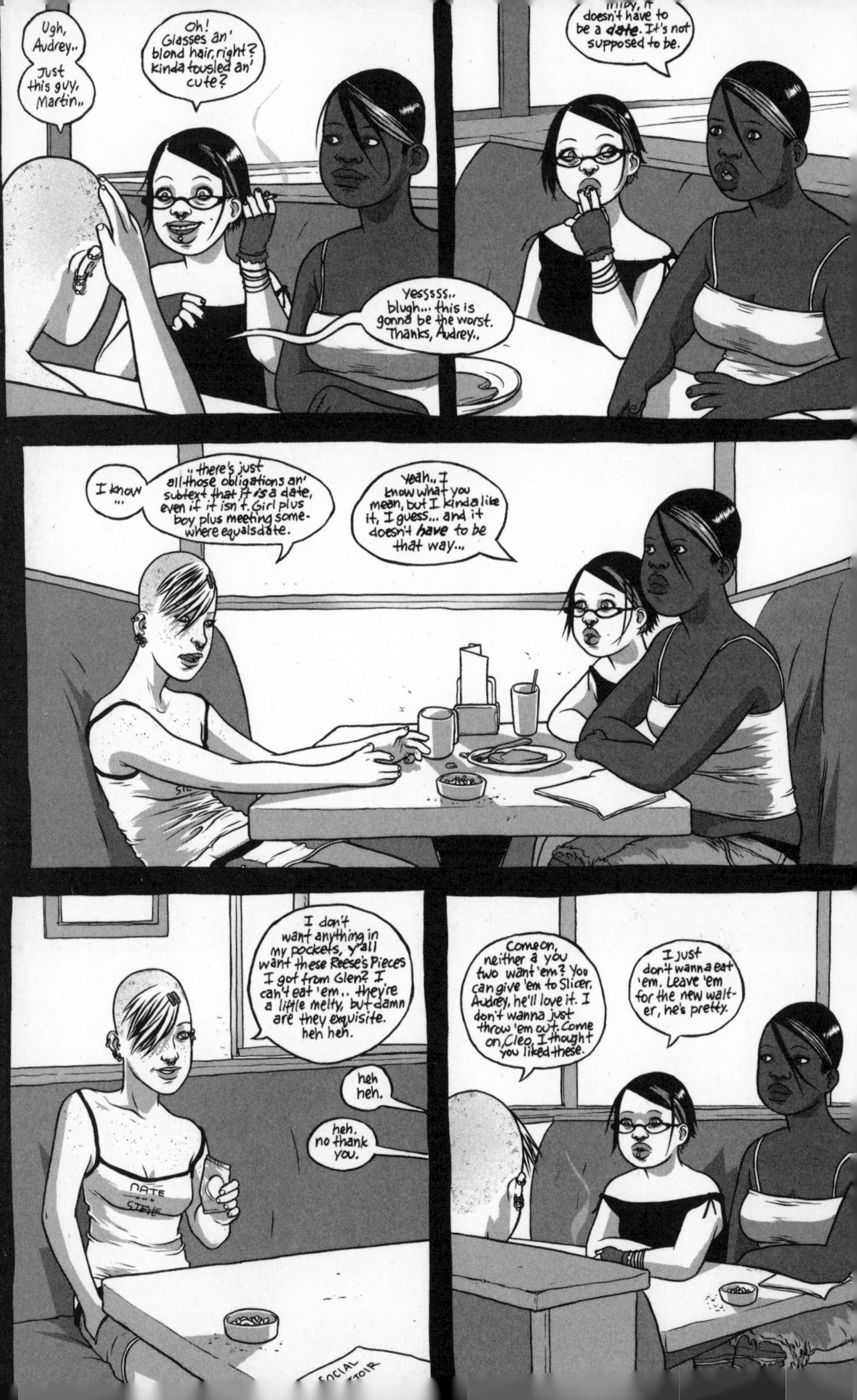

Ugh, Audrey..
Just this guy, Martin..
Oh! Glasses an' blond hair, right? Kinda tousled an' cute?
Yessss.. blugh... this is gonna be the worst. Thanks, Audrey..
doesn't have to be a date. It's not supposed to be.
I know ...
.. there's just all those obligations an' subtext that it is a date, even if it isn't. Girl plus boy plus meeting somewhere equals date.
Yeah.. I know what you mean, but I kinda like it, I guess... and it doesn't have to be that way...
I don't want anything in my pockets, y'all want these Reese's Pieces I got from Glen? I can't eat 'em.. they're a little melty, but damn are they exquisite. heh heh.
heh heh.
heh. no thank you.
Come on, neither a you two want 'em? You can give 'em to Slicer, Audrey, he'll love it. I don't wanna just throw 'em out. Come on, Cleo. I thought you liked these.
I just don't wanna eat 'em. Leave 'em for the new waiter, he's pretty.
NATE
STEVE
SOCIAL

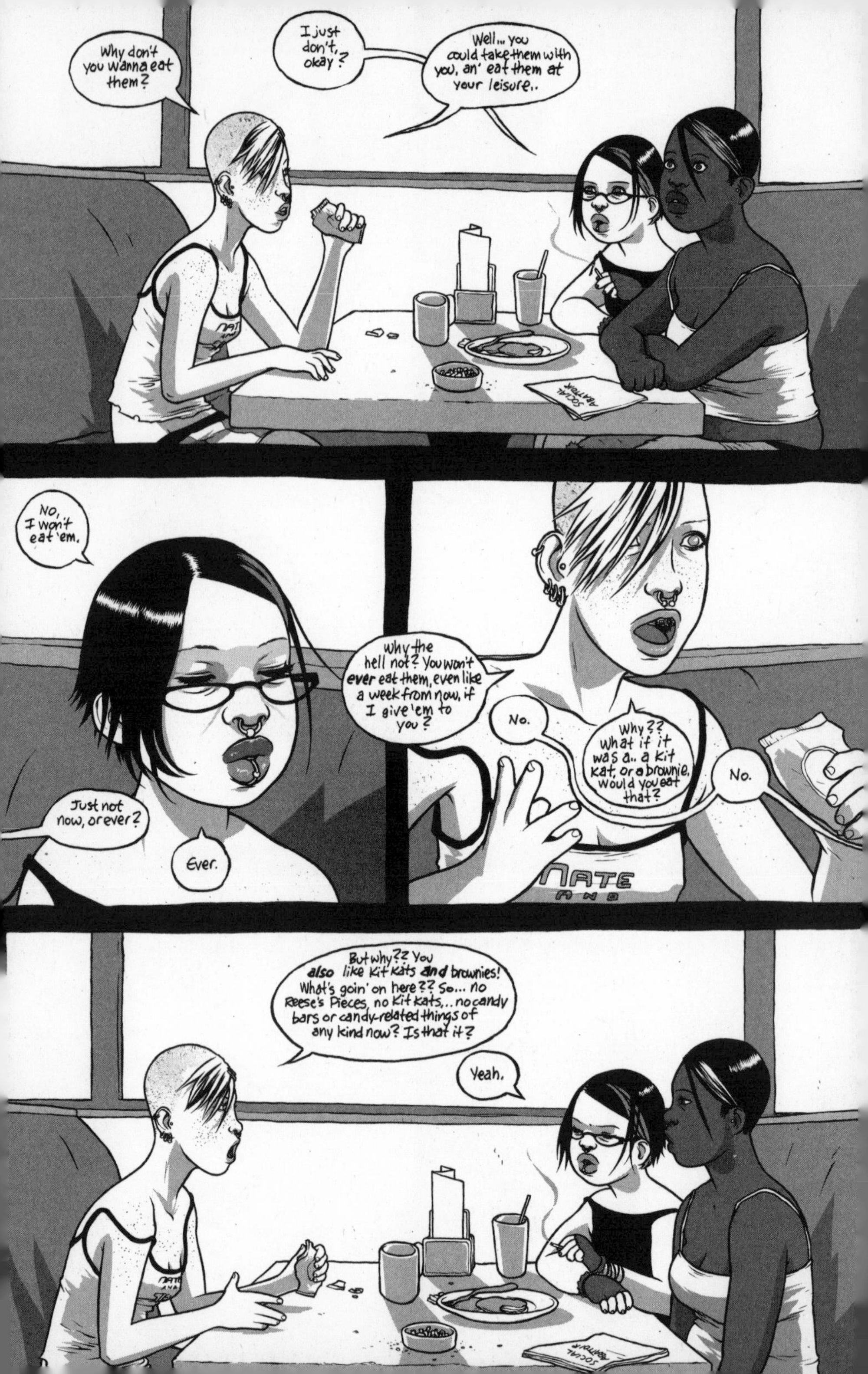

Why don't you wanna eat them?
I just don't, okay?
Well... you could take them with you, an' eat them at your leisure..
SOCIAL ABATTOIR
No, I won't eat 'em.
Just not now, or ever?
Ever.
Why the hell not? You won't **ever** eat them, even like a week from now, if I give 'em to you?
No.
Why?? What if it was a.. a Kit Kat, or a brownie, would you eat that?
No.
NATE AND
But why?? You **also** like Kit Kats **and** brownies! What's goin' on here?? So... no Reese's Pieces, no Kit Kats,.. no candy bars or candy-related things of any kind now? Is that it?
Yeah.
SOCIAL ABATTOIR

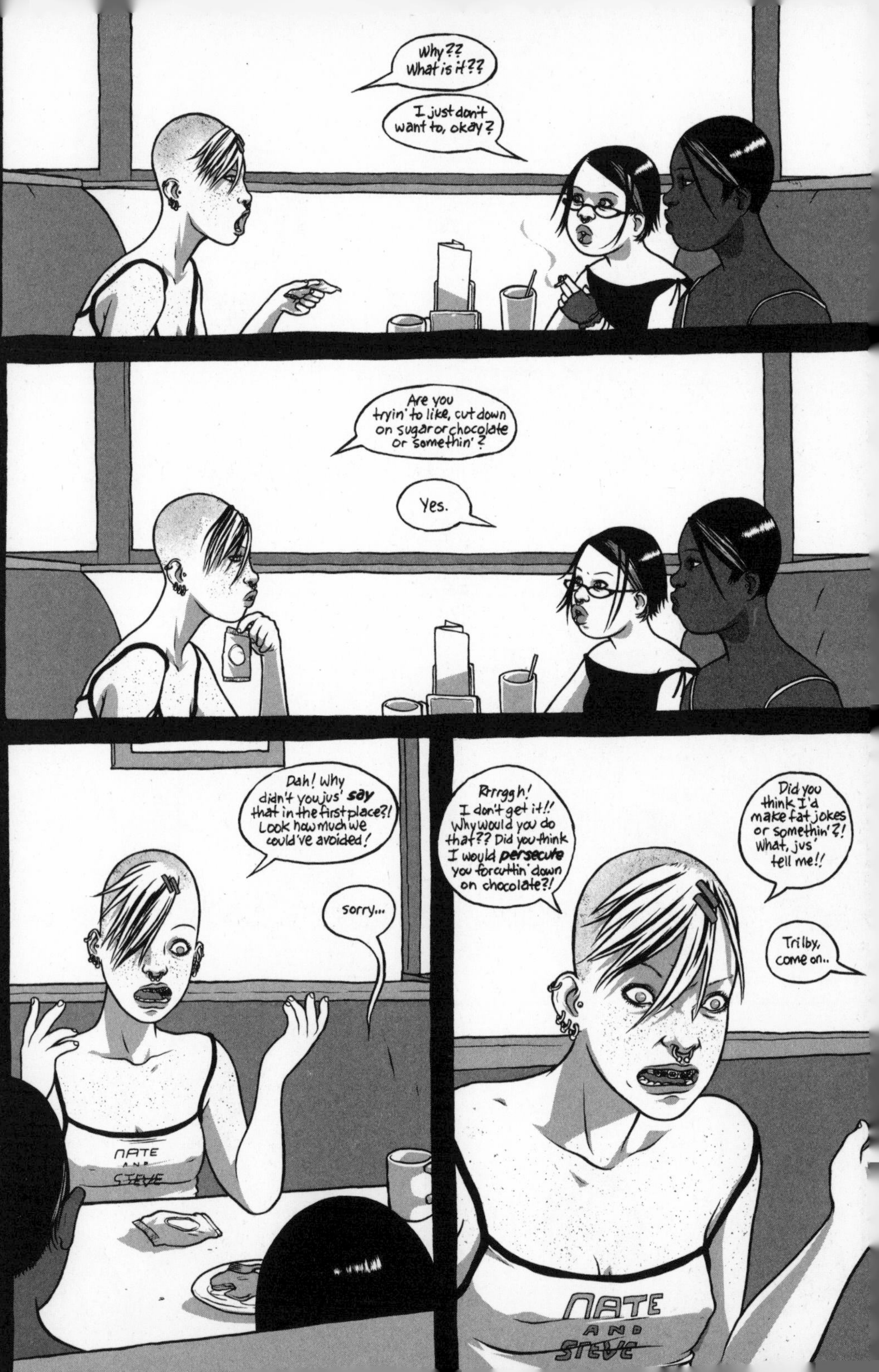
Why?? What is it??
I just don't want to, okay?
Are you tryin' to like, cut down on sugar or chocolate or somethin'?
Yes.
Dah! Why didn't you jus' **say** that in the first place?! Look how much we could've avoided!
sorry...
NATE AND STEVE
Rrrrggh! I don't get it!! Why would you do that?? Did you think I would **persecute** you for cuttin' down on chocolate?!
Did you think I'd make fat jokes or somethin'?! What, jus' tell me!!
Trilby, come on..
NATE AND STEVE

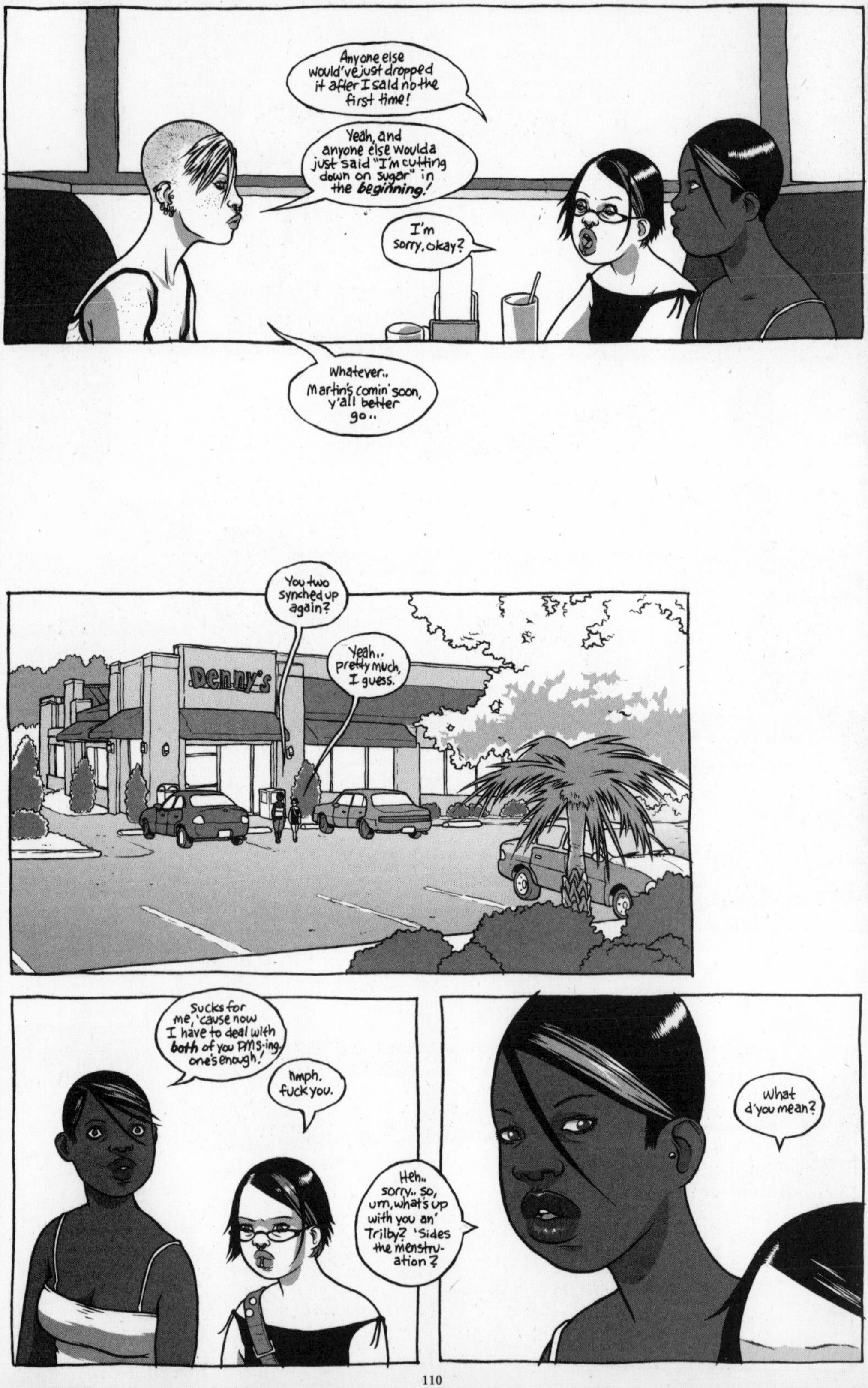
Anyone else would've just dropped it after I said no the first time!
Yeah, and anyone else woulda just said "I'm cutting down on sugar" in the *beginning!*
I'm sorry, okay?
Whatever.. Martin's comin' soon, y'all better go..
You two synched up again?
Yeah.. pretty much, I guess.
Denny's
Sucks for me, 'cause now I have to deal with *both* of you PMS-ing. one's enough!
hmph. fuck you.
Heh.. sorry.. so, um, what's up with you an' Trilby? 'Sides the menstru-ation?
What d'you mean?

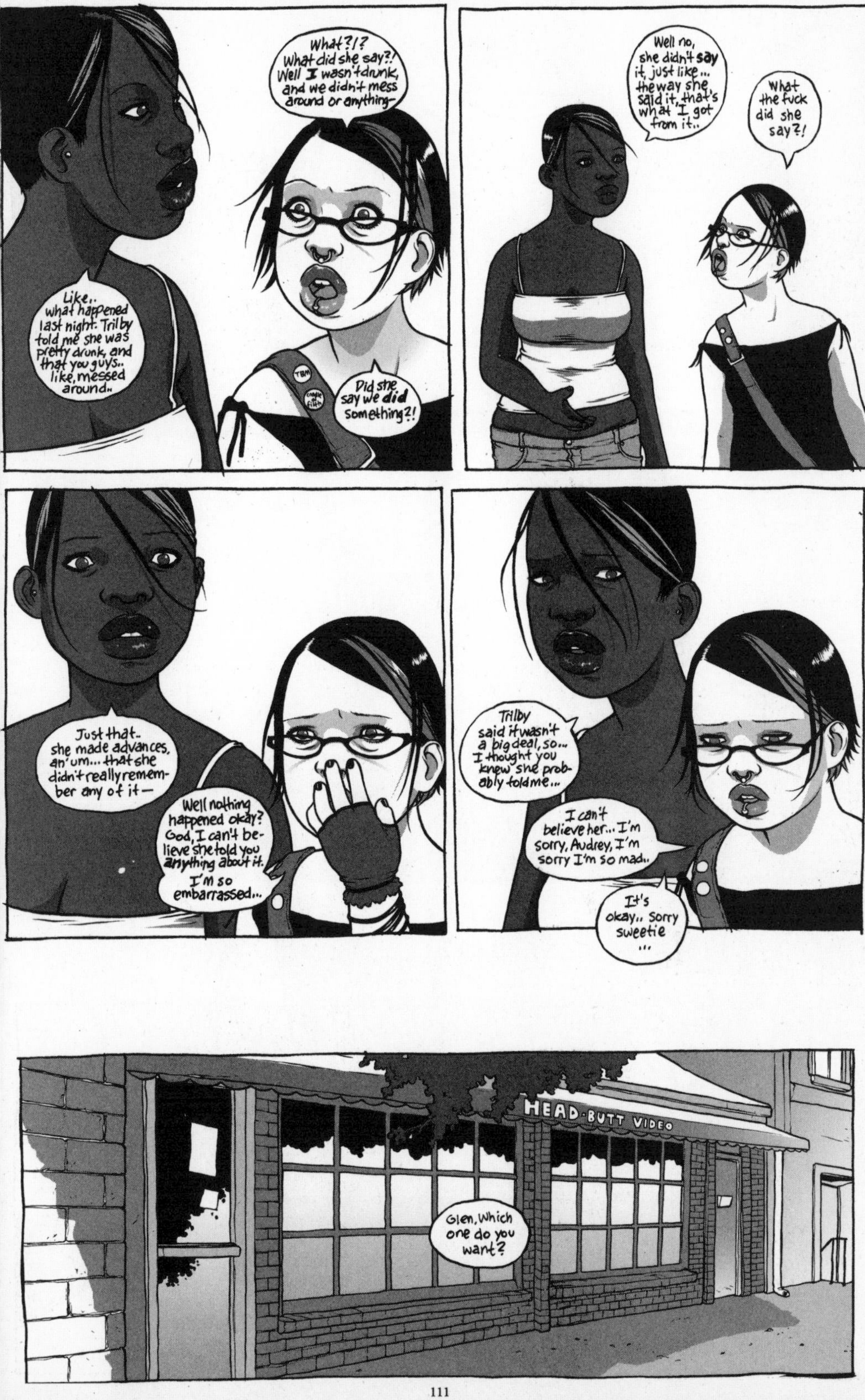
What?!?
What did she say?!
Well I wasn't drunk,
and we didn't mess
around or anything—
Like..
what happened
last night. Trilby
told me she was
pretty drunk, and
that you guys..
like, messed
around..
Did she
say we did
something?!
Well no,
she didn't say
it, just like...
the way she
said it, that's
what I got
from it..
What
the fuck
did she
say?!
Just that..
she made advances,
an'um... that she
didn't really remem-
ber any of it—
Well nothing
happened okay?
God, I can't be-
lieve she told you
anything about it.
I'm so
embarrassed...
Trilby
said it wasn't
a big deal, so..
I thought you
knew she prob-
ably told me...
I can't
believe her... I'm
sorry, Audrey, I'm
sorry I'm so mad..
It's
okay.. Sorry
sweetie
...
HEAD-BUTT VIDEO
Glen, Which
one do you
want?

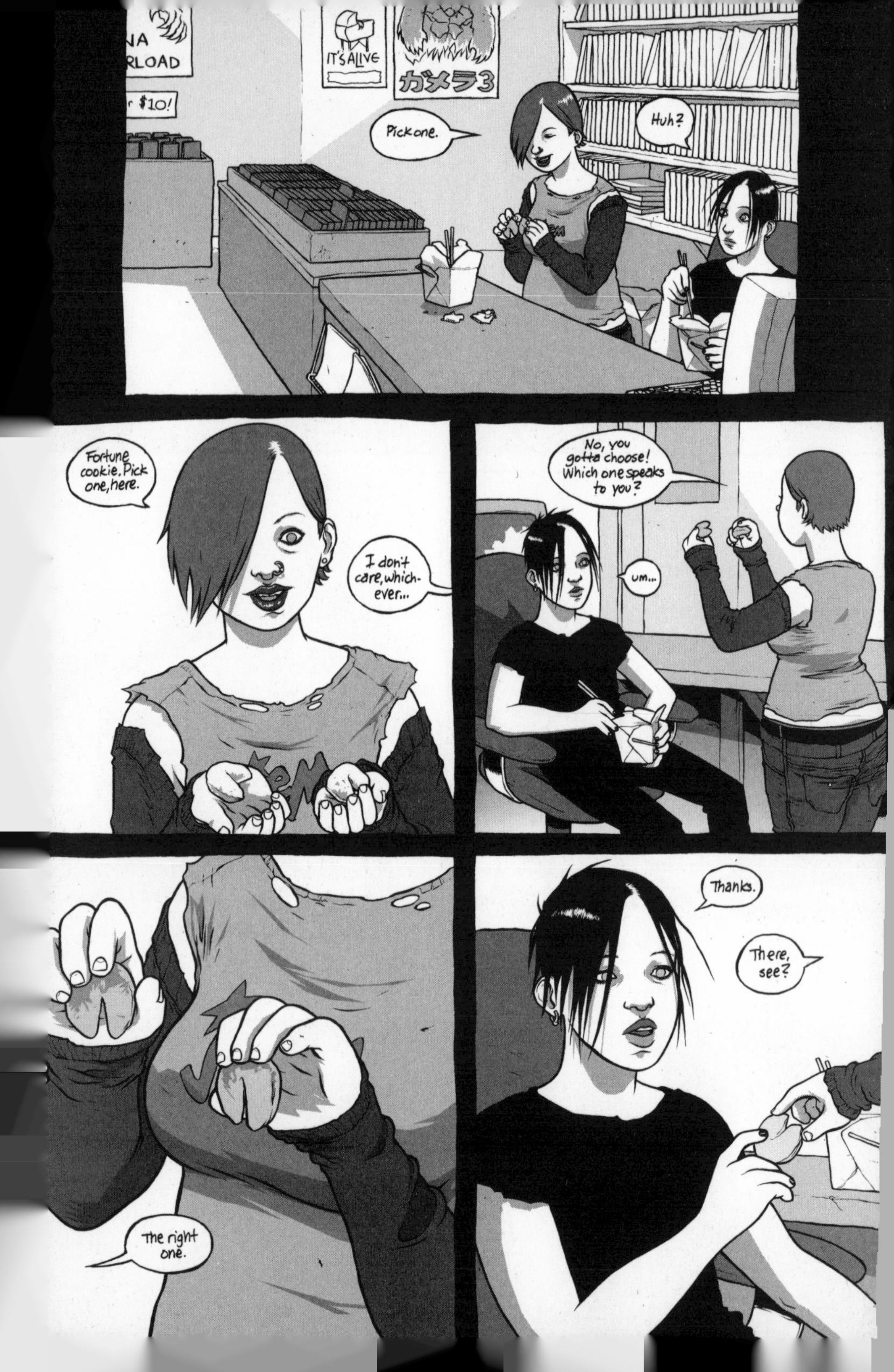
NA
RLOAD
r $10!
IT'S ALIVE
ガメラ3
Pick one.
Huh?
Fortune cookie. Pick one, here.
I don't care, which-ever...
No, you gotta choose! Which one speaks to you?
um...
The right one.
Thanks.
There, see?

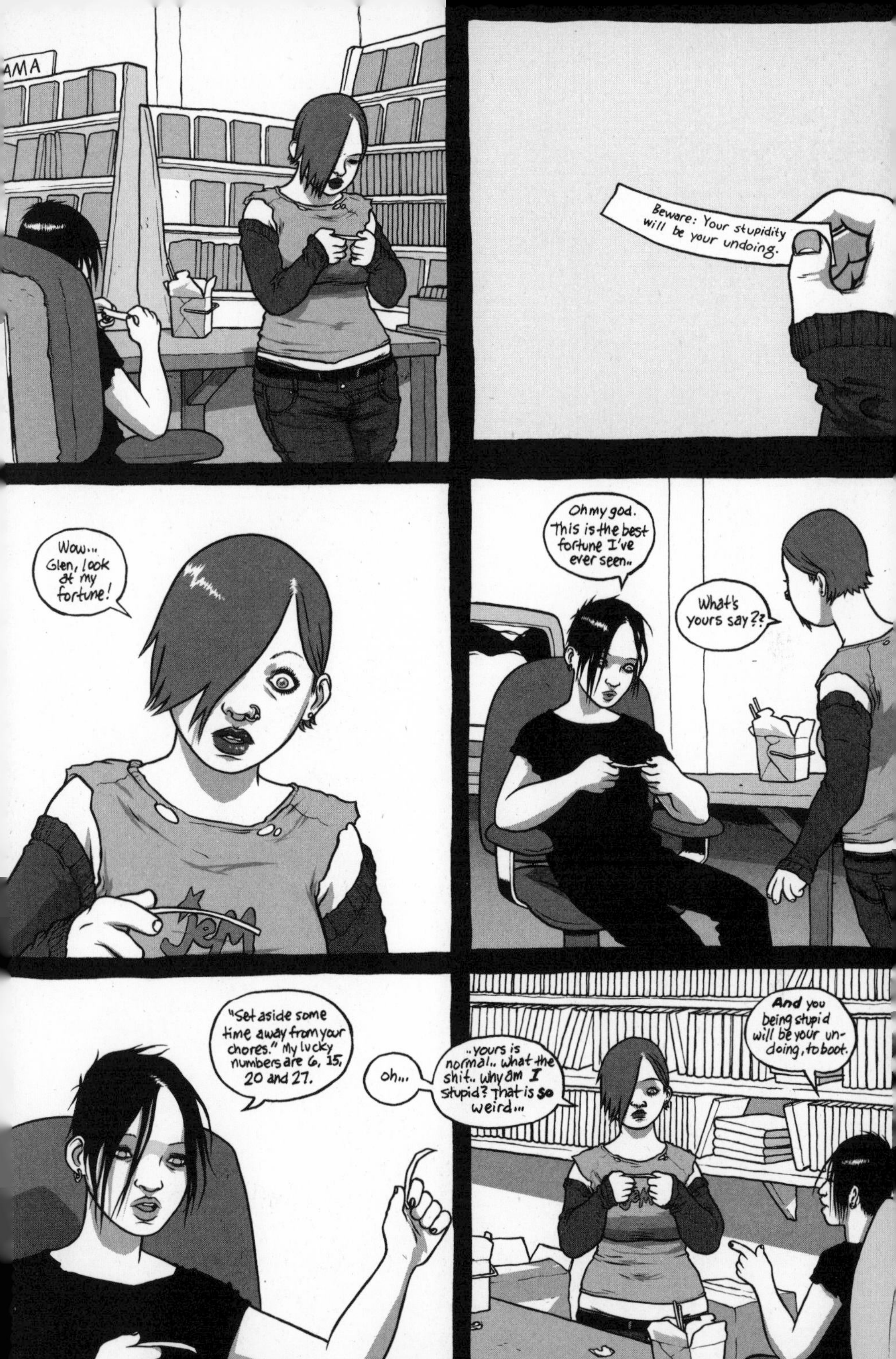

AMA
Beware: Your stupidity will be your undoing.
Wow... Glen, look at my fortune!
Oh my god. This is the best fortune I've ever seen..
What's yours say??
"Set aside some time away from your chores." My lucky numbers are 6, 15, 20 and 27.
oh...
..yours is normal.. what the shit.. why am I stupid? That is so weird...
And you being stupid will be your undoing, to boot.

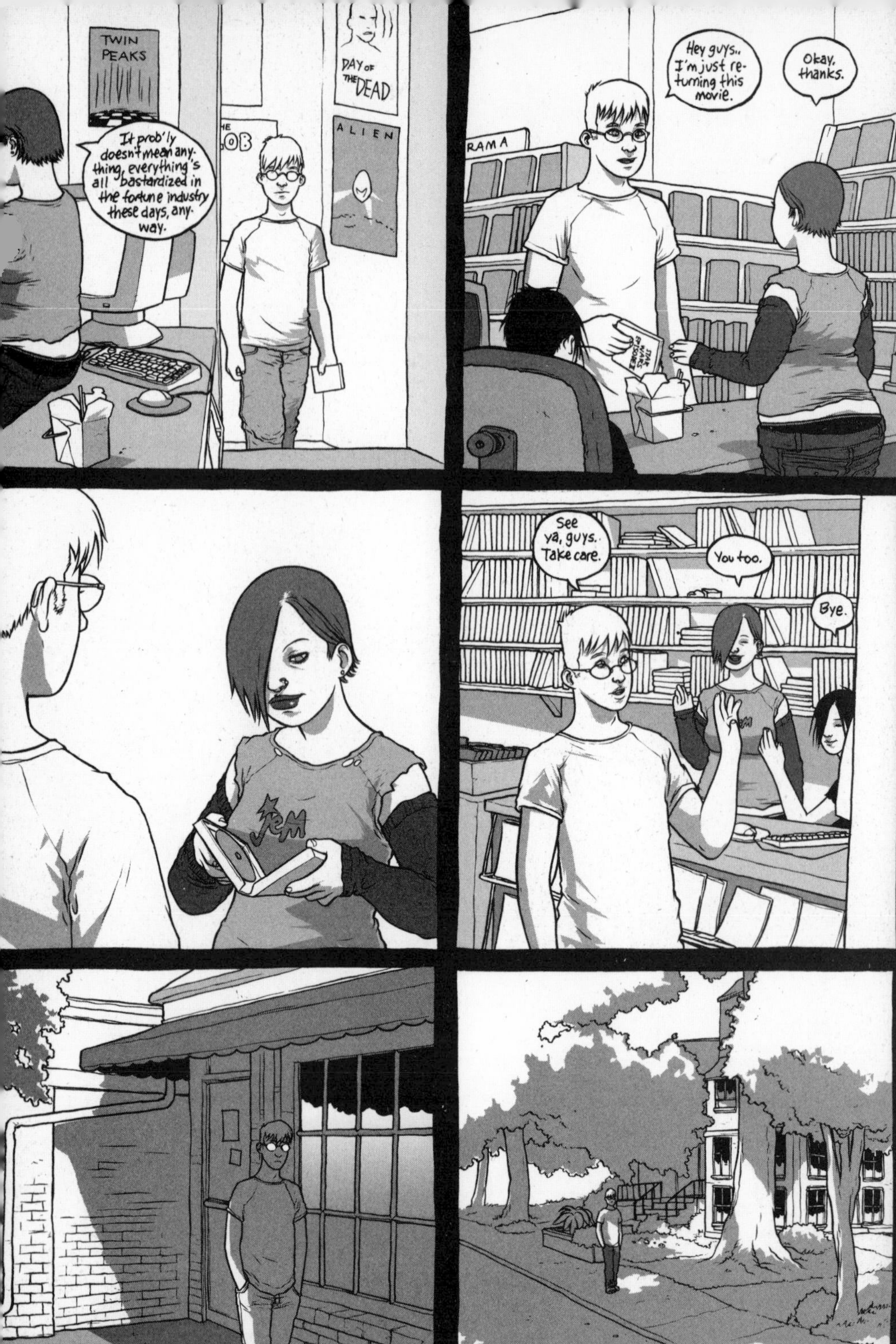
TWIN PEAKS
DAY OF THE DEAD
ALIEN
It prob'ly doesn't mean anything, everything's all bastardized in the fortune industry these days, anyway.
Hey guys.. I'm just returning this movie.
Okay. thanks.
See ya, guys. Take care.
You too.
Bye.

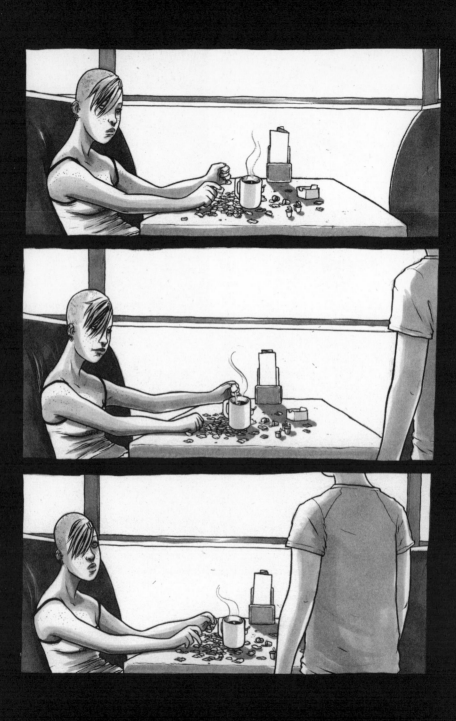

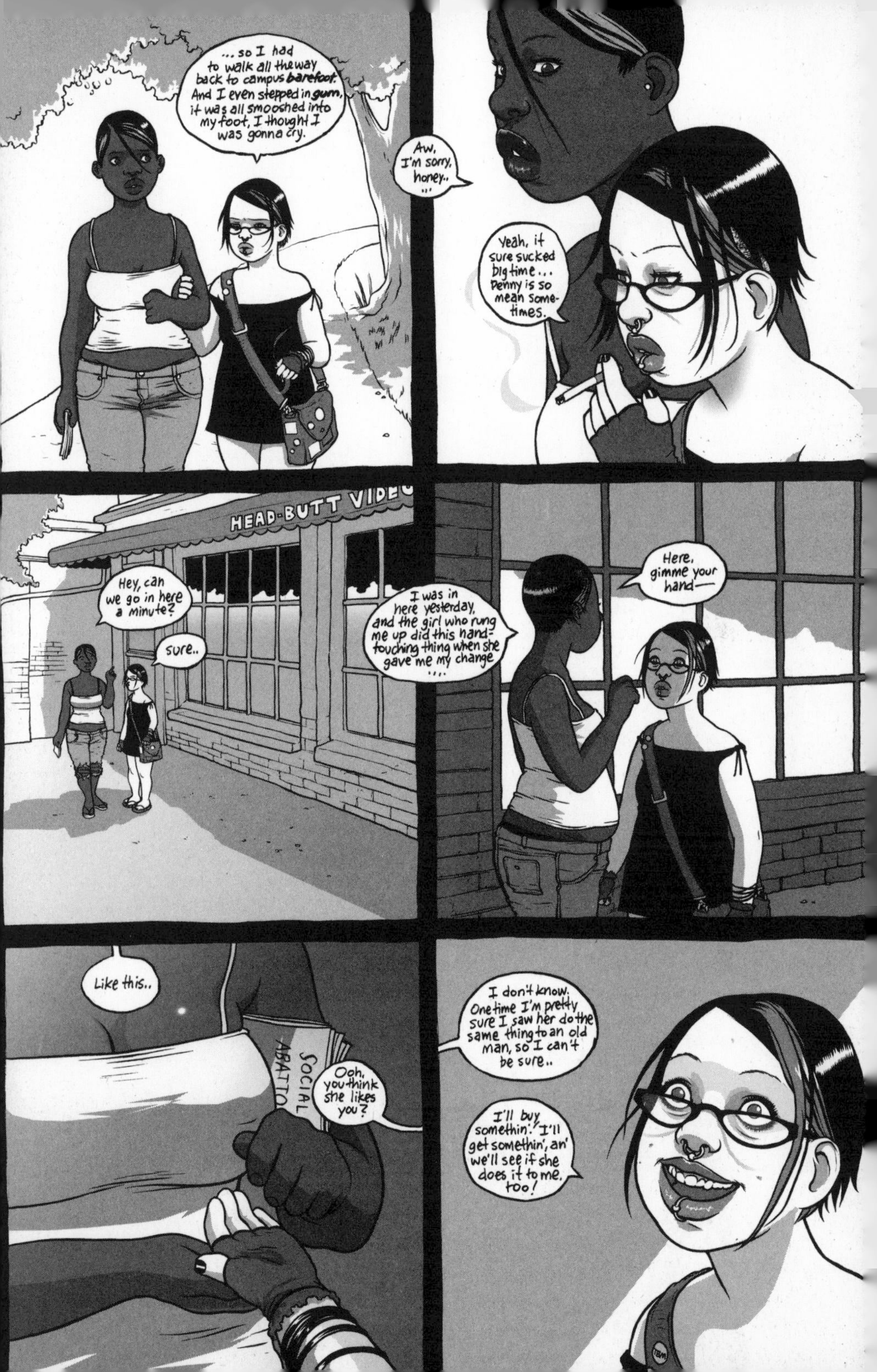
...so I had to walk all the way back to campus barefoot. And I even stepped in gum, it was all smooshed into my foot, I thought I was gonna cry.
Aw, I'm sorry, honey.. ...
Yeah, it sure sucked big time... Denny is so mean sometimes.
HEAD-BUTT VIDEO
Hey, can we go in here a minute?
sure..
I was in here yesterday, and the girl who rung me up did this hand-touching thing when she gave me my change ....
Here, gimme your hand—
Like this..
SOCIAL ABATTO
Ooh, you think she likes you?
I don't know. One time I'm pretty sure I saw her do the same thing to an old man, so I can't be sure..
I'll buy somethin'. I'll get somethin', an' we'll see if she does it to me, too!

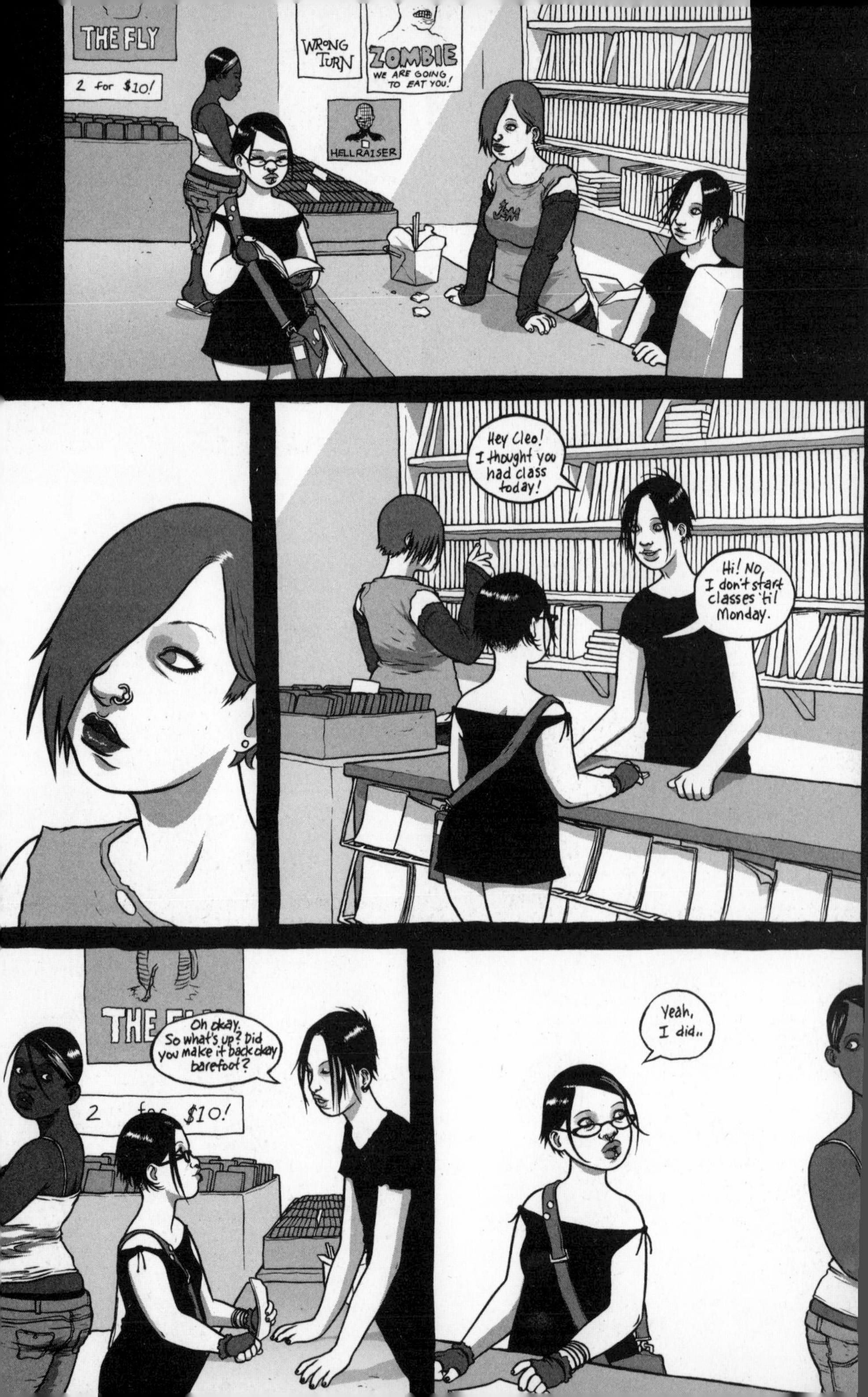
THE FLY
2 for $10!
WRONG TURN
ZOMBIE
WE ARE GOING TO EAT YOU!
HELLRAISER
Hey Cleo! I thought you had class today!
Hi! No, I don't start classes 'til Monday.
Oh okay. So what's up? Did you make it back okay barefoot?
2 for $10!
Yeah, I did..

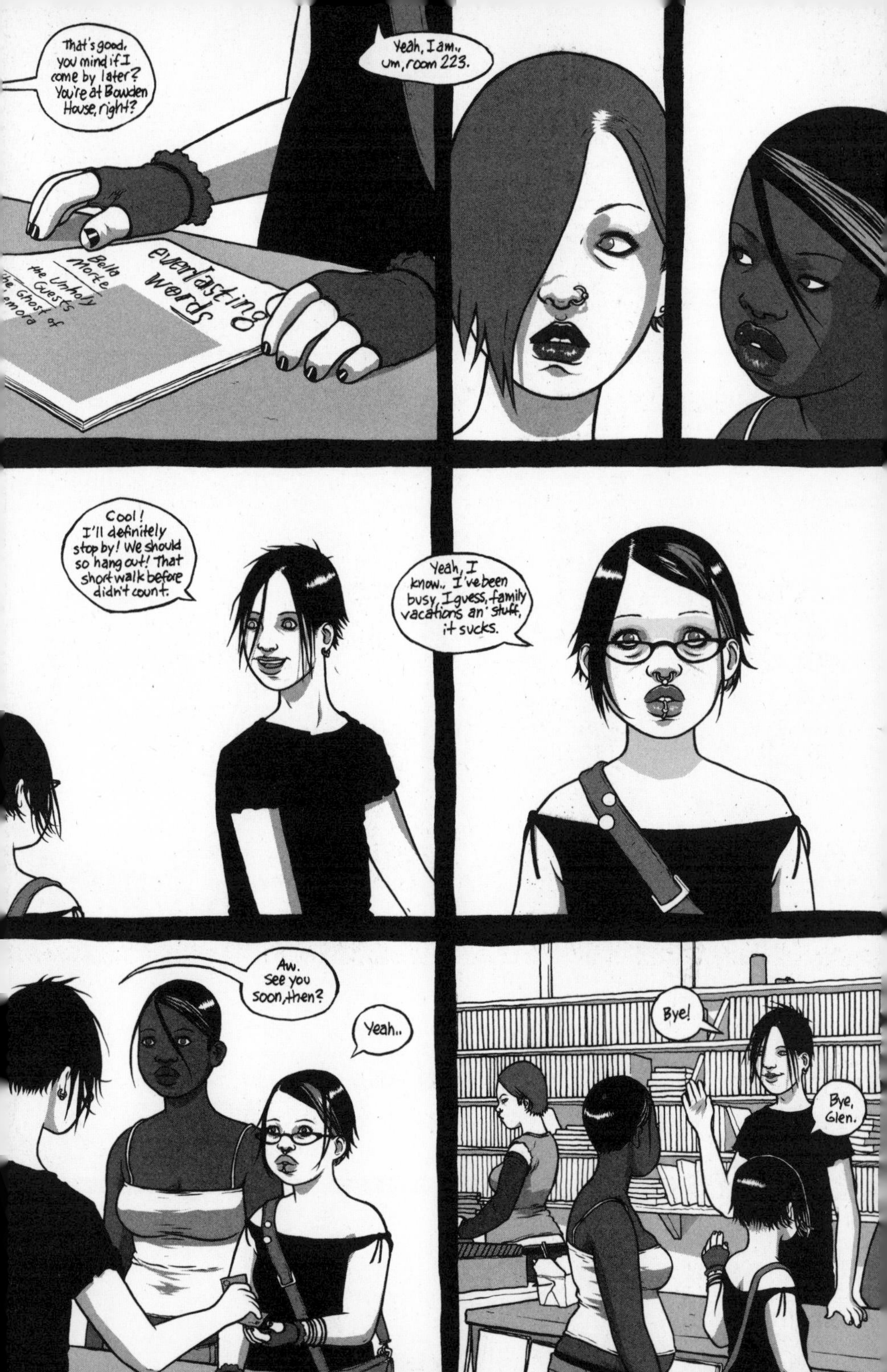
That's good. you mind if I come by later? You're at Bowden House, right?
everlasting words
Bella Morte
the Unholy Guests
the Ghost of Lemora
Yeah, I am.. um, room 223.
Cool! I'll definitely stop by! We should so hang out! That short walk before didn't count.
Yeah, I know.. I've been busy, I guess, family vacations an' stuff, it sucks.
Aw. see you soon, then?
Yeah..
Bye!
Bye, Glen.

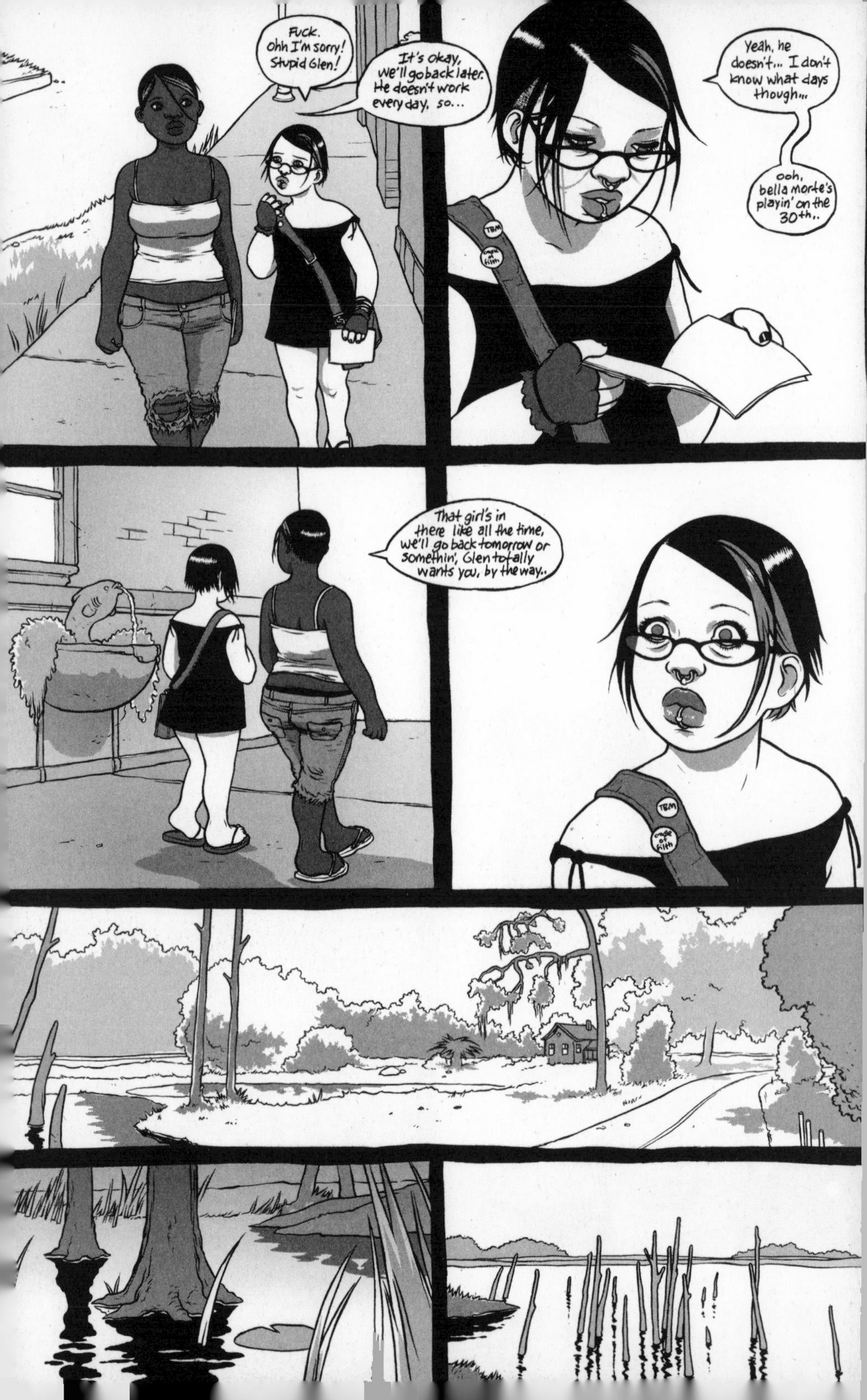

Fuck. Ohh I'm sorry! Stupid Glen!
It's okay, we'll go back later. He doesn't work every day, so...
Yeah, he doesn't... I don't know what days though...
ooh, bella morte's playin' on the 30th..
TBM
That girl's in there like all the time, we'll go back tomorrow or somethin', Glen totally wants you, by the way..
TBM

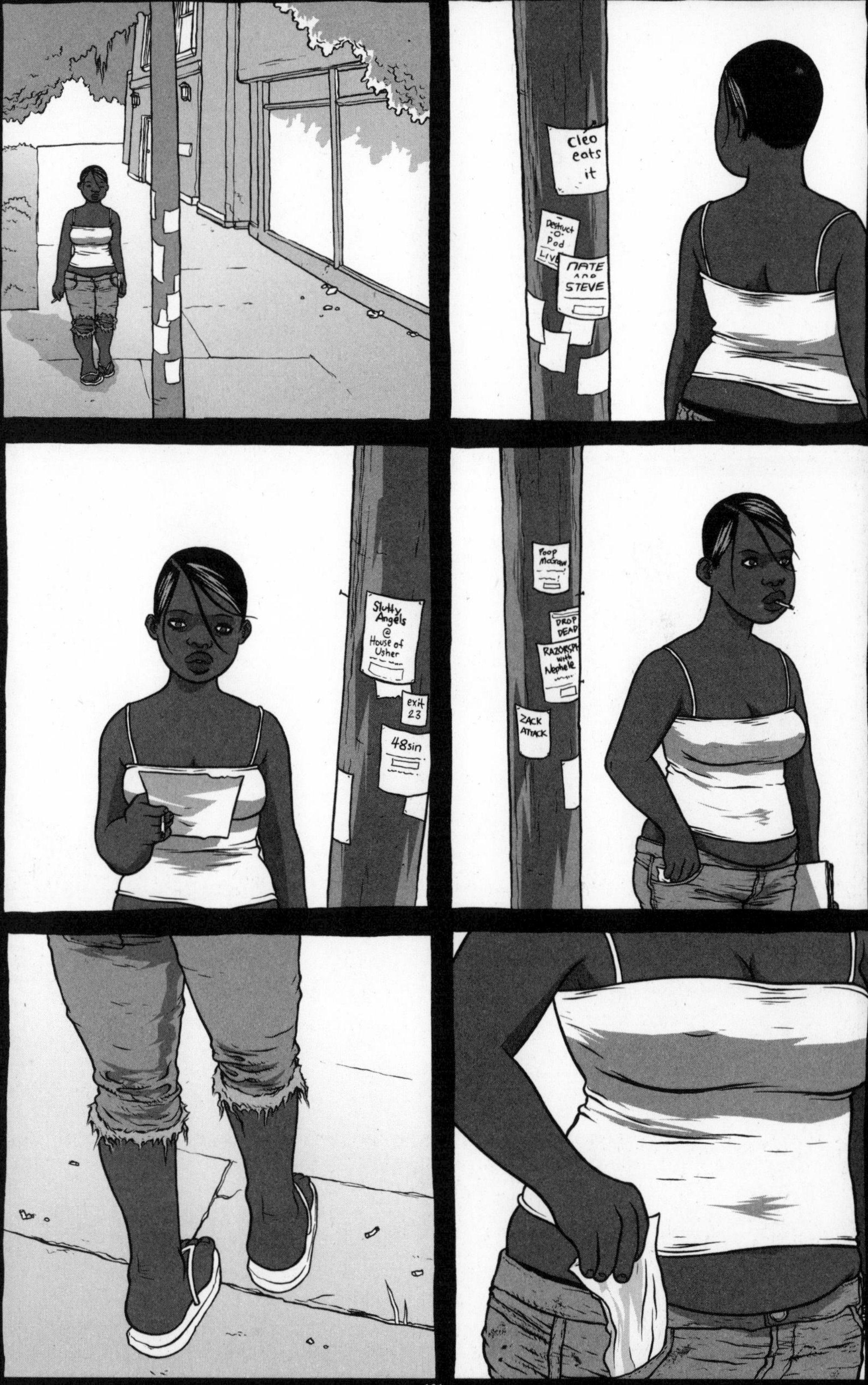
Cleo eats it
Destruct -O- Pod LIVE
NATE AND STEVE
Slutty Angels @ House of Usher
exit 23
48sin
Poop McGraw
DROP DEAD
with Nephele
ZACK ATTACK

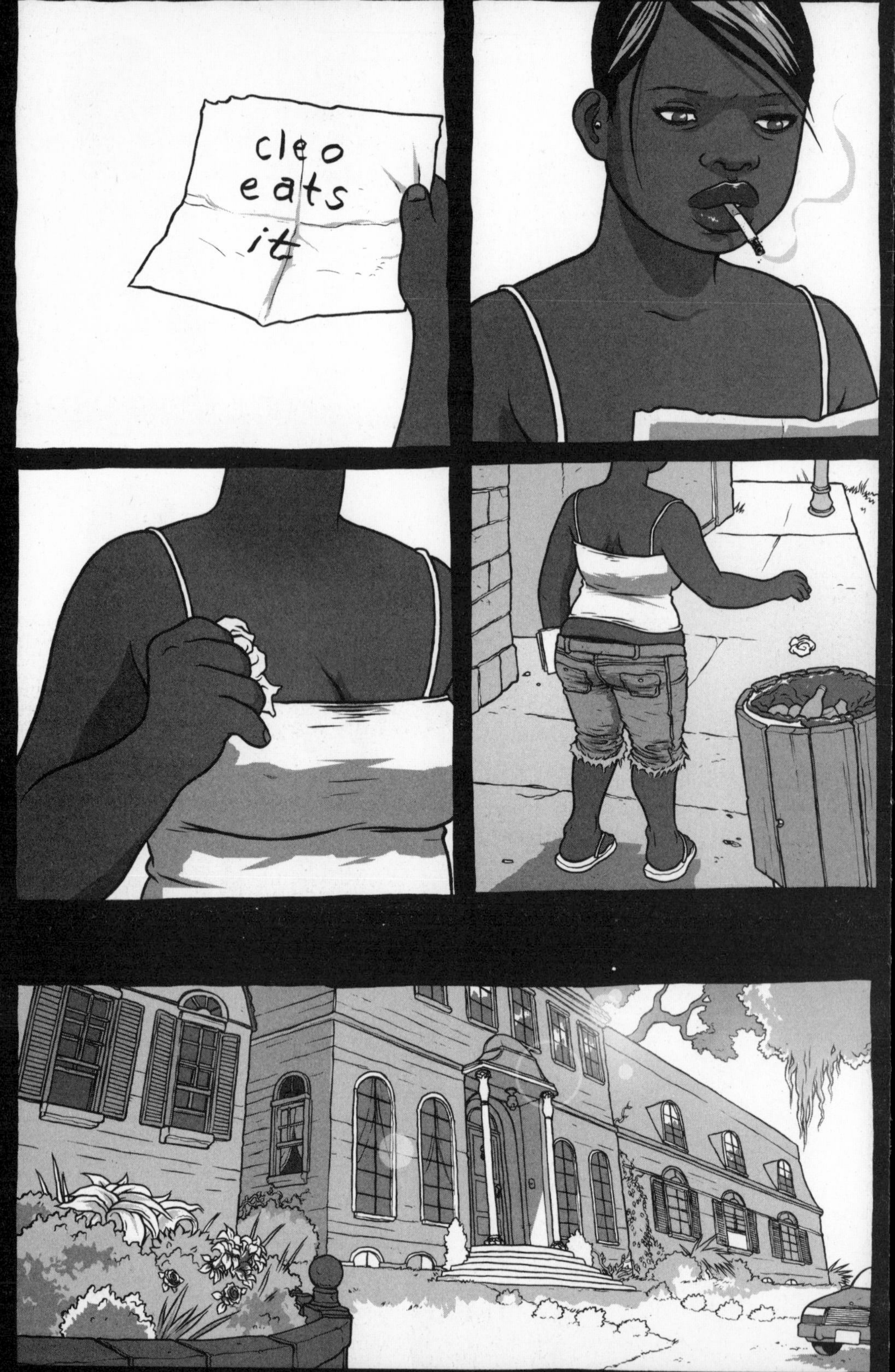
cleo eats it

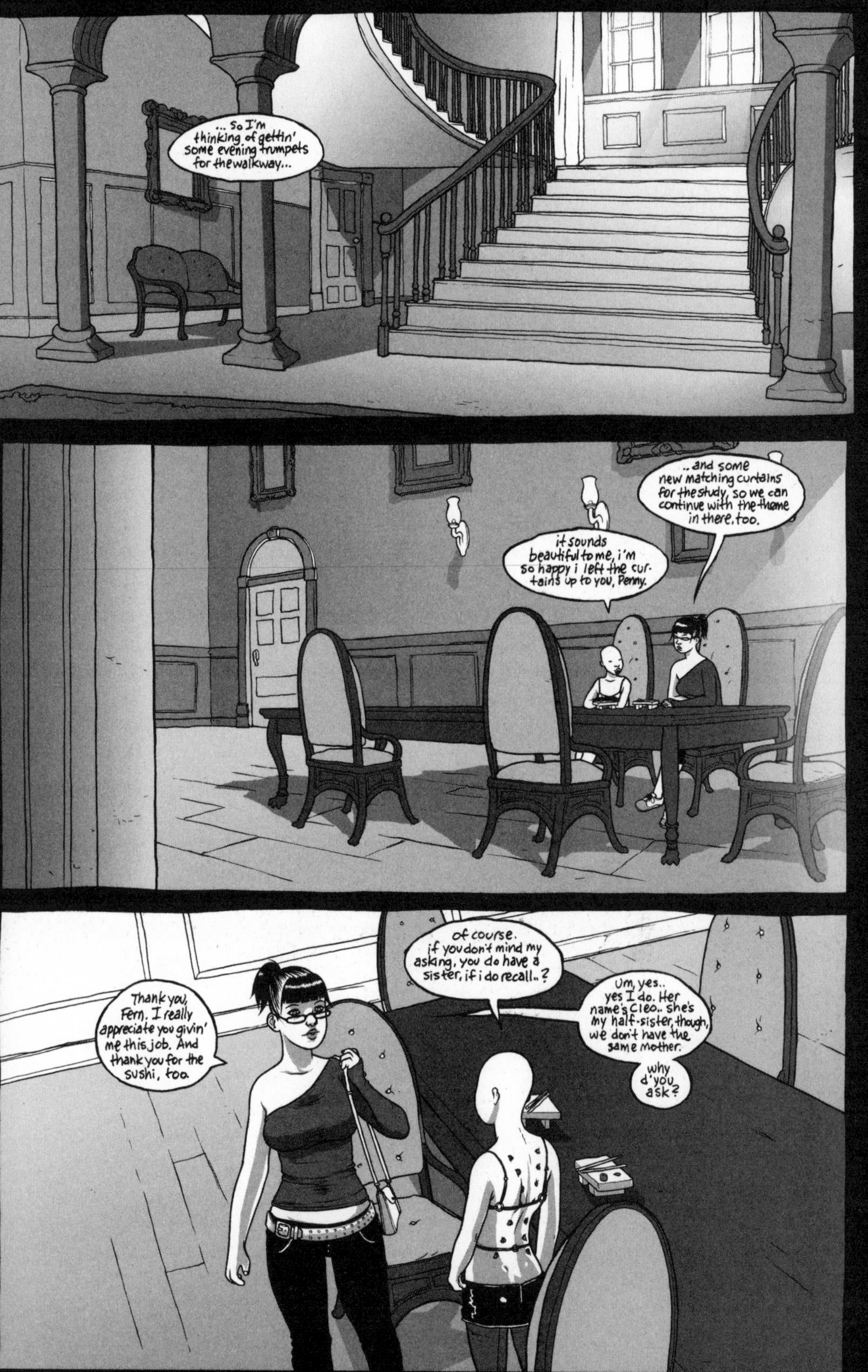
... So I'm thinking of gettin' some evening trumpets for the walkway...
.. and some new matching curtains for the study, so we can continue with the theme in there, too.
it sounds beautiful to me, i'm so happy i left the curtains up to you, Penny.
Thank you, Fern. I really appreciate you givin' me this job. And thank you for the sushi, too.
of course. if you don't mind my asking, you do have a sister, if i do recall..?
Um, yes.. yes I do. Her name's Cleo.. she's my half-sister, though, we don't have the same mother.
why d'you ask?

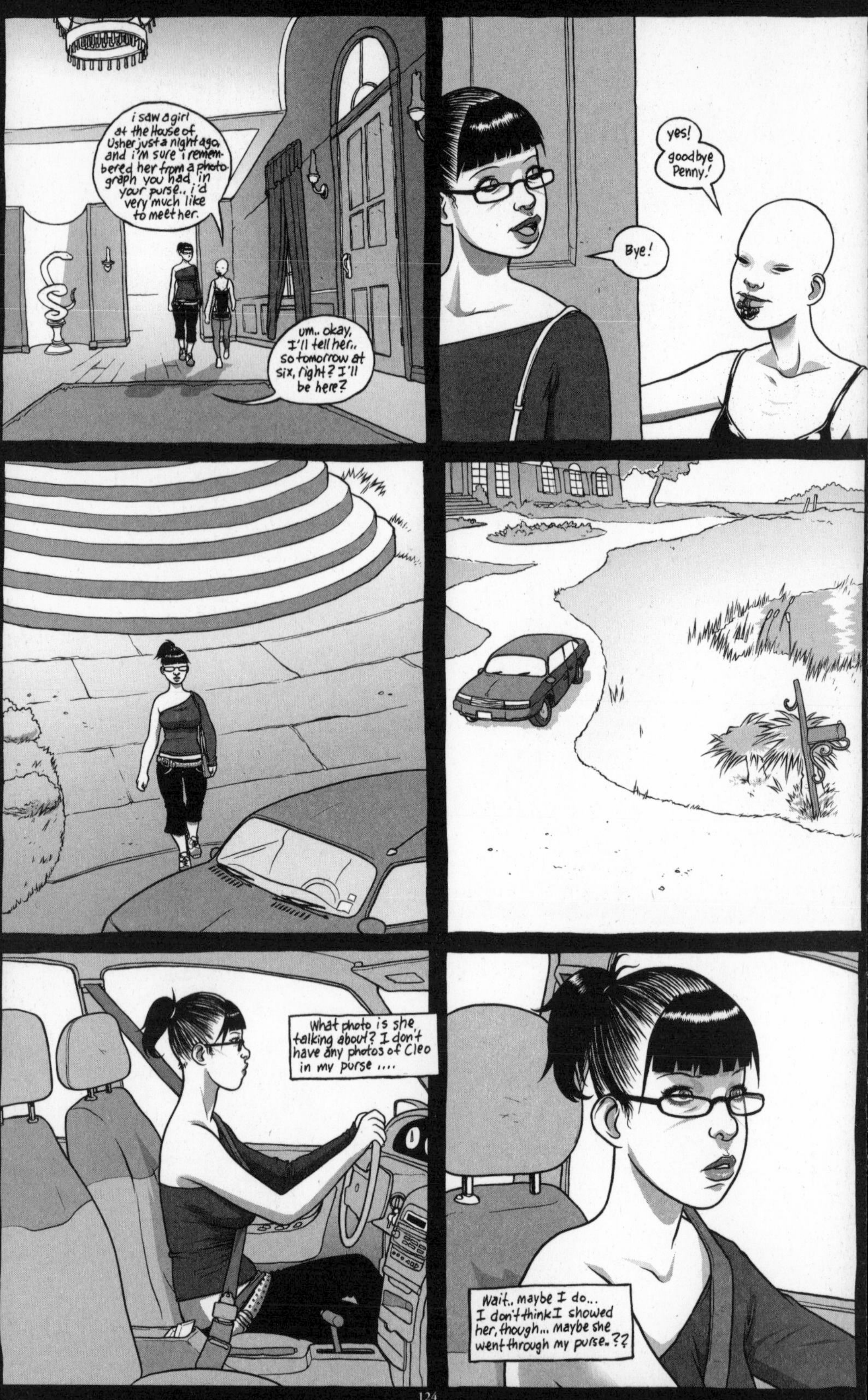
i saw a girl at the House of Usher just a night ago, and i'm sure i remembered her from a photograph you had in your purse.. i'd very much like to meet her.
um.. okay, I'll tell her.. so tomorrow at six, right? I'll be here?
yes! goodbye Penny!
Bye!
What photo is she talking about? I don't have any photos of Cleo in my purse ....
Wait.. maybe I do... I don't think I showed her, though... maybe she went through my purse.. ??

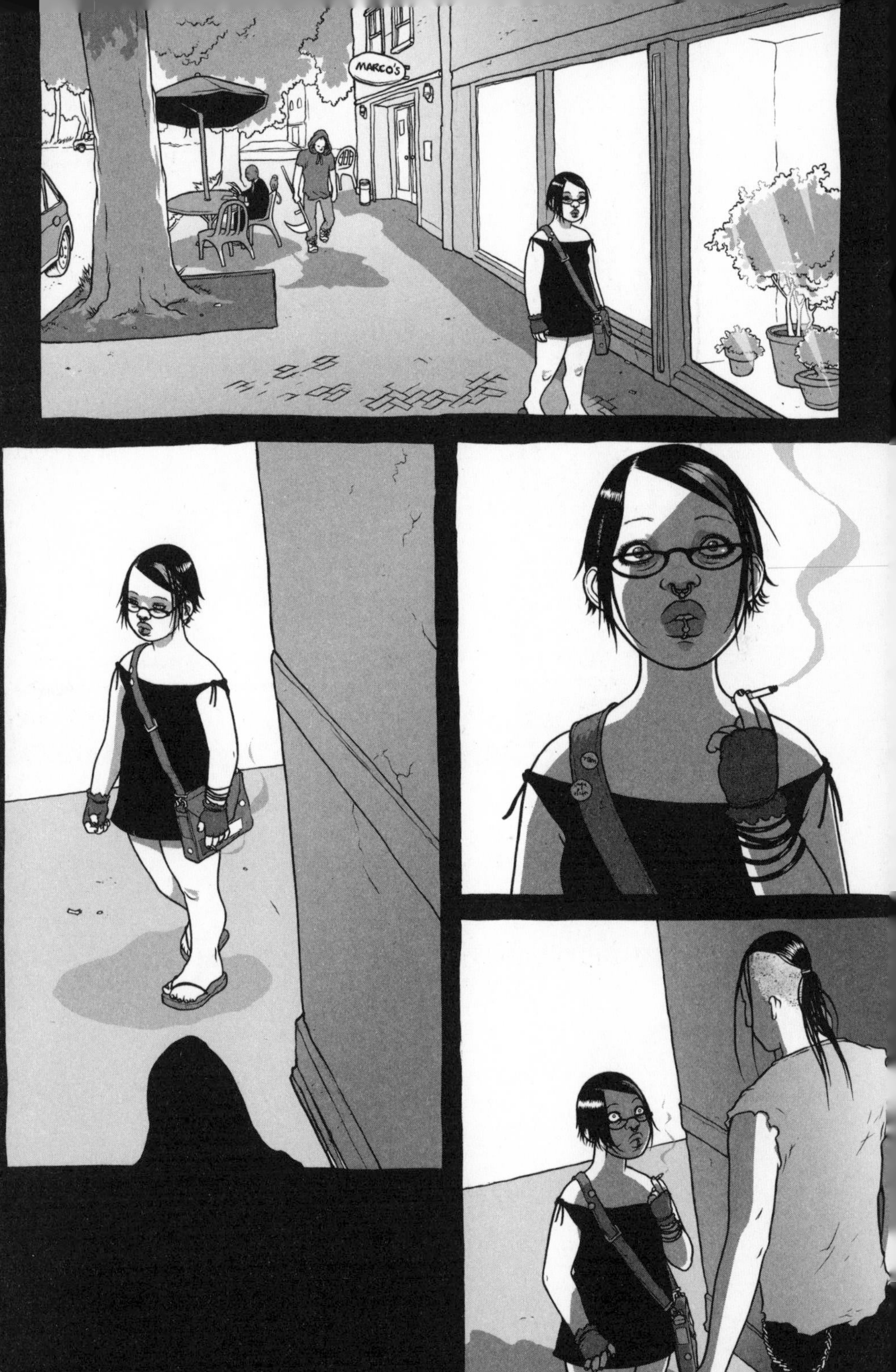
MARCO'S

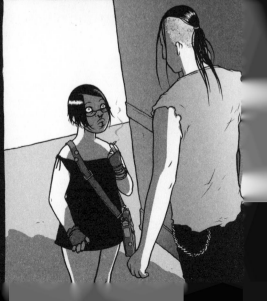

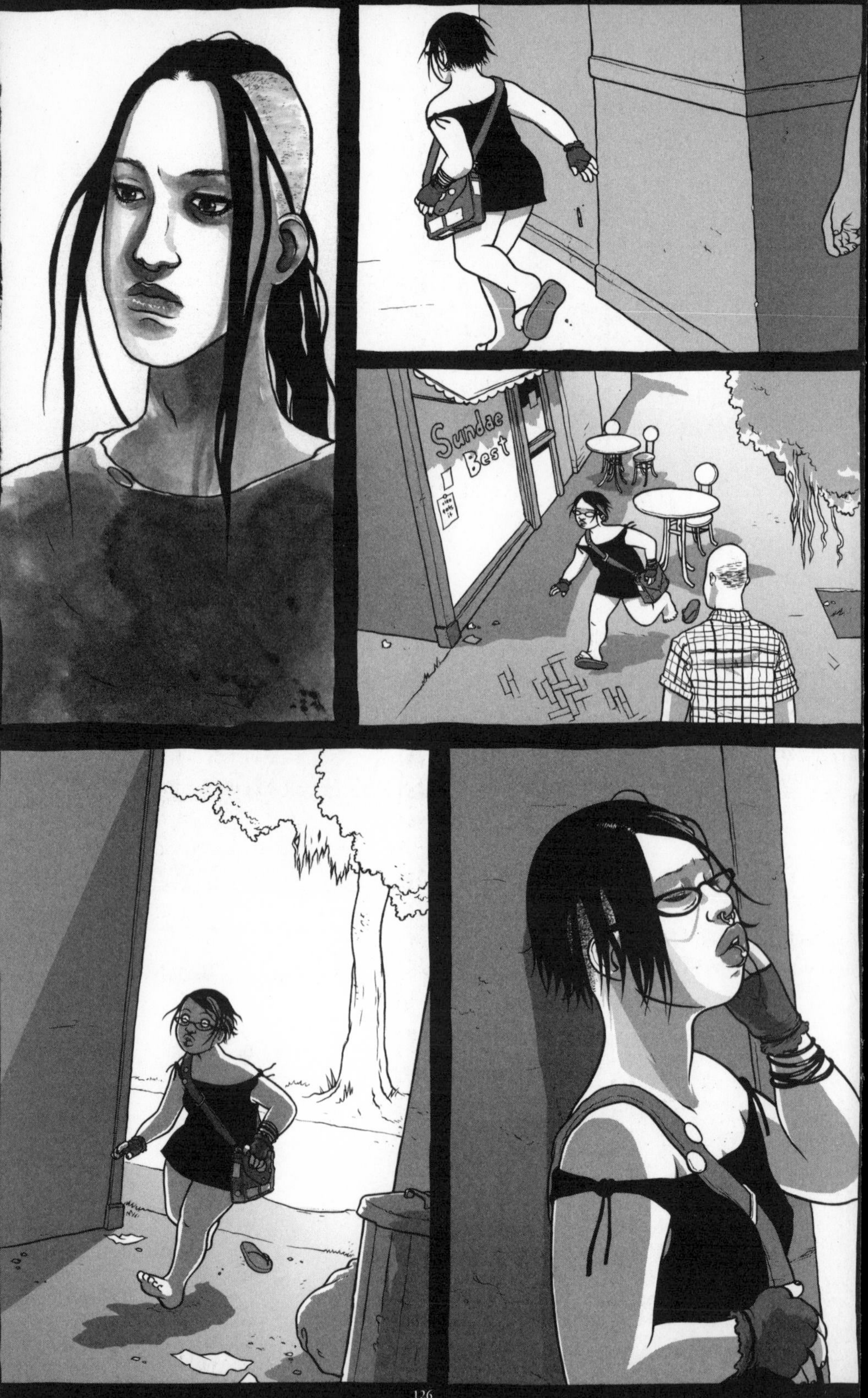
Sundae Best

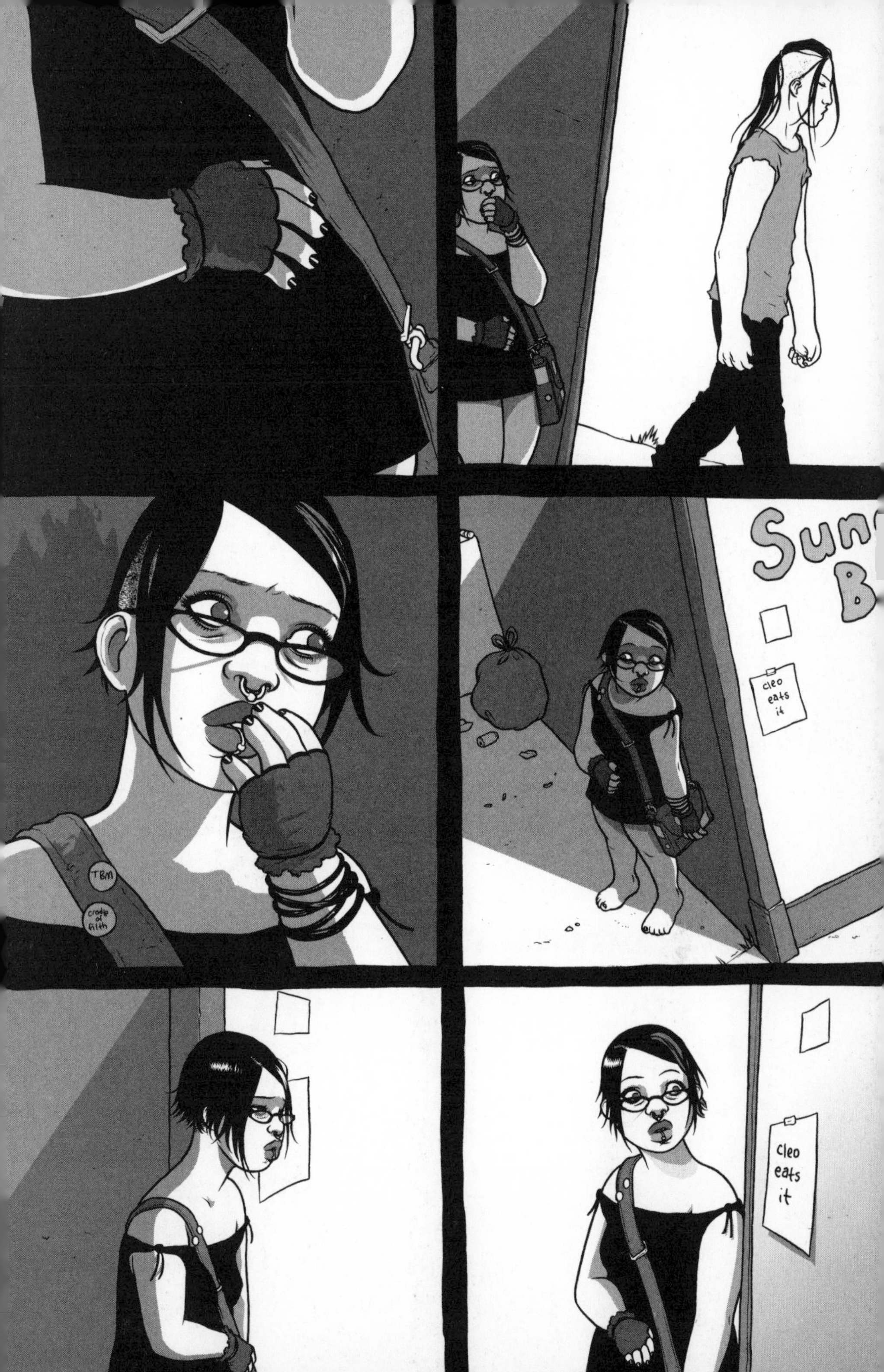
TBM
cradle of filth
cleo eats it
cleo eats it

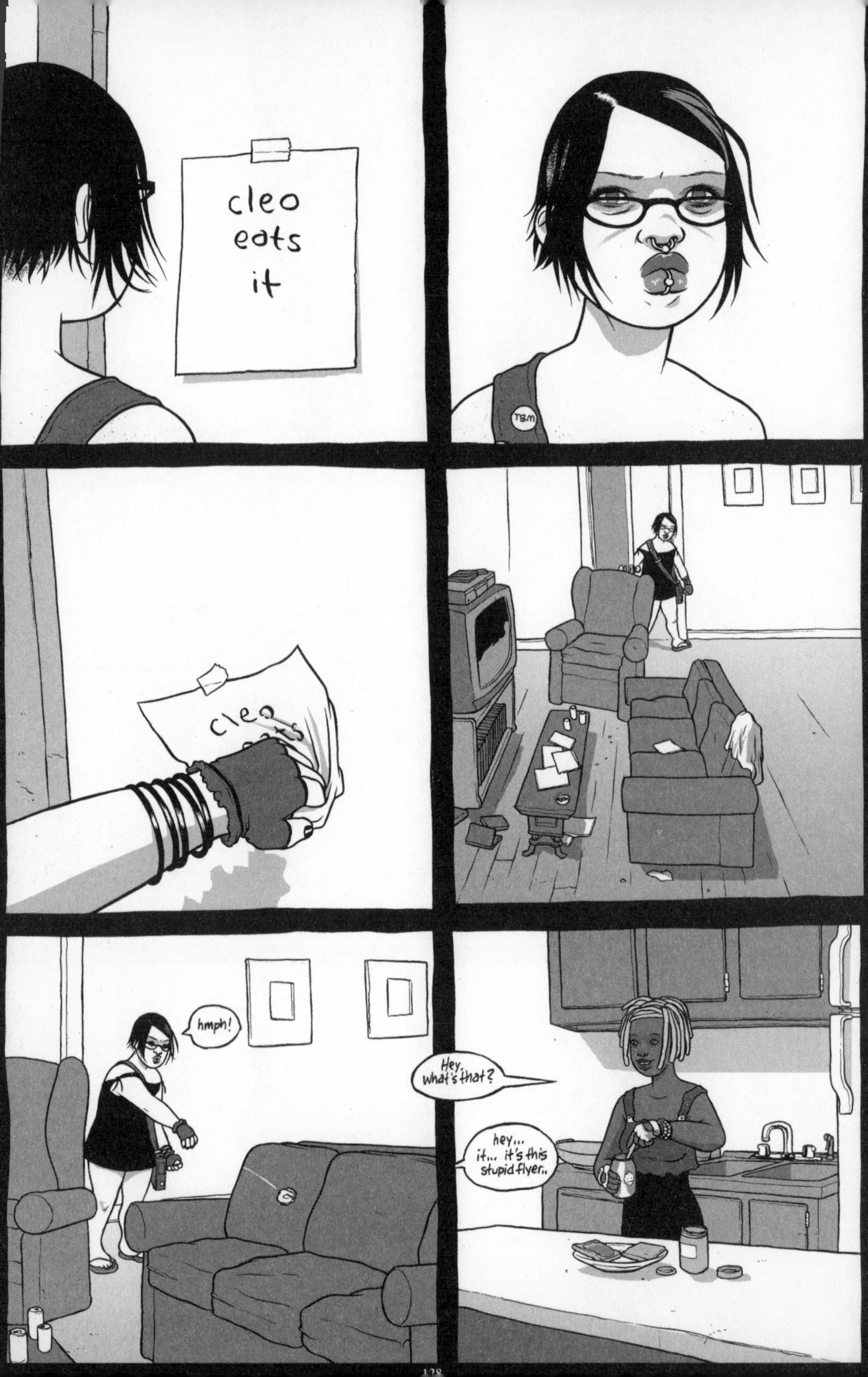
cleo
eats
it
TBM
cleo
hmph!
Hey, what's that?
hey... it... it's this stupid flyer..

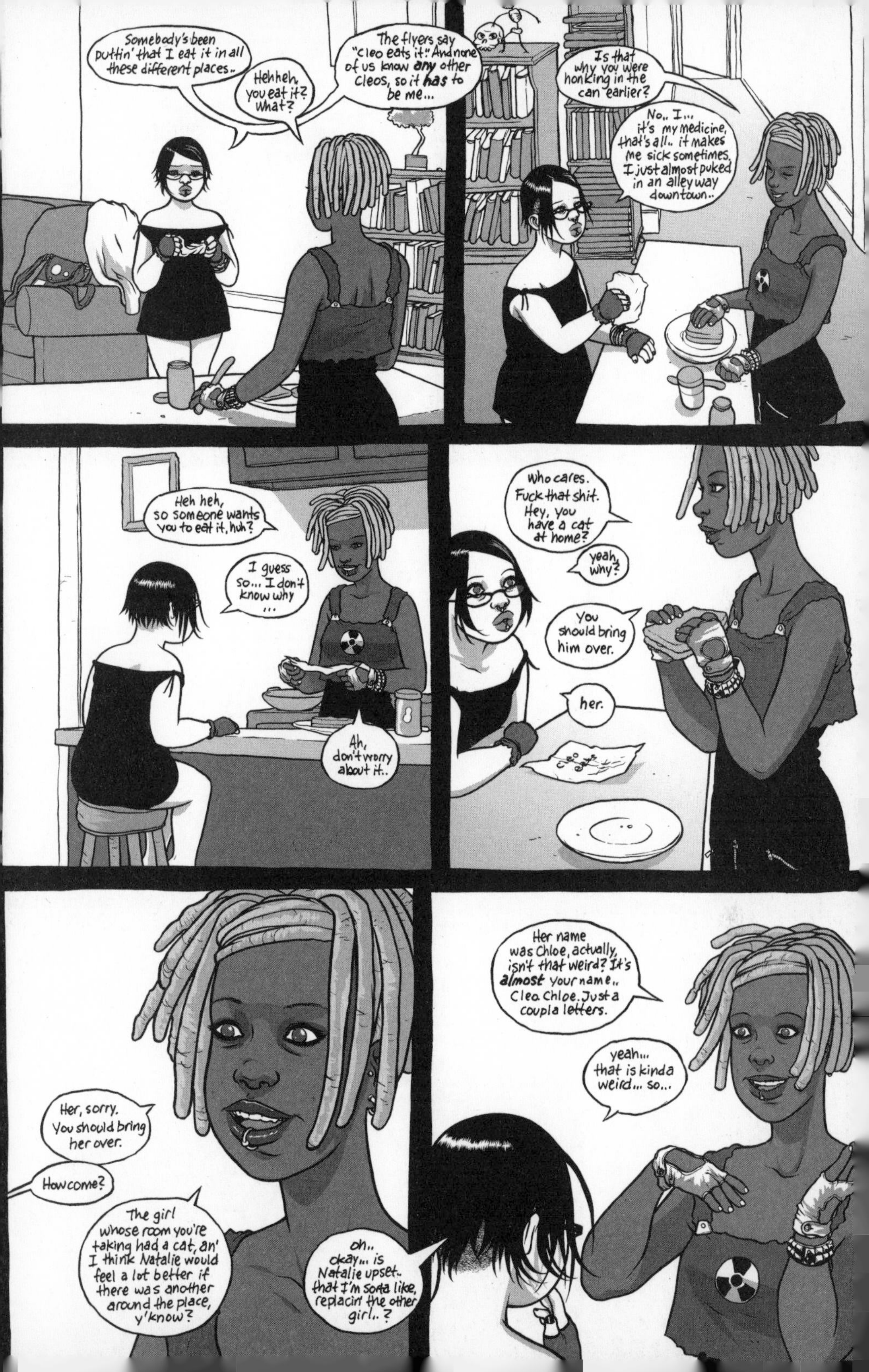
Somebody's been puttin' that I eat it in all these different places..
Hehheh, you eat it? What?
The flyers say "Cleo eats it!" And none of us know any other Cleos, so it has to be me...
Is that why you were honking in the can earlier?
No.. I... it's my medicine, that's all.. it makes me sick sometimes. I just almost puked in an alleyway downtown..
Heh heh, so someone wants you to eat it, huh?
I guess so... I don't know why ...
Ah, don't worry about it..
Who cares. Fuck that shit. Hey, you have a cat at home?
yeah, why?
You should bring him over.
her.
Her, sorry. You should bring her over.
How come?
The girl whose room you're taking had a cat, an' I think Natalie would feel a lot better if there was another around the place, y'know?
oh.. okay... is Natalie upset.. that I'm sorta like, replacin' the other girl..?
Her name was Chloe, actually, isn't that weird? It's almost your name.. Cleo. Chloe. Just a coupla letters.
yeah... that is kinda weird... so...

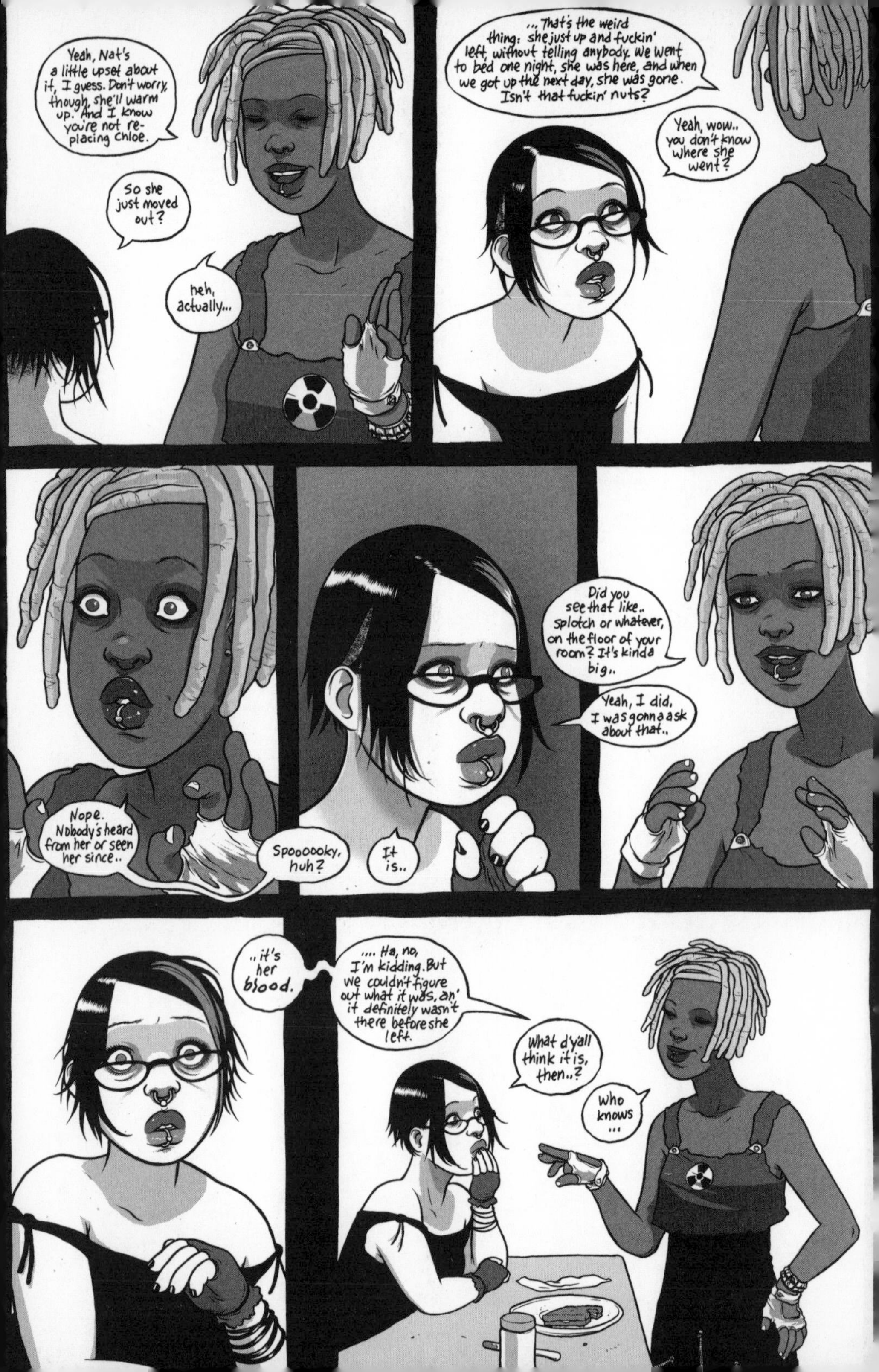
Yeah, Nat's a little upset about it, I guess. Don't worry, though, she'll warm up. And I know you're not replacing Chloe.
So she just moved out?
heh, actually...
... That's the weird thing: she just up and fuckin' left, without telling anybody. We went to bed one night, she was here, and when we got up the next day, she was gone. Isn't that fuckin' nuts?
Yeah, wow.. you don't know where she went?
Nope. Nobody's heard from her or seen her since..
Spoooooky, huh?
It is..
Did you see that like.. splotch or whatever, on the floor of your room? It's kinda big..
Yeah, I did, I was gonna ask about that..
.. it's her blood.
.... Ha, no, I'm kidding. But we couldn't figure out what it was, an' it definitely wasn't there before she left.
What d'yall think it is, then..?
Who knows ...

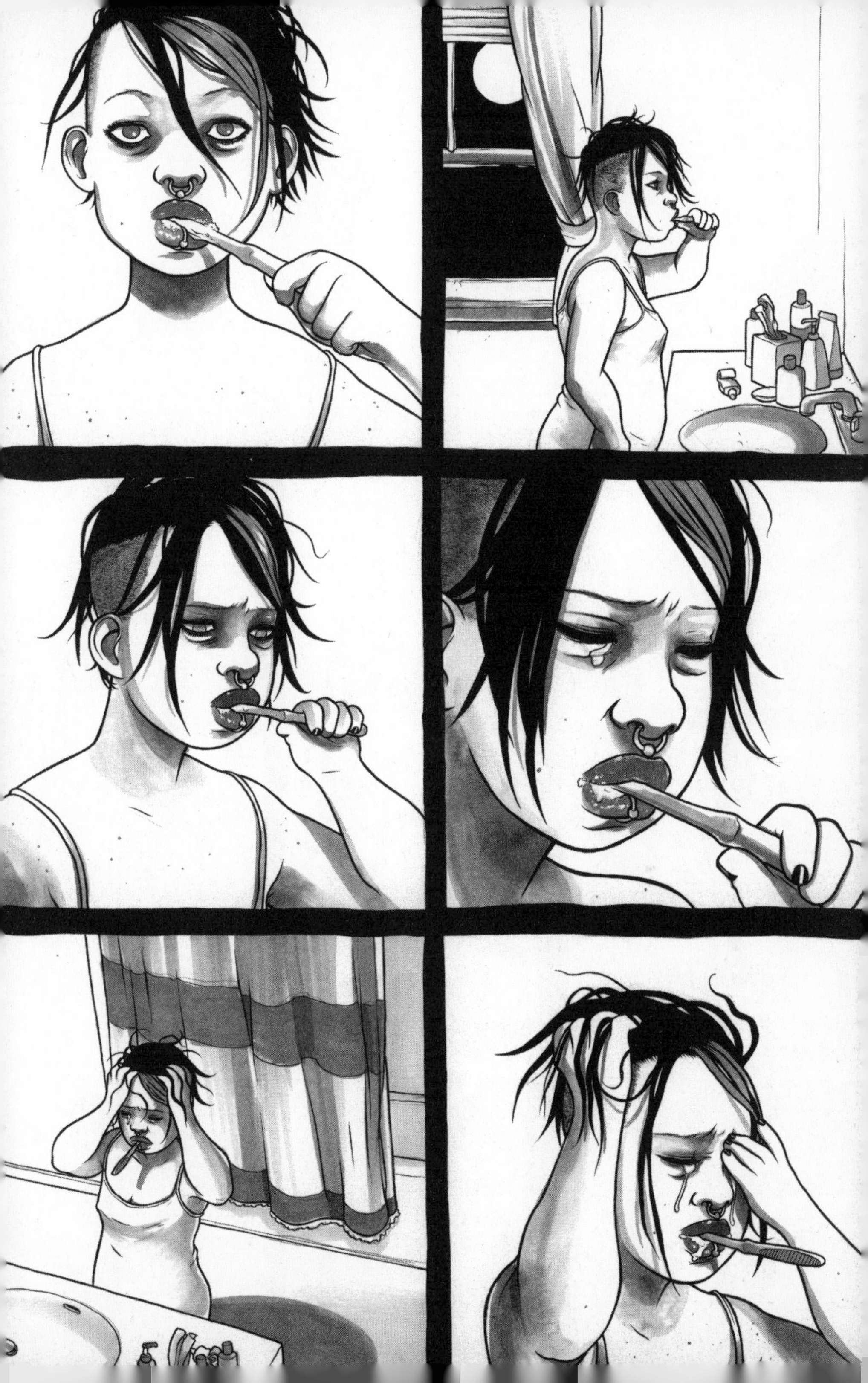

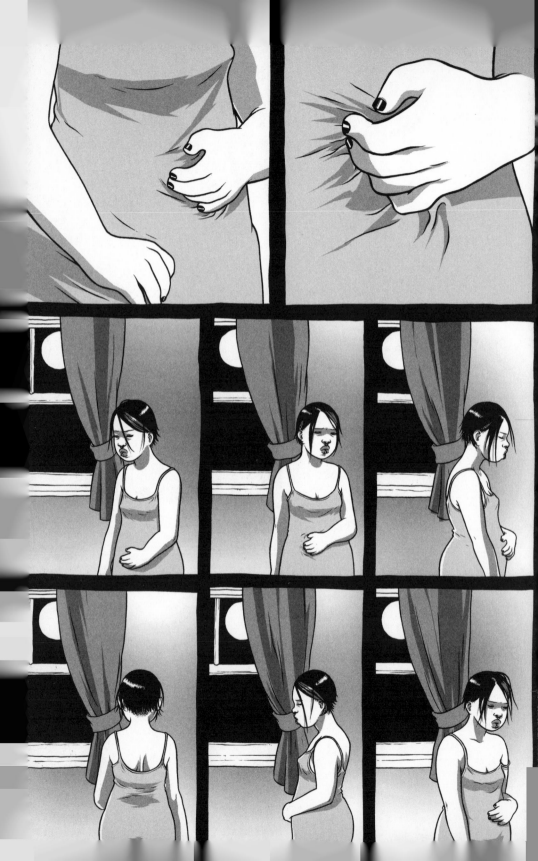

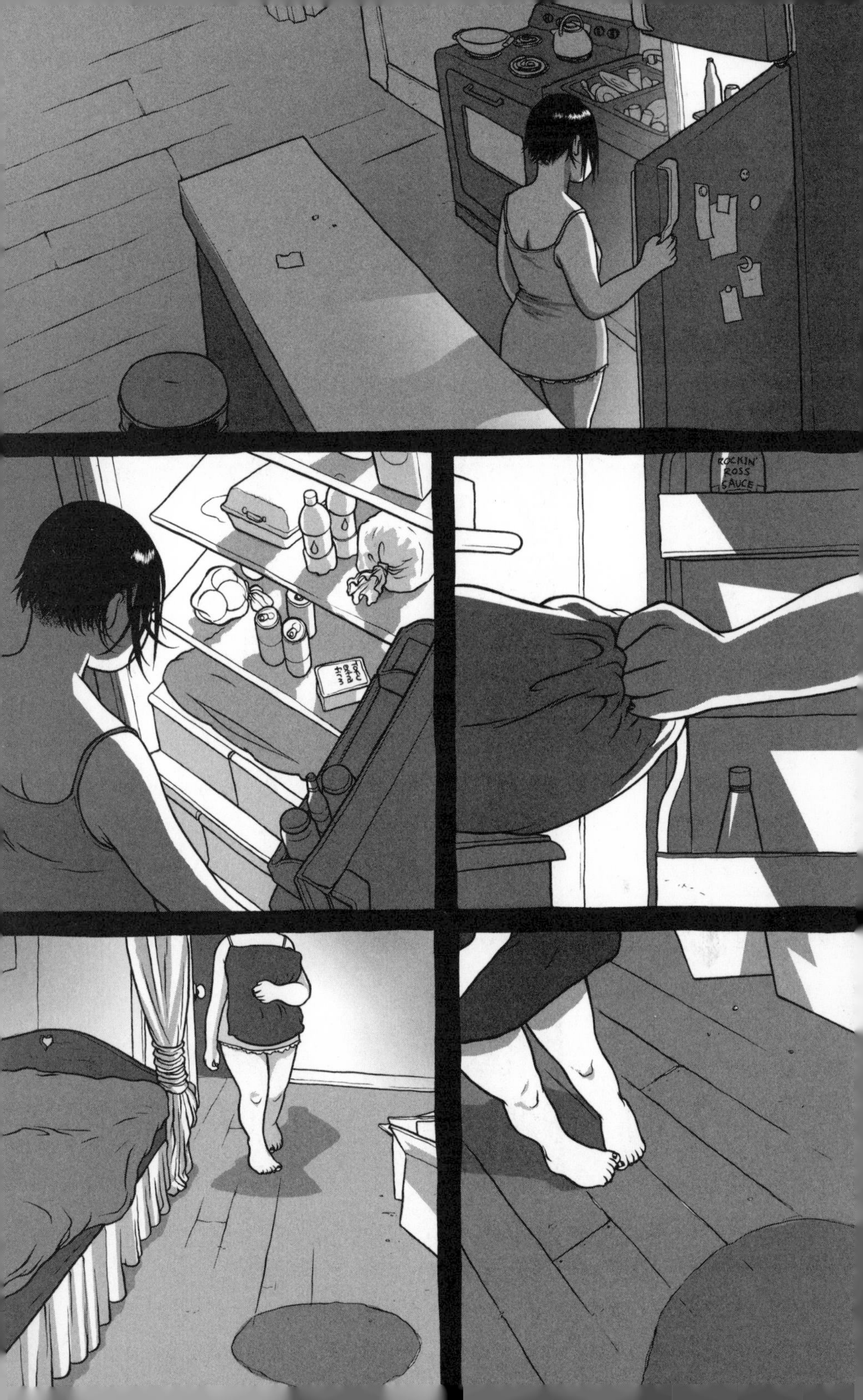
Tofu extra firm
ROCKIN' ROSS SAUCE

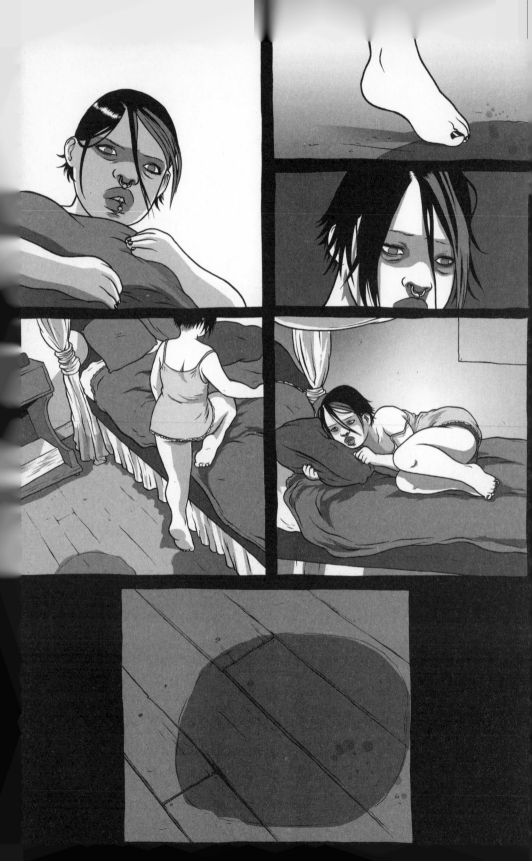

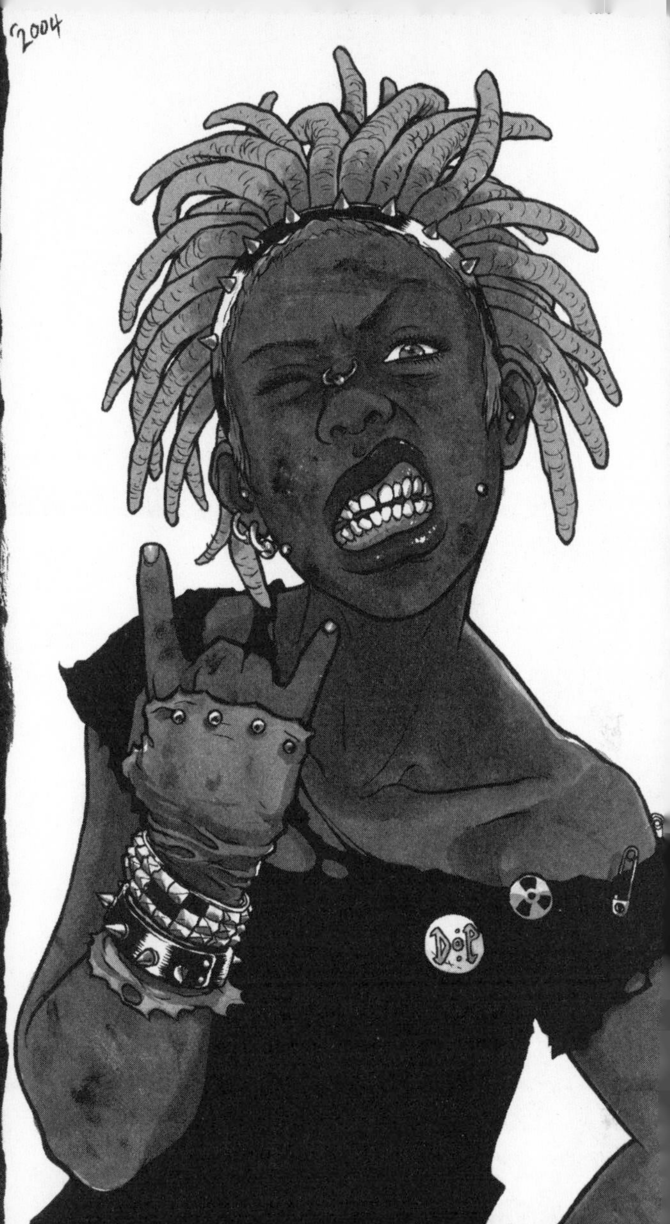

"And your face seems somehow altered; something swims b
If I live to be much older I fear I'll be al
For your stare speaks something so in
And I know you won't be saved ton
-Bella Morte

east coast rising

NATE and STEVE FUCKIN' ROCK

echoes in the ashes

INDIANA ...ES

promise of shade meadows

SPOOKED

FRUIT BRUTE

I'm s'posed to meet Martin later on for lunch I think..

oh.. okay.. will you be free later, then..?

I dunno, I don't think so... you'll be okay by yourself for one day, okay hon?

Yeah... guess I'll go get some school supplies or somethin'...

What's your first class?

...RUIT

YUM

European Gothic Literature.

hehheh. of course.

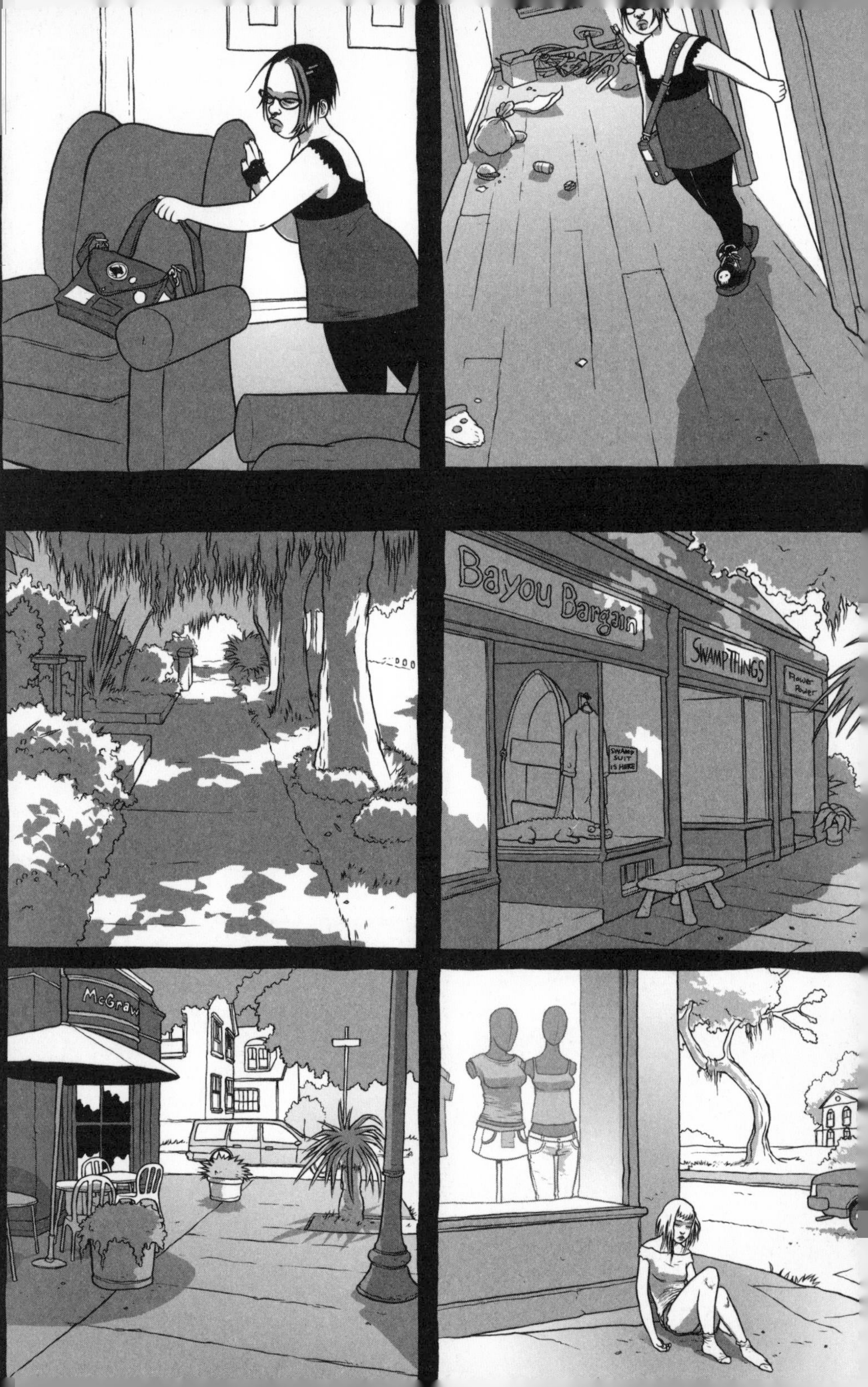
Bayou Bargain
SWAMP THINGS
Flower Power
SWAMP SUIT IS HERE
McGraw

september 19th

class starts temorrow. I'm nervous. I wish trilby and I were in the same major program, then at least I'd have someone in class that I know. I wonder when my evil fortune is supposed to come true... like how long it'll be before my stupidity ~~takes~~ takes over and causes my undoing. Maybe it's already causing it... maybe my undoing is already in progress, and temorrow I'll wake up undone. Maybe going to class temorrow is stupid, and I'll be undone by that... but I'd think I'd more likely be undone by not going to class, because that would be stupider than going, definitely.

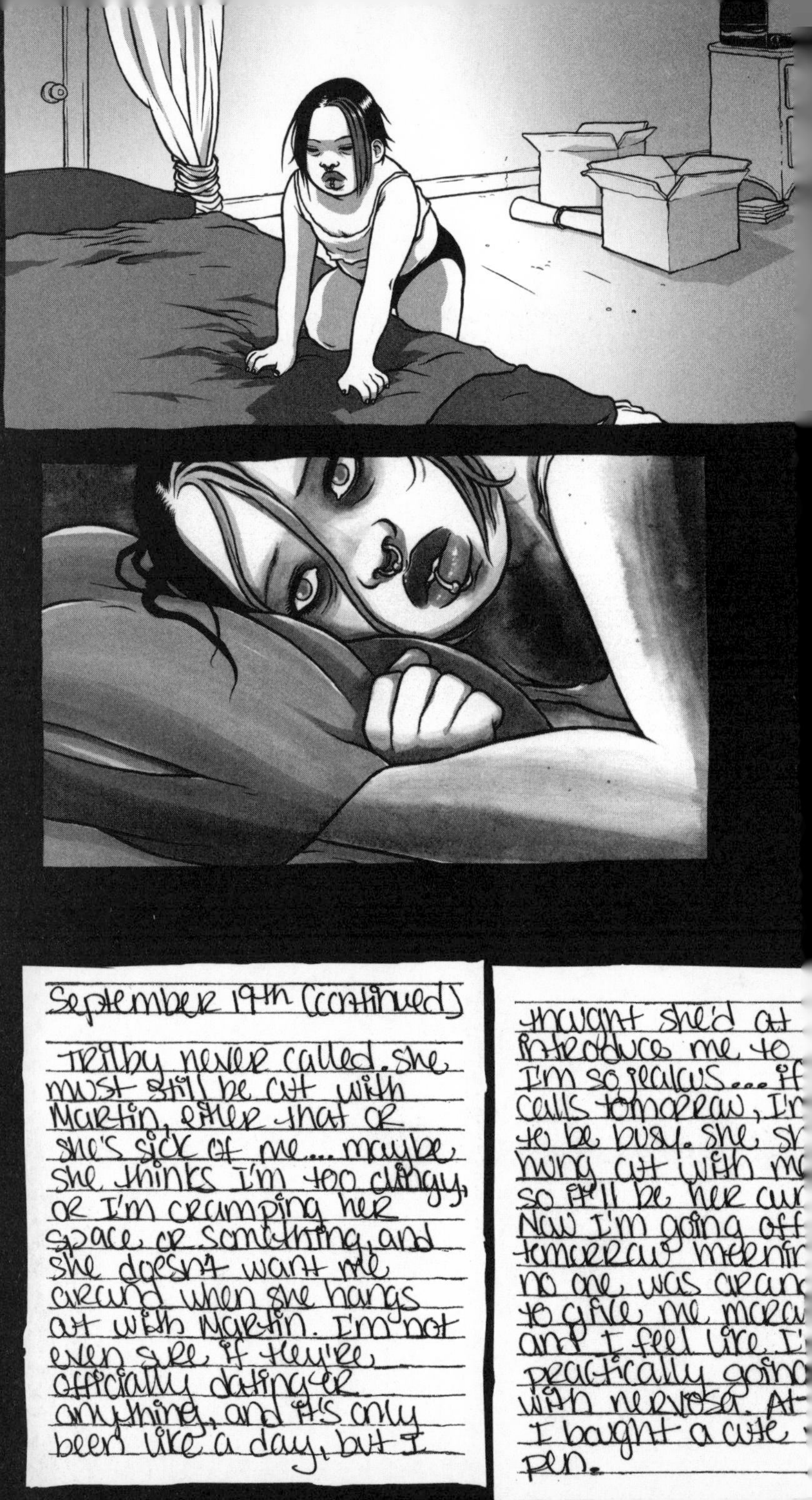

September 19th (continued)
Tribby never called. She must still be out with Martin, either that or she's sick of me... maybe she thinks I'm too clingy, or I'm cramping her space or something, and she doesn't want me around when she hangs out with Martin. I'm not even sure if they're officially dating or anything, and it's only been like a day, but I
thought she'd at
introduce me to
I'm so jealous... if
calls tomorrow, I'
to be busy. She s
hang out with m
so it'll be her ow
Now I'm going off
tomorrow mornin
no one was aroun
to give me mora
and I feel like I'
practically goin
with nervosa. At
I bought a cute
pen.

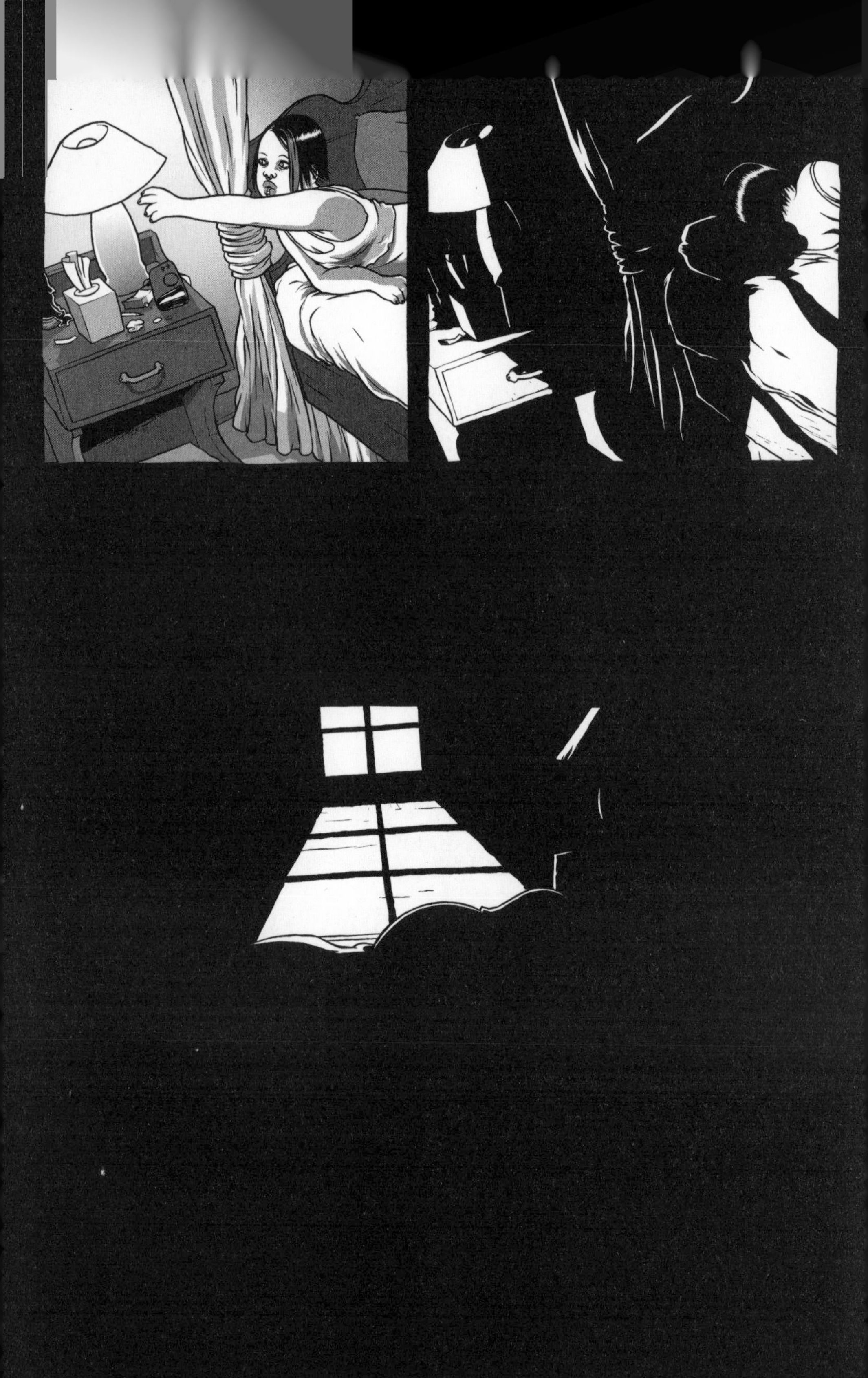

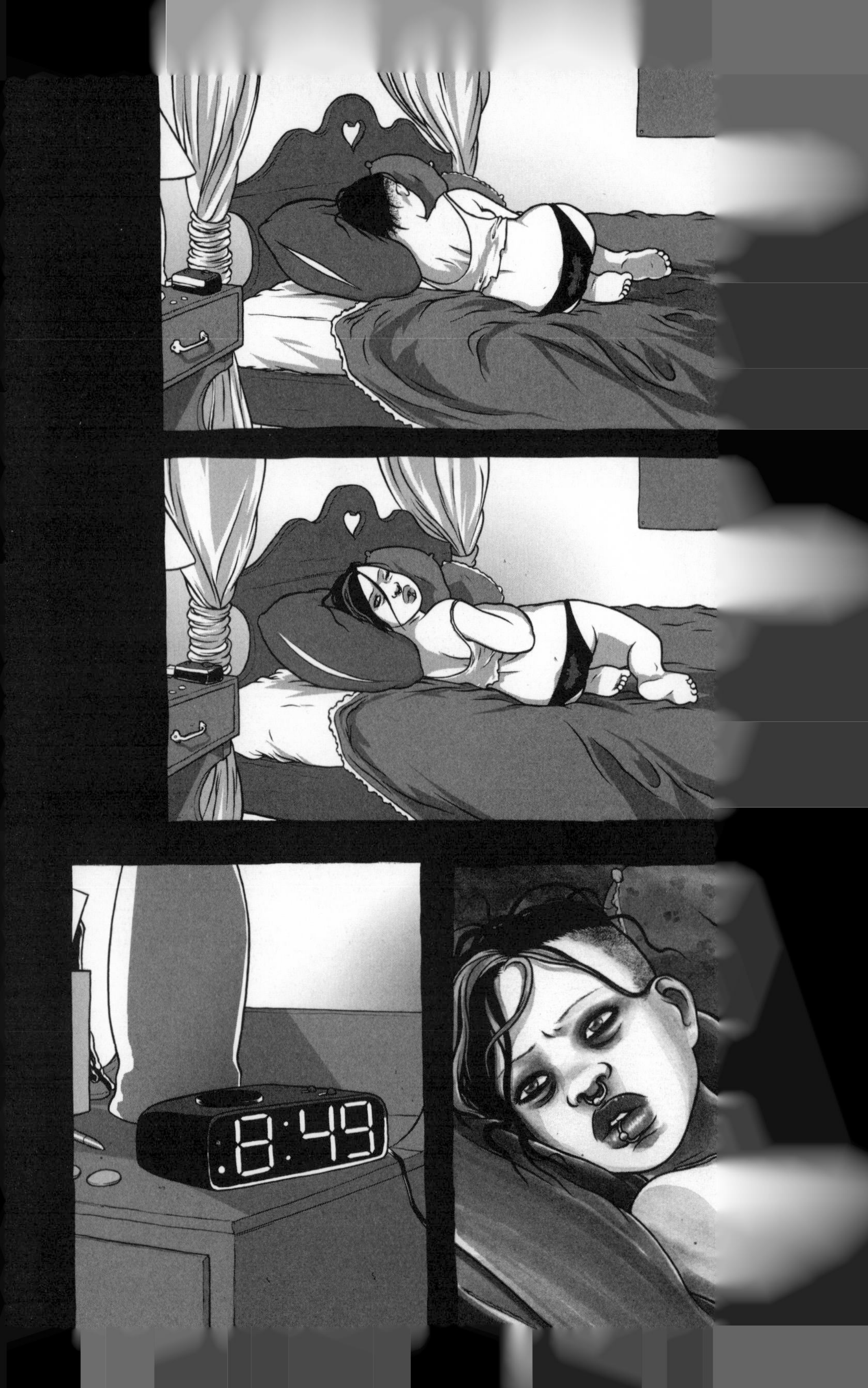
8:49

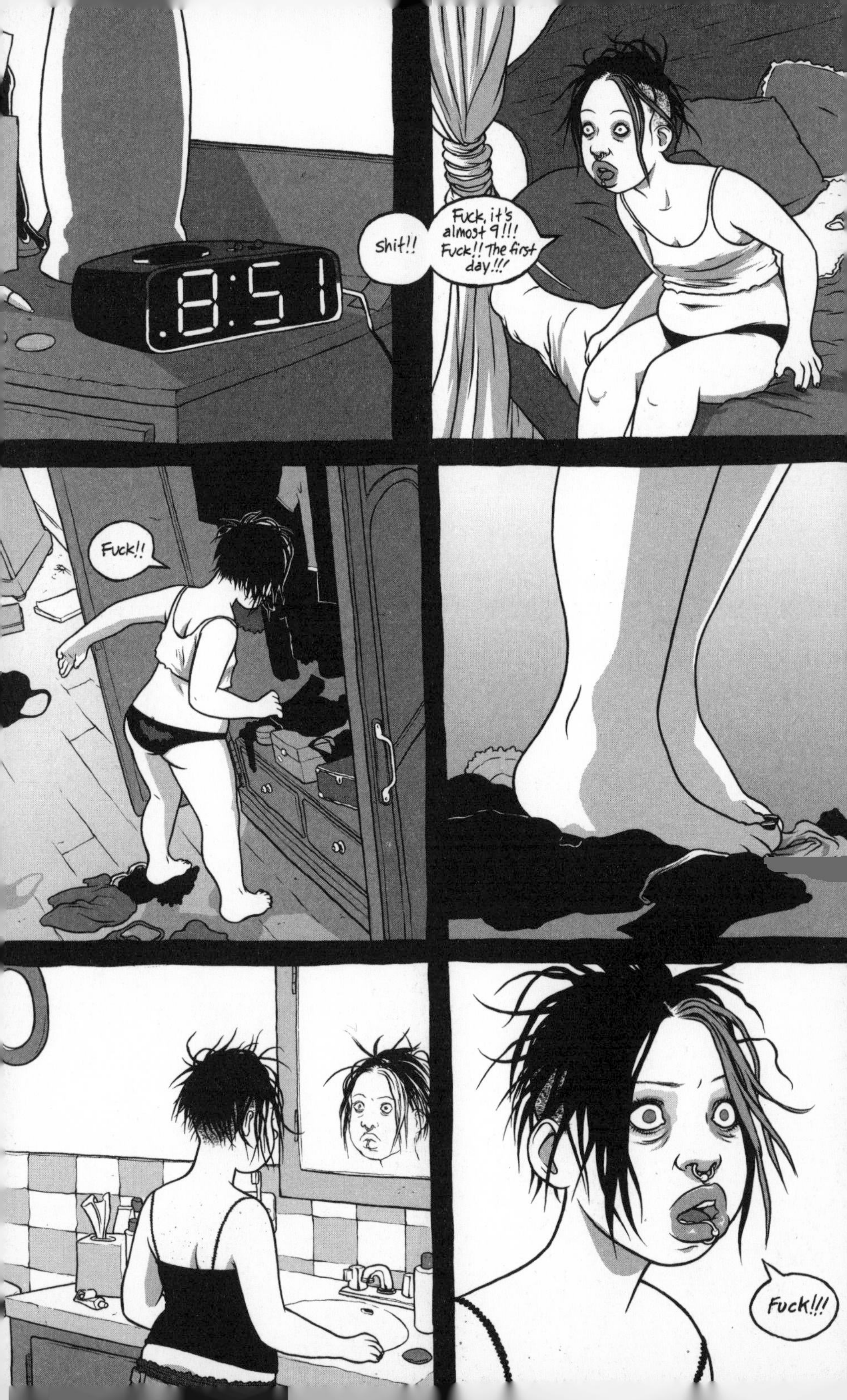
8:51
shit!!
Fuck, it's almost 9!!! Fuck!! The first day!!!
Fuck!!
Fuck!!!

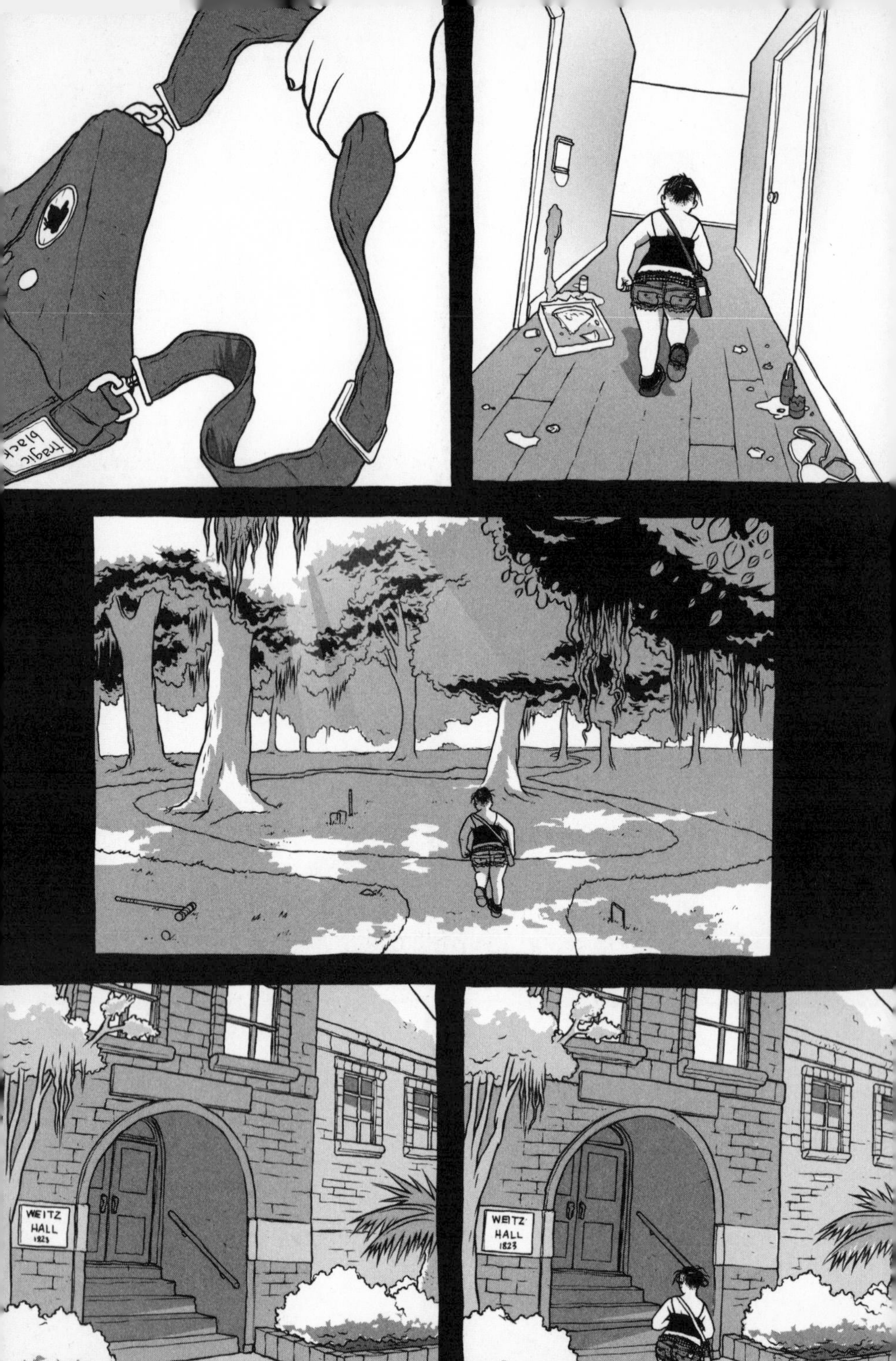
tragic black
WEITZ HALL 1823
WEITZ HALL 1823

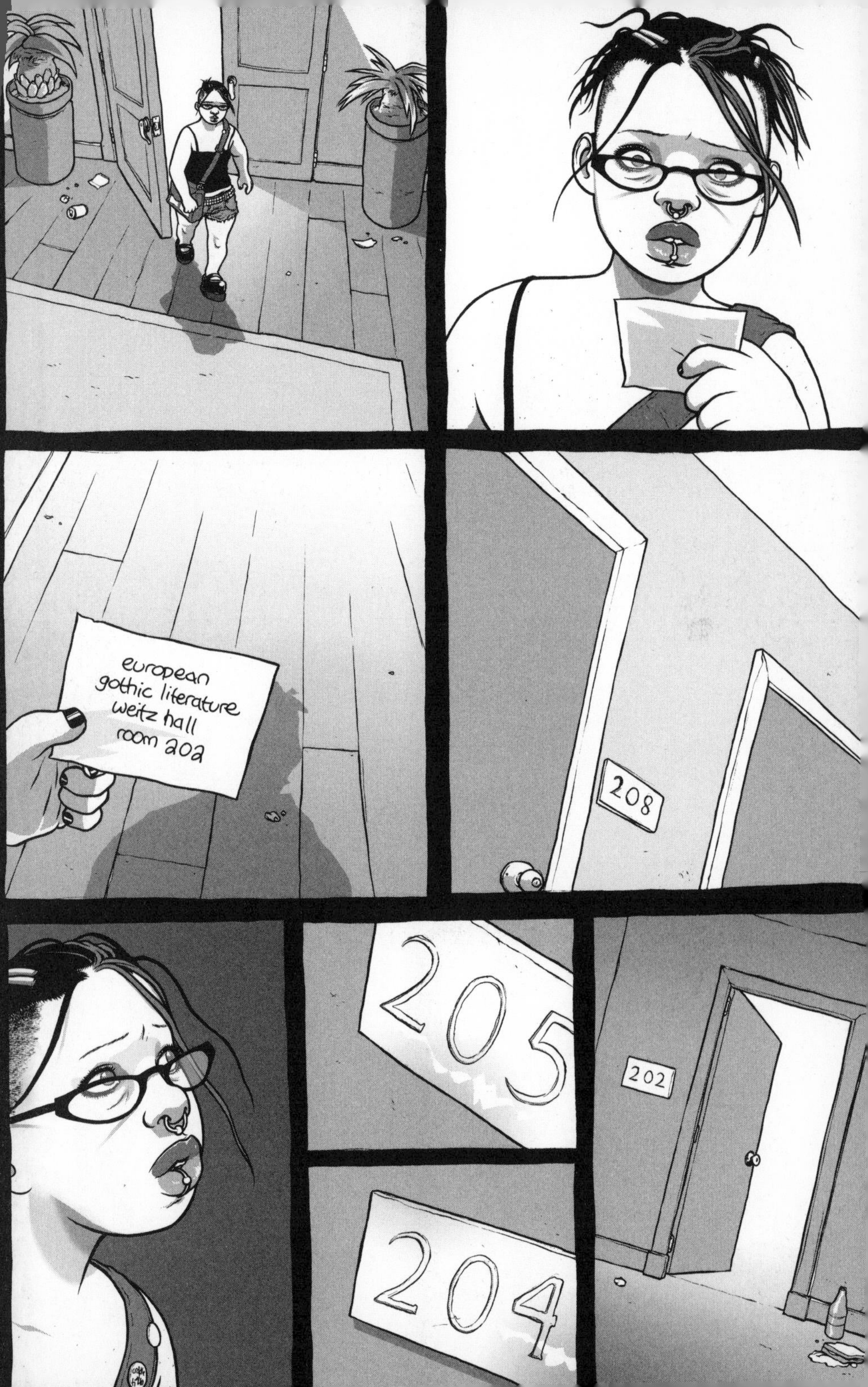
european
gothic literature
weitz hall
room 202
208
205
204
202

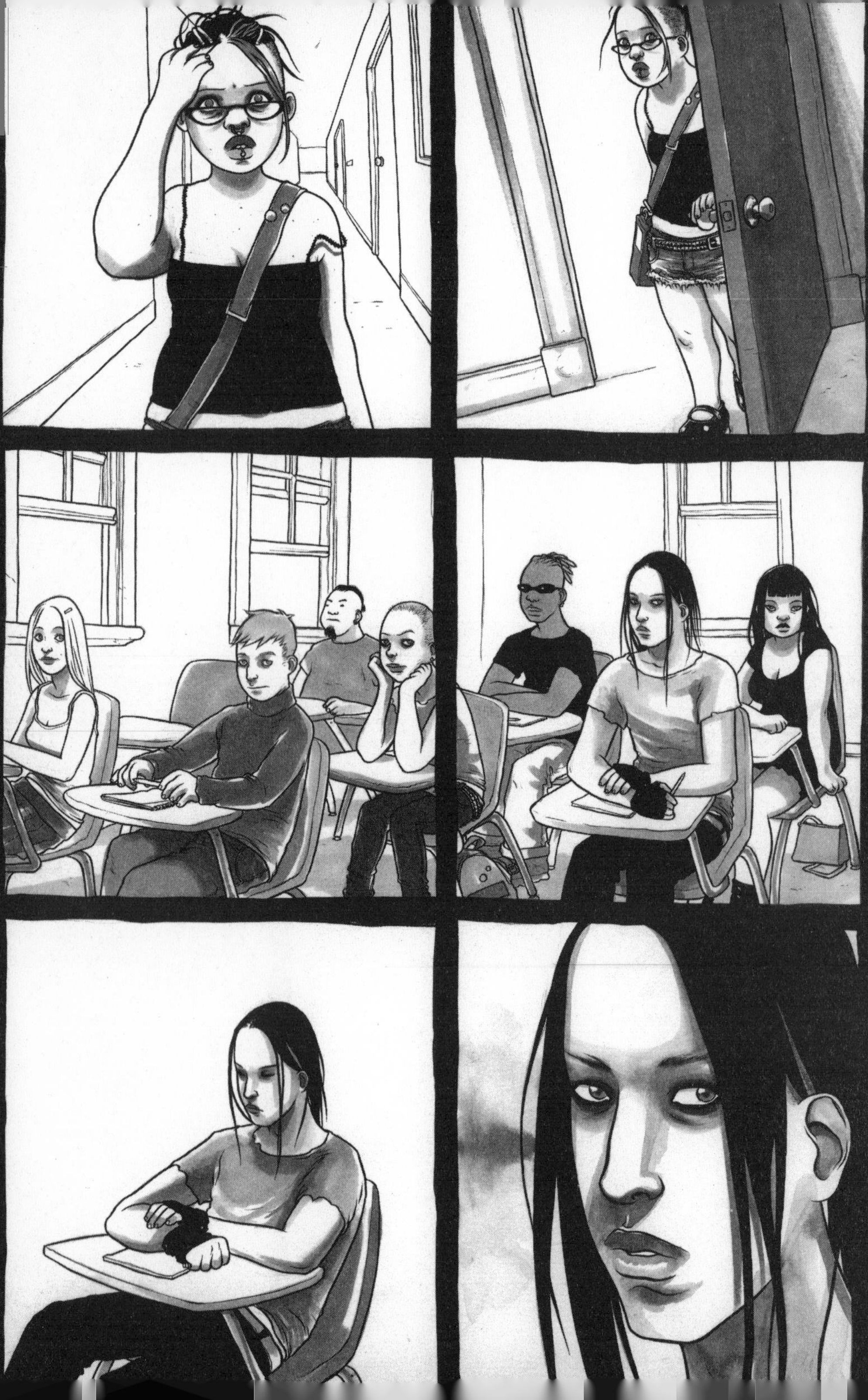

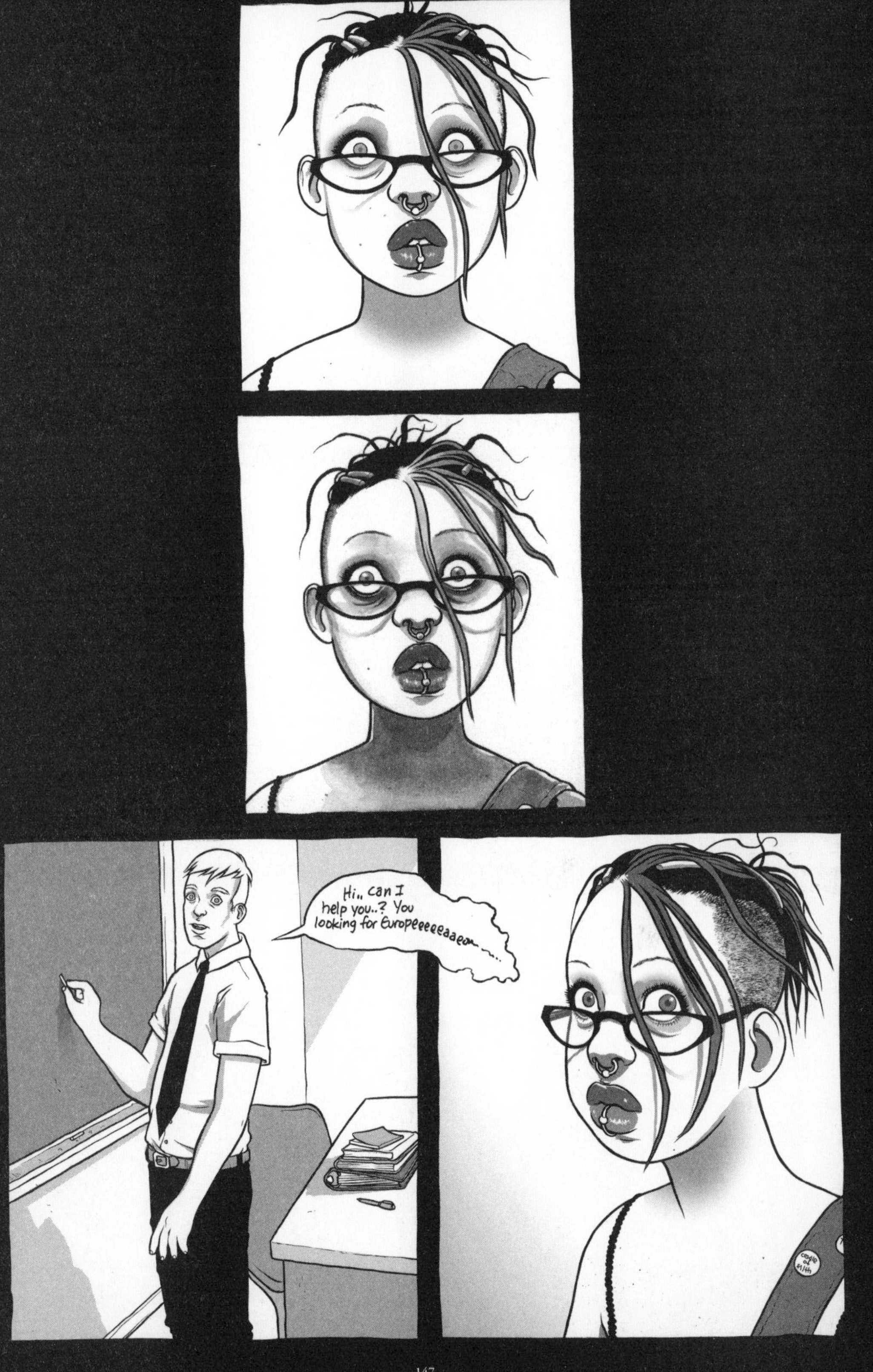
Hi.. can I help you..? You looking for Europeeeeeaaeea.....
cradle of filth

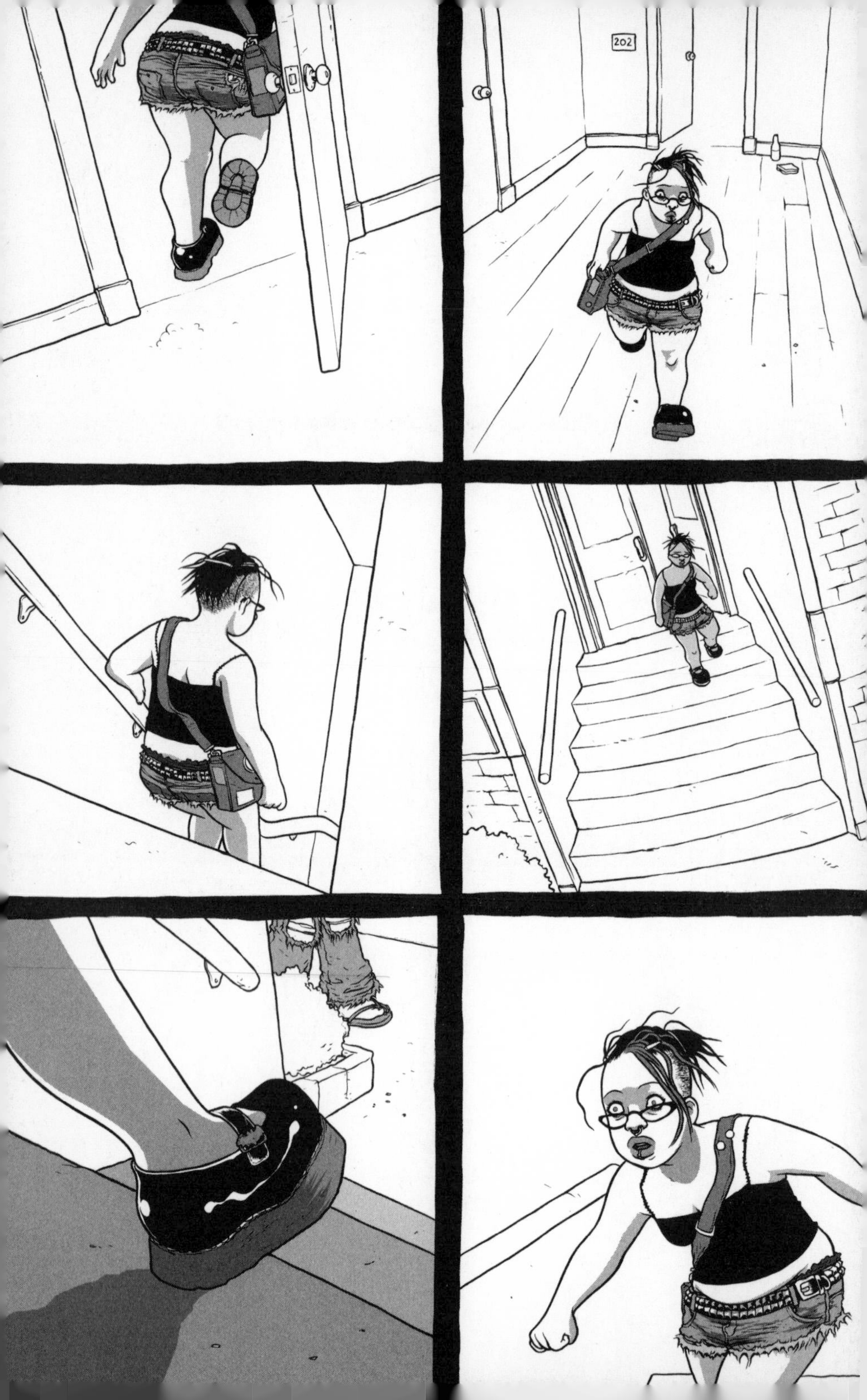
202

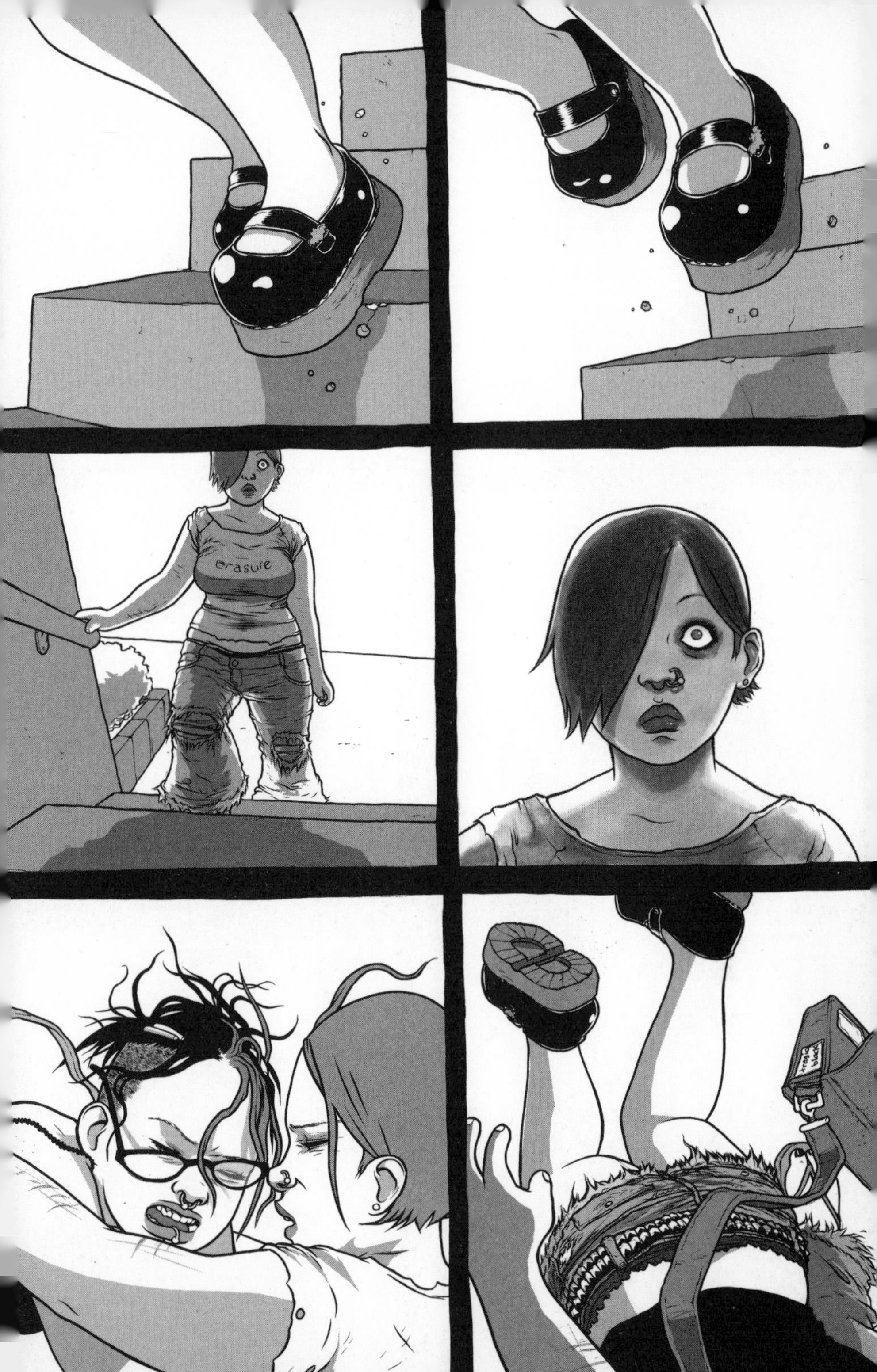
erasure
tragic black

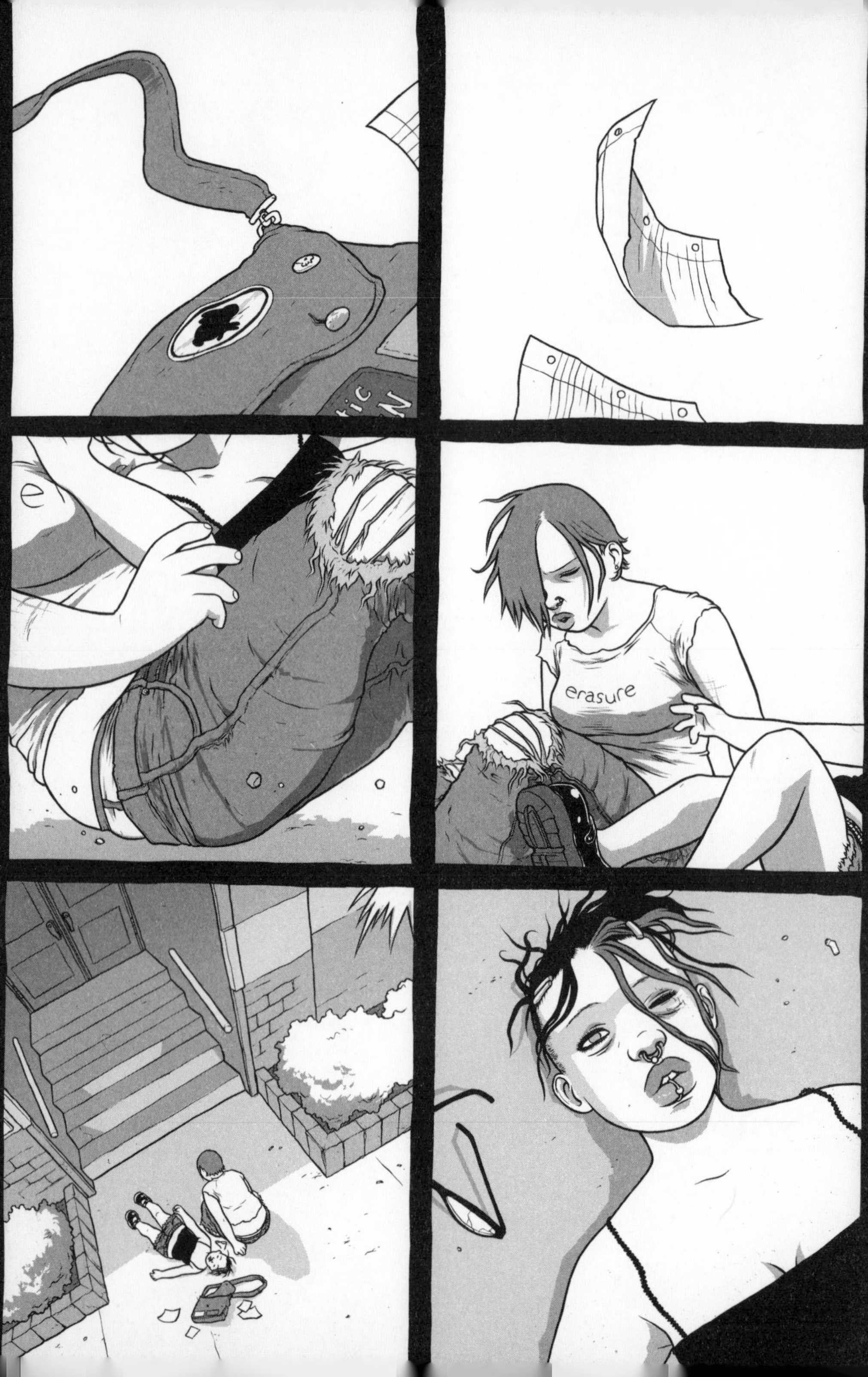
erasure

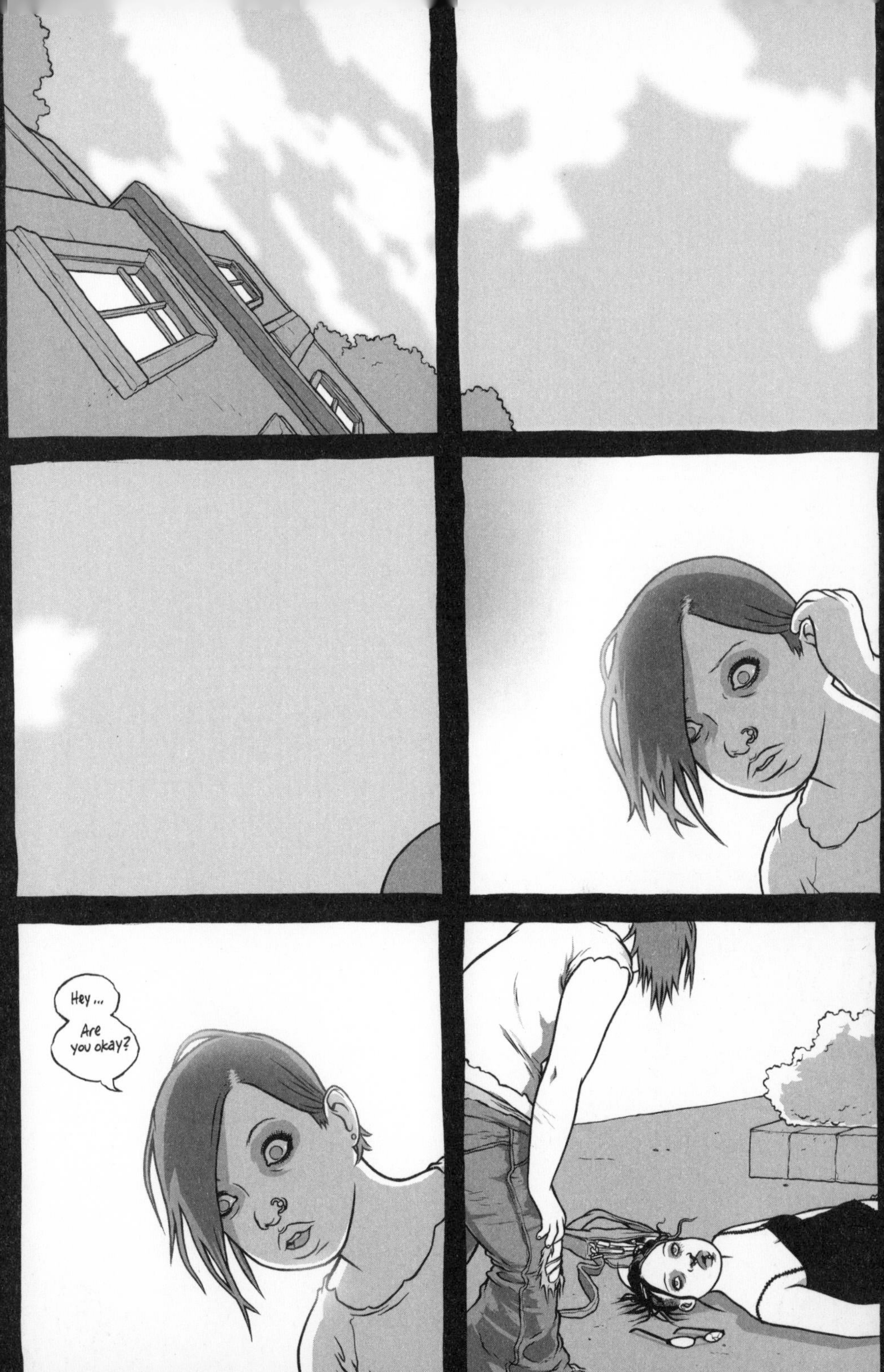
Hey...
Are you okay?

oh....

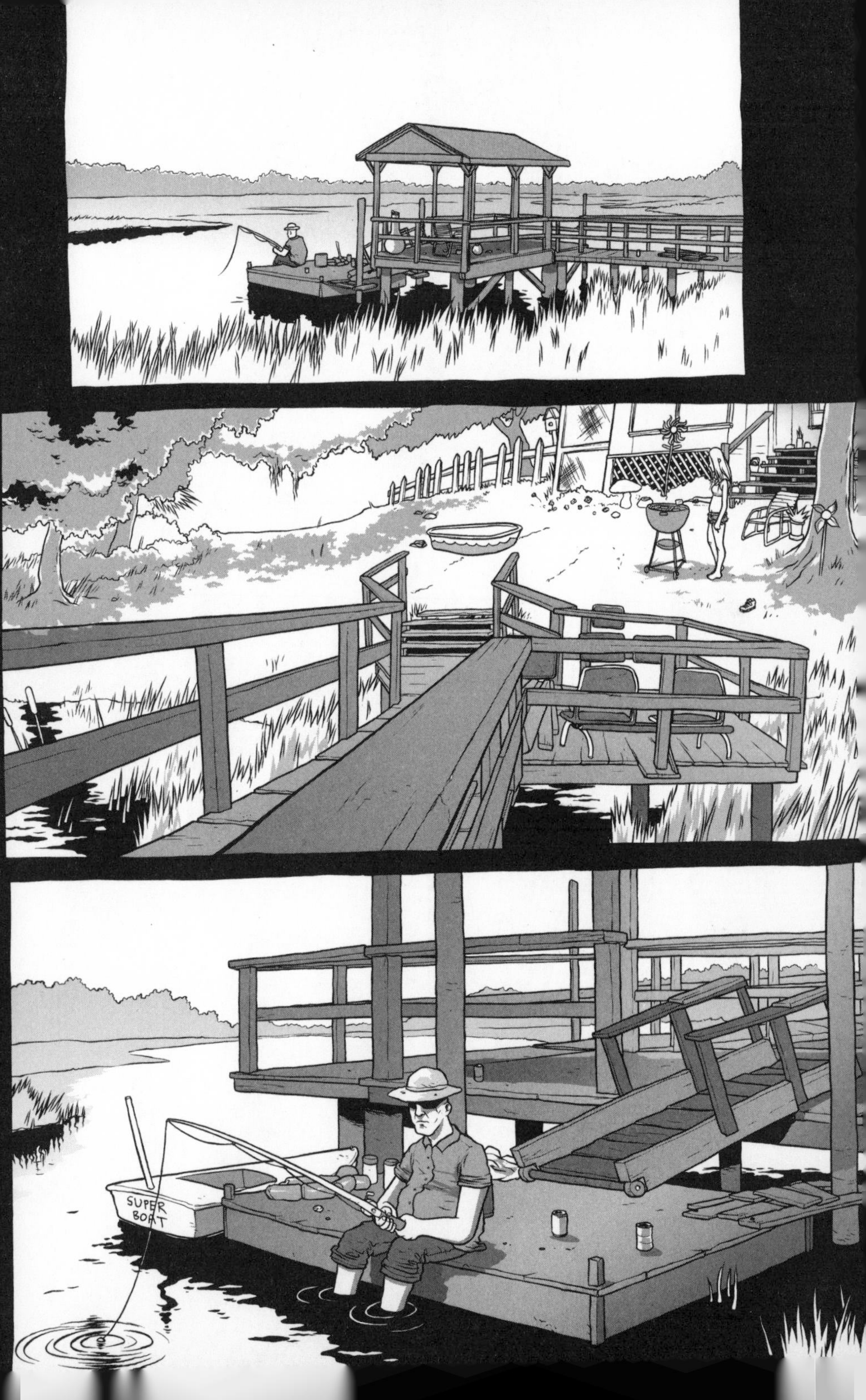
SUPER BOAT

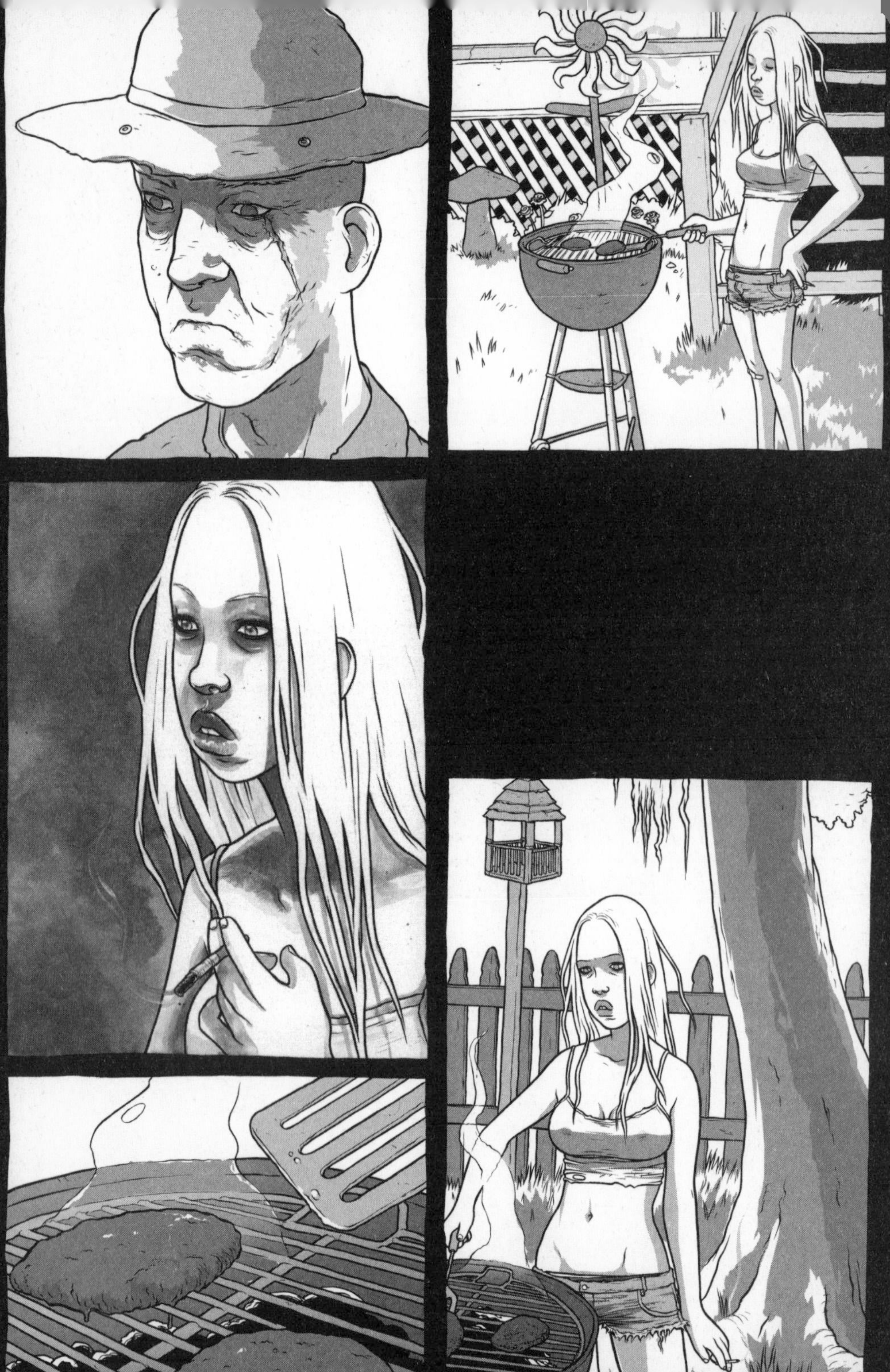

Hey Paw, burgers're dunnn!

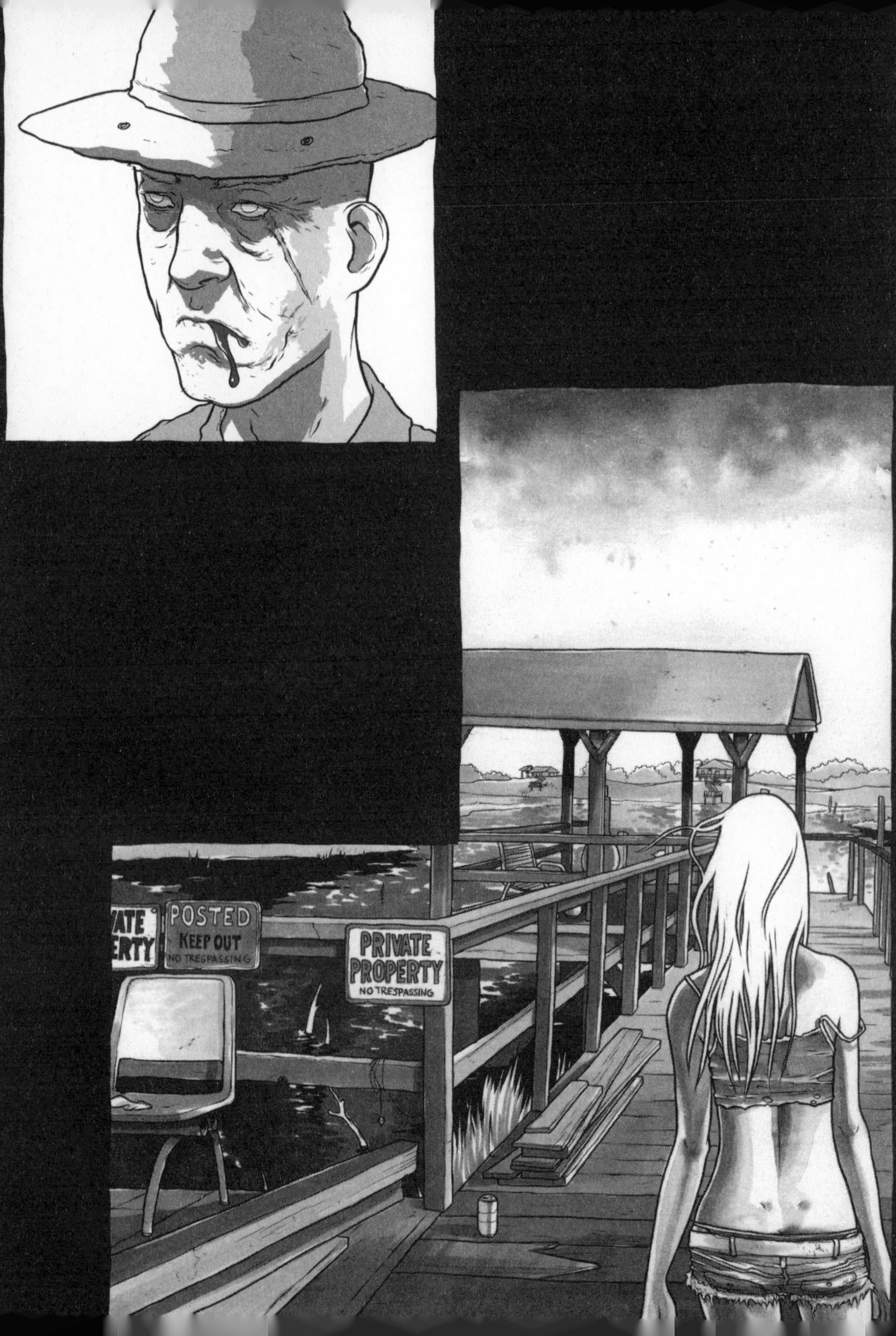
POSTED
KEEP OUT
NO TRESPASSING
PRIVATE PROPERTY
NO TRESPASSING

to be continued

older wet moon artwork

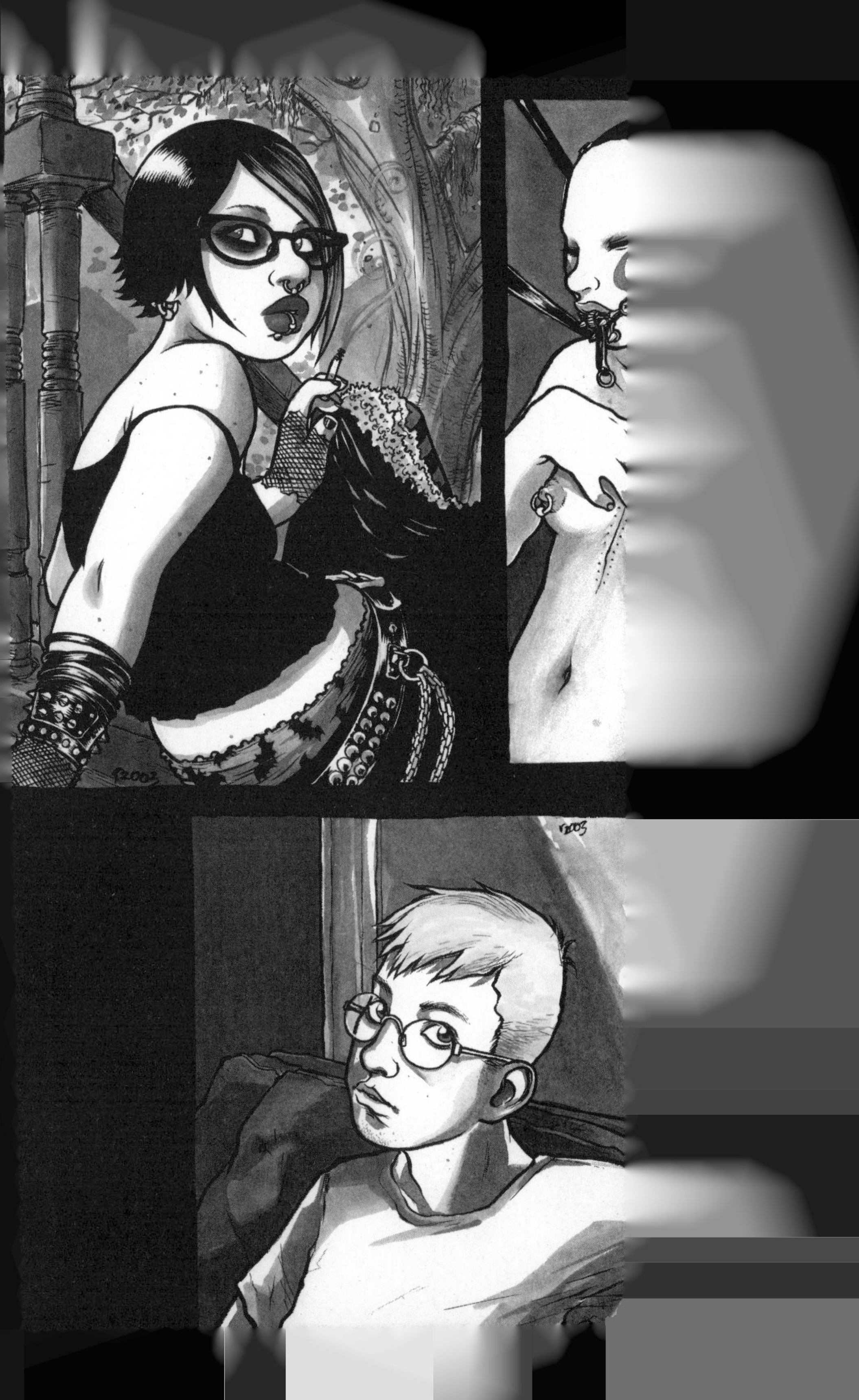

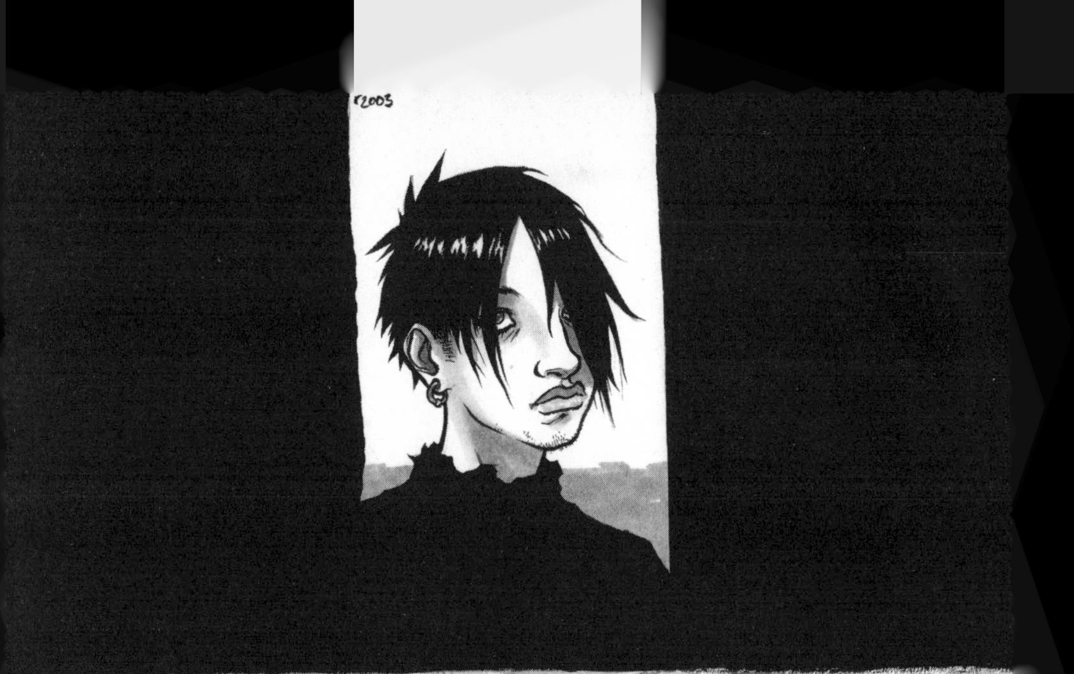

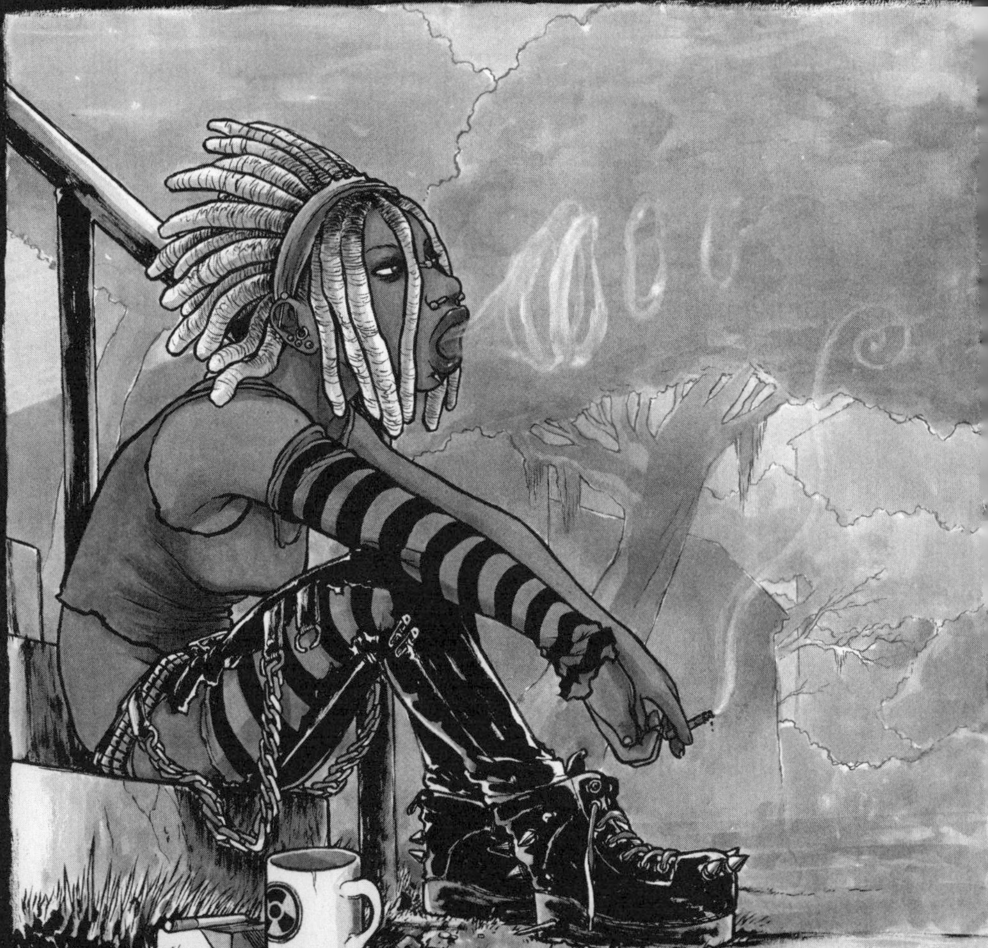

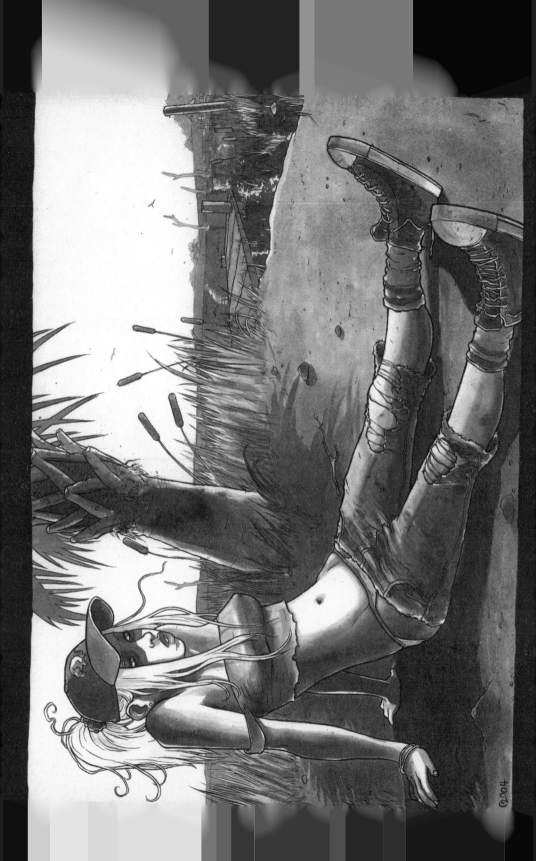

following are the first five pages
of what was originally supposed
to be *wet moon* volume 1, done
sometime between december 2002
and the end of january 2003.

i never finished it, but i think it
works well as a short story all by
itself. it takes place before the events
in this book, in senior year of
high school.

cleo has since gotten herself a
digital clock, and i'm guessing
she dropped her skull lamp
when packing for college.

-r.

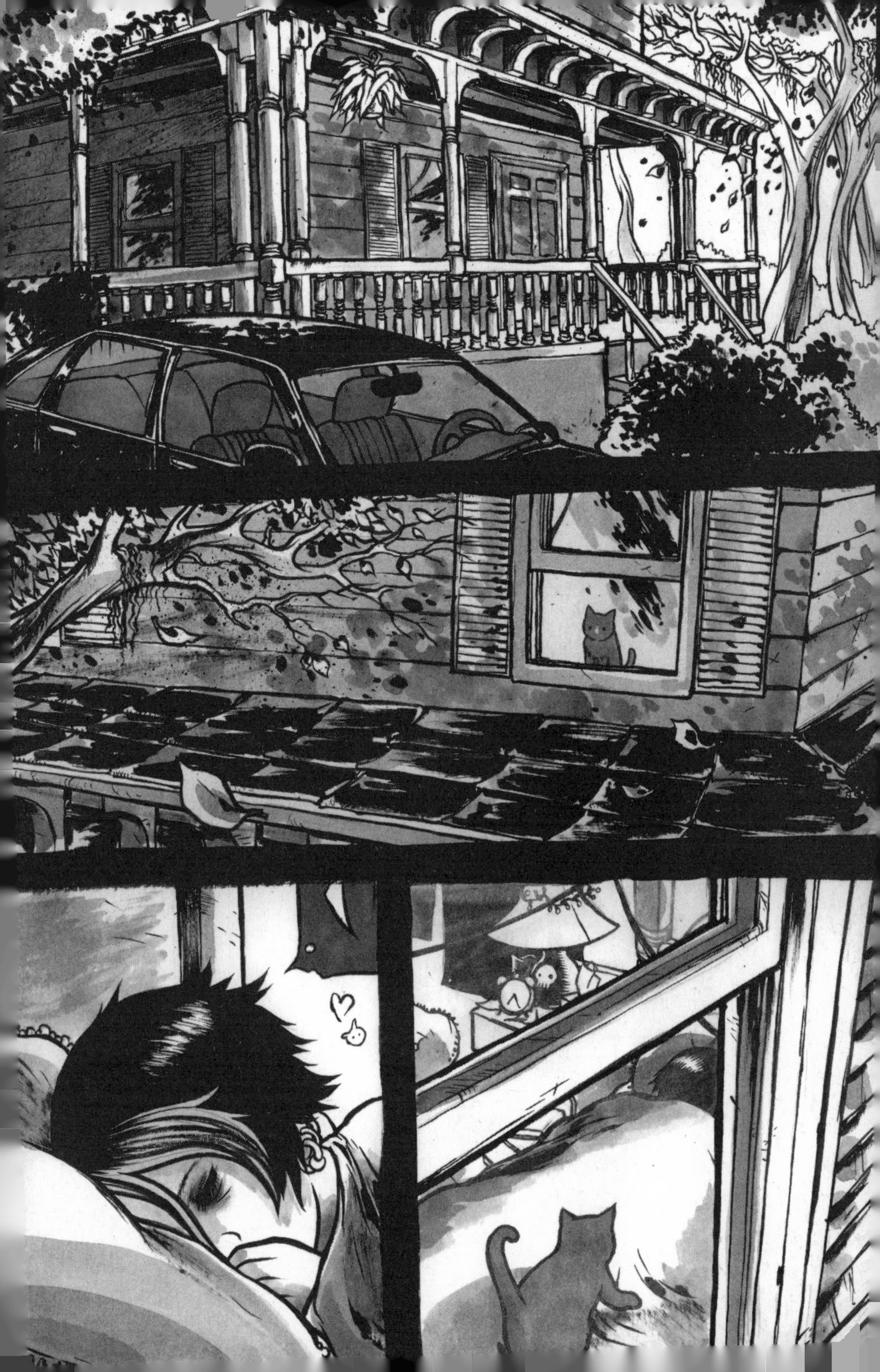

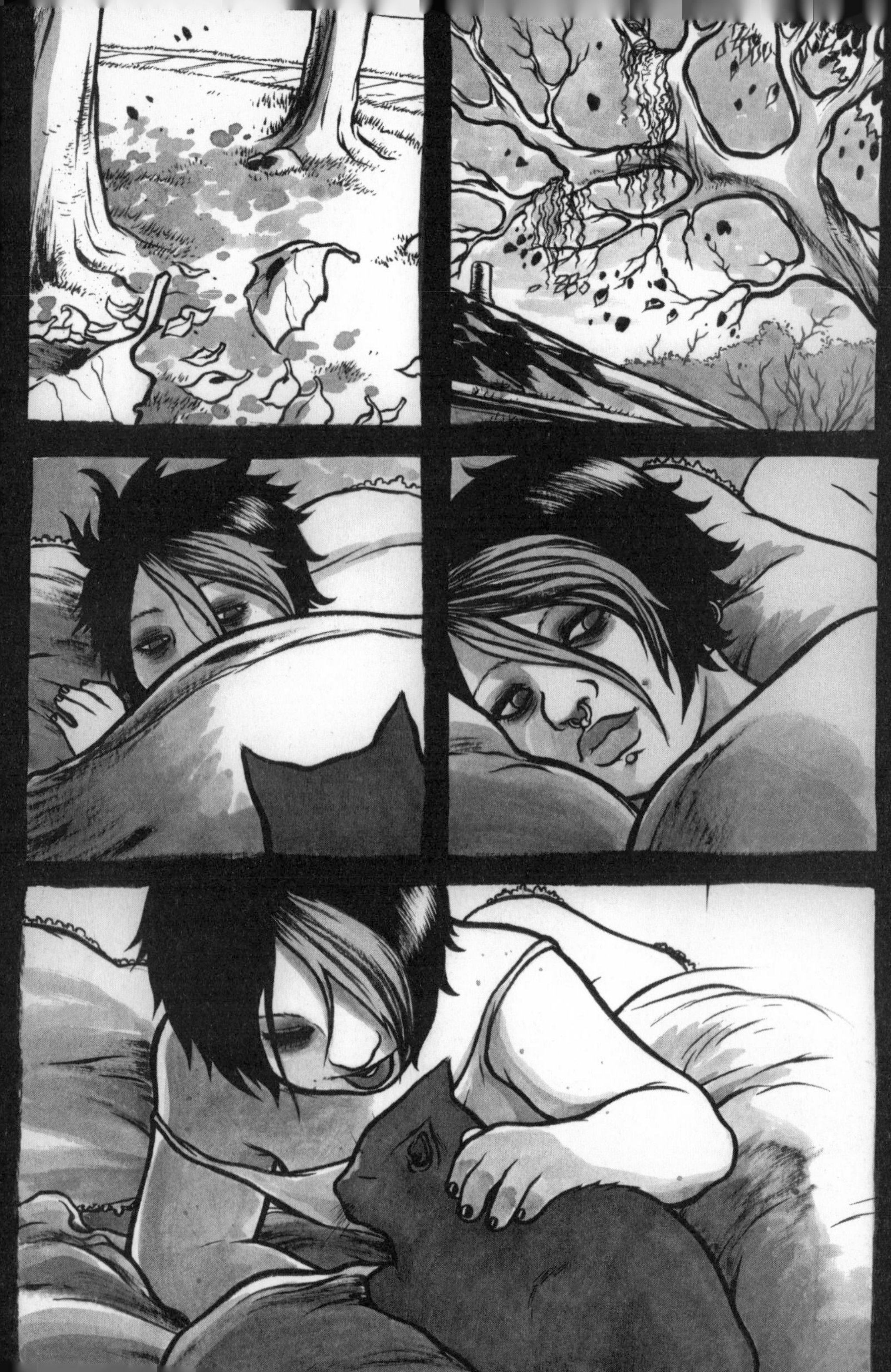

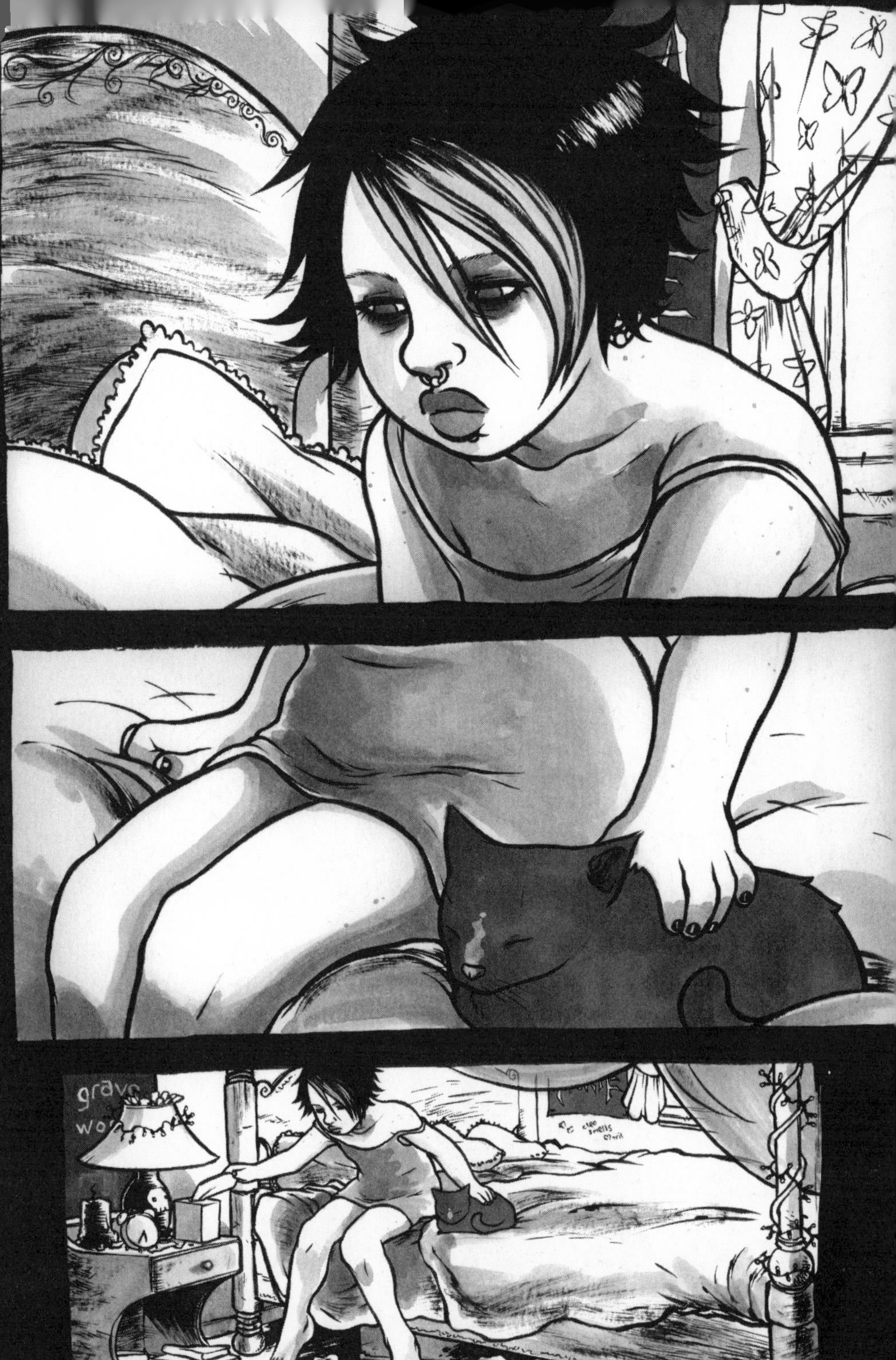
cleo smells evil

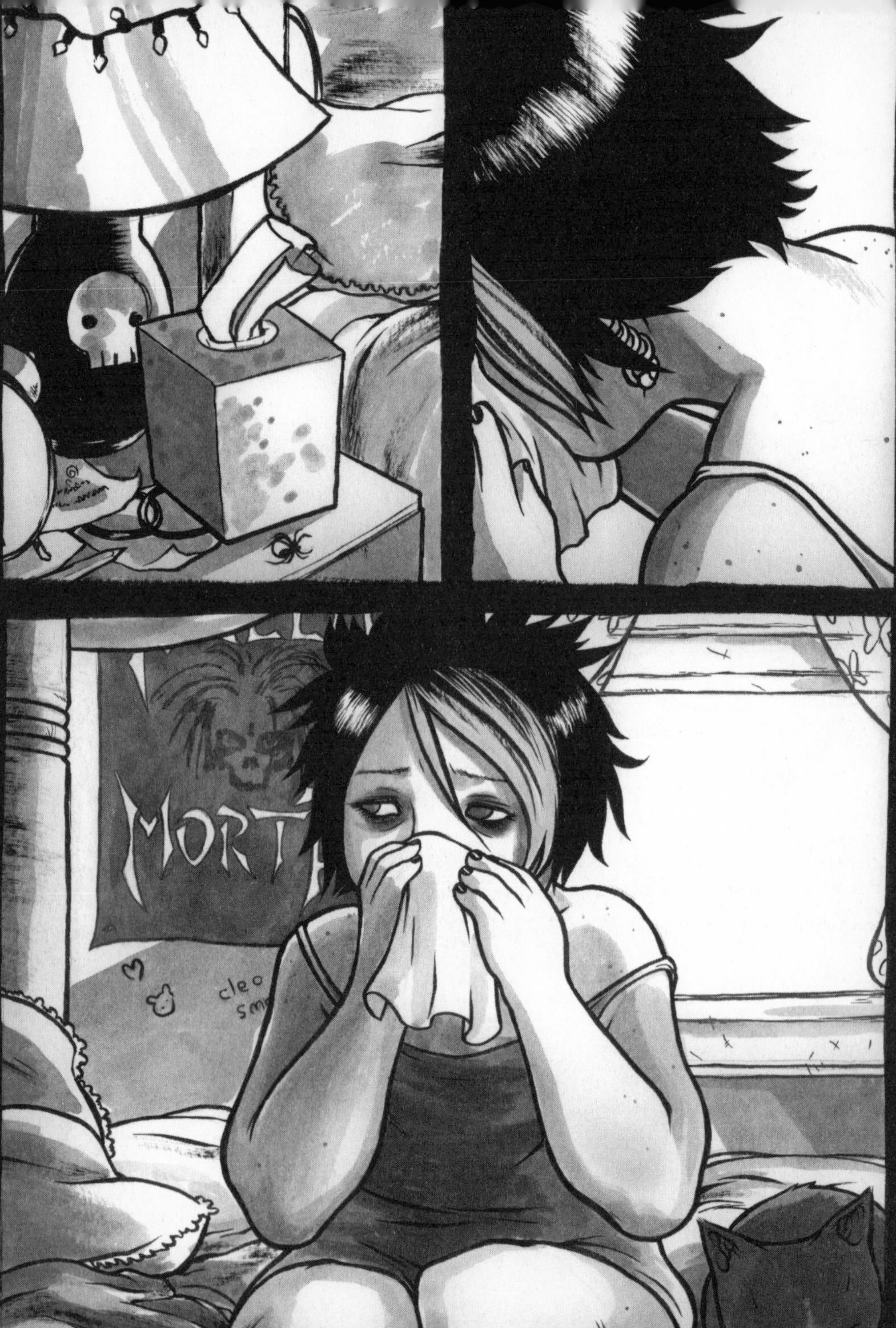
MORT
cleo

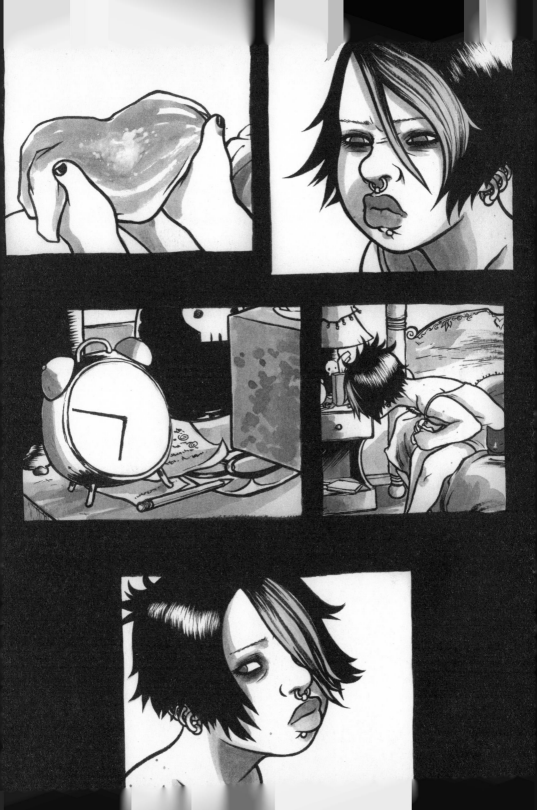

who's who in wet moon

 cleo lovedrop

 penny lovedrop

 trilby bernarde

 audrey richter

 mara zuzanny

 fern

 natalie ringtree

 myrtle turenne

 martin samson

 malady mayapple

 glen neuhoff

 slicer

 meiko

 marissa lyons

 connor eakle

 the pringles guy

 fall swanhilde

 vincent verrier

 ben viola

Thanks to: Mom, Dad, Julie, Dan, Zach, Dee, Mandy, Steve, Nate, Tracy, Brandon, Ker, Bub, Gork, Krog, Nano, Carlie, Lance, Lydia, Rain, Pat, Ron, Roger, Adam, Dave H., Katie, Dave D., Jamaica, the Oni folks (James, Jen, Jamie, & Joe*), Antony, everyone at deviantart, all my SCAD sequential professors, Brian G. at White Wolf, Mysterious Hick Girl #2, Eileen at Kinko's, Jeremy, Sarah, Sean, Chris, Don for being profoundly weird, the Porn Guy, Mysterious Bagger Girl at Wilmington Island Kroger, no1super for changing my life, and everyone who's ever supported me and my work in one way or another.

Special thanks to: Becky C., Jess, Andy & the Bella Morte guys (Gopal, Tony, & Micah), Orenda & Maria from Azure Ray, the Birthday Massacre (Chibi, Rainbow, M. Falcore, Aslan, ADM & Rhim), Tut, Jenny, Laurie, and the Wishmaster: my faithful chariot, may a flock of angels sing thee to thy rest.

Extra-special thanks to: my awesome scanner.

No thanks to: Bill Goodin, Global DVD, Victor Denny's management staff, in2art.com.

Honorable mention: Keith.

Plugs: www.bellamorte.com, www.azureraymusic.com, www.nothingandnowhere.com, www.tinycreature.com, www.nateandsteve.com, www.jamaicad.com, www.greenoblivion.com

* all J's... weird.

Other great books available from Oni Press:

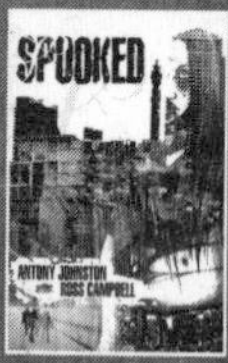
SPOOKED
ANTONY JOHNSTON
ROSS CAMPBELL

SPOOKED™
by Antony Johnston & Ross Campbell
168 pages, black-and-white interiors
$14.95 US
ISBN 1-929998-79-1

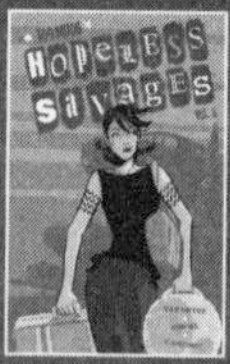
Hopeless Savages

HOPELESS SAVAGES™, VOL. 3: TOO MUCH HOPELESS SAVAGES
By Jen Van Meter, Christine Norrie, & Ross Campbell
128 pages, black-and-white interiors
$11.95 US
ISBN 1-929998-85-6

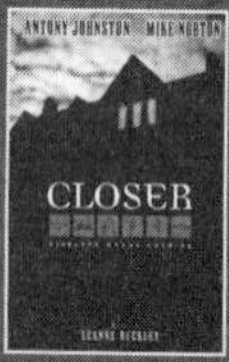
ANTONY JOHNSTON
MIKE NORTON
CLOSER

CLOSER™
by Antony Johnston, Mike Norton, & Leanne Buckley
144 pages, black-and-white interiors
$14.95 US
ISBN 1-929998-81-3

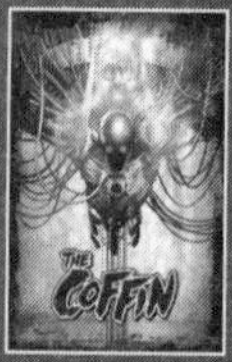
THE COFFIN

THE COFFIN™
by Phil Hester & Mike Huddleston
120 pages, black-and-white interiors
$11.95 US
ISBN 1-929998-16-3

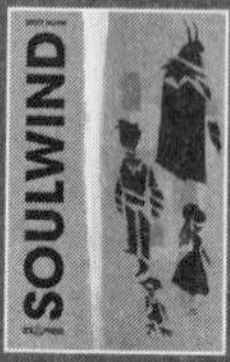
SOULWIND

THE COMPLETE SOULWIND™
by Scott Morse
520 pages, black-and-white interiors
$11.95 US
ISBN 1-929998-73-2

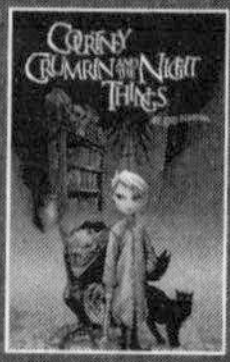

COURTNEY CRUMRIN™, VOL. 1: THE NIGHT THINGS
by Ted Naifeh
128 pages, black-and-white interiors
$11.95 US
ISBN 1-929998-60-0

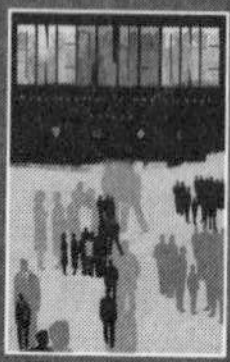
ONE PLUS ONE

ONE PLUS ONE™
by Neal Shaffer & Daniel Krall
160 pages, black-and-white interiors
$14.95 US
ISBN 1-929998-65-1

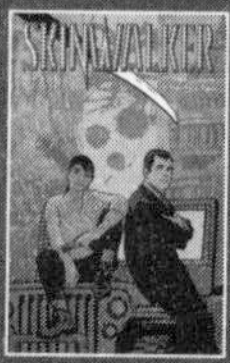
SKINWALKER

SKINWALKER™
By Defilippis, Weir, Hurtt, & Dela Cruz
128 pages, black-and-white interiors
$11.95 US
ISBN 1-929998-16-3

Available at finer comics shops everywhere. For a comics store near you, call 1-888-COMIC-BOOK or visit www.the-master-list.com.

For additional Oni Press books and information visit www.onipress.com.